The Precarious Homestead

*Trading Ceremony at York Factory, 1780's
by Adam Sherriff Scott, R.C.A.
(courtesy of the Hudson's Bay Company).*

The Precarious Homestead

ESSAYS ON
ECONOMICS, TECHNOLOGY AND NATIONALISM

Abraham Rotstein

new press   Toronto   1973

ISBN   0-88770-710-6   cloth
ISBN   0-88770-711-4   paper

First printing

123456   77   76   75   74   73

new press

Order Department
553 Richmond Street West
Toronto, Ontario
M5V 1Y6

Design: Pamela Patrick
Typeset by House of Letters, Toronto
Printed by Web Offset, Toronto
Manufactured in Canada

for
Diane

Contents

Acknowledgements····································ix

Preface··xiii

Part I Concession Lines

1   The Precarious Society····························3

2   Innocents at Home·······························8
    The Economist's Quandary······················8
    The Political Economy of the Multinational
        Corporation·······························15

3   One Forest—Two Flags··························26

4   Journeys of the Magi···························37
    The Watkins Report···························37
    The Wahn Report·····························49
    The Gray Report·····························53

5   Functional Socialism···························58

6   The Search for Independence·····················69
    Fractured Nationalism·························69
    Clearing the Smog····························78

7   Homesteading on Bay Street······················82
    Conspicuous Absence: Regional Development········82
    Canadian Business and the Eternal No·············88
    Last Chance·······························99

8 La Survivance   102
      The B & B Report   102
      Every Count but the Crucial One: Trudeau and
         the Constitution   107
      Les Juifs Montréalais   111
      After the Fall   118

9 Beyond the Pale: Canada's Foreign Policy   125
      Pearson   125
      Trudeau   127
      Strategies   131

10 Trade and Politics   135
      The Fur Trade   135
      Economic Coexistence: Canada's Trade
         Relations with the Soviet Bloc   159

11 Binding Prometheus   183

Part II Ark Welding

12 Secondary Relays   199
      The Outer Man: Technology and Alienation   199
      Nationalism in a Technological Society   203

13 Voices of Wisdom   218
      Robert Owen   218
      George Grant   241
      Karl Polanyi   249

14 Points of Departure   253
      Watts: An American Dilemma   253
      Chile   259
      Italy: The Strike at Fiat   278
      A Summer on the Island   282

15 University and Society   286
      University and Society   286
      The Toronto Teach-Ins   296
      The Makings of a President   306
      The Right to Survive   315

16 The Unknown Student   321

Acknowledgements

The essays in this volume first appeared in the form indicated below. I am indebted to the respective publishers for permission to reprint.

"The Precarious Society" appeared as the Introduction to *The Prospect of Change: Proposals for Canada's Future*, by the University League for Social Reform, Abraham Rotstein (ed.), McGraw-Hill Company of Canada, Toronto, 1965. "Economic Coexistence: Canada's Trade Relations With the Soviet Bloc" also appeared in the latter volume. "The Political Economy of the Multinational Corporation" is being published in the volume *Nationalism and the Multinational Enterprise*, H.R. Hahlo, J. Graham Smith and Richard W. Wright (eds.), A.W. Sijthoff Publishing Company N.V. of Leiden, and Oceana Publications, Inc. of New York, 1972. "The Watkins Report" appeared as "Foreign Ownership of Industry, A New Canadian Approach" in *The Round Table* (London), no. 231, July 1968. "Functional Socialism" appeared as the Introduction to *Reclaiming the Canadian Economy* by Gunnar Adler-Karlsson, House of Anansi, Toronto, 1970. "Clearing the Smog" is a revised version of a review of *Gordon To Watkins To You* (Dave Godfrey with Mel Watkins (eds.), New Press, 1970) in the magazine of *The Globe and Mail*, Toronto, June 13, 1970. "Conspicuous Absence: Regional Development" appeared as the

ACKNOWLEDGEMENTS

Introduction to *Forced Growth, Five Studies of Government Involvement in the Development of Canada* by Philip Mathias, James Lewis and Samuel, Toronto, 1971. "Les Juifs Montréalais" was first delivered as a talk to the Jewish Public Library of Montreal and appeared in *Maintenant* (Montreal) no. 85, April 1969. "Strategies" appeared as part of a round-table discussion "Retaliation: The Price of Independence?" in *An Independent Foreign Policy for Canada?*, by the University League for Social Reform, Stephen Clarkson (ed.), McClelland and Stewart, Toronto, 1968. "The Fur Trade" appeared as "Trade and Politics: An Institutional Approach" in *Western Canadian Journal of Anthropology*, Special Issue: The Fur Trade in Canada, Vol. III, No. 1, 1972. The original version contains additional documentation. "Binding Prometheus" appeared in *Close the 49th Parallel Etc., The Americanization of Canada*, by the University League for Social Reform, Ian Lumsden (ed.), University of Toronto Press, 1970. "Nationalism in a Technological Society" is a shortened version of "The 20th Century Prospect: Nationalism in a Technological Society" which appeared in *Nationalism in Canada,* by the University League for Social Reform, Peter Russell (ed.), McGraw-Hill Company of Canada, Toronto, 1966. "University and Society" is an address delivered to the African Youth Conference sponsored by The Program of East African Studies of Syracuse University, October 8, 1966. "The Right to Survive" is the text of the opening remarks made to the conference on The Canadianization of Post-Secondary Education sponsored by the Committee for an Independent Canada and The Graduate Students' Association of the Ontario Institute for Studies in Education, March 5-6, 1971, Toronto. The Proceedings of the conference will be published in 1973, edited by Gesta J. Abols and Bruce Rusk. "The Unknown Student" was given as the Annual Spring Lecture to The Thomas More Institute, Montreal, May 15, 1967.

The essays "Robert Owen," "University and Society," "The Right to Survive," and "The Unknown Student" are published here for the first time.

All other articles originally appeared in *The Canadian*

Forum on the respective dates indicated.

I should also like to thank Mel Watkins who is co-author of "The Outer Man: Technology and Alienation," "Watts: An American Dilemma," and "The Toronto Teach-Ins: Communication in a New Key"; Stephen Clarkson, who is co-author of "The Toronto Teach-Ins: The Ivory Microphone"; and Viv Nelles who is co-author of "Canadian Business and the Eternal No."

The book has been published with the help of a grant from the Social Science Research Council of Canada, using funds provided by the Canada Council.

Preface

The imprint of the 1960's is clearly apparent in this collection of articles and essays. But Canadian problems have a continuity of their own and we are still very far from having dealt adequately with the issues that lie at the heart of our survival as an independent nation. The debate continues.

In the summer of 1964, I entered the fray with an attack on the *doyen* of economic liberalism in this country, Professor Harry Johnson. It appeared in a small magazine, *The Canadian Forum* but it made the rounds. I was quite sure that I was destined to remain a maverick in my views on the foreign ownership question, but I was wrong. Expressions of support came slowly at first, but gradually the climate of public opinion began to shift. The problem of Canadian survival was too patently obvious to be obscured indefinitely even by the distorted perspectives in which we had been nurtured: initially the political liberalism inculcated among our best students at Oxbridge and the economic liberalism dispensed to our postwar graduate students at Harvard, the University of Chicago and M.I.T.

My own task, as I saw it throughout these years, was to find an intellectual toehold for an alternative position. Every doctrine and fashion in the current textbooks proclaimed that we were wrong. Nationalists were, apparently, protectionists—defenders of the narrow interests of a selfserving Canadian middle class, destined to wreck the economy by interfering with the 'free market' for capital and for goods with the United States. They were, moreover, chauvinists in an era of budding internationalism and the universal 'free flow of ideas'. Not infrequently the charge was levied—the ultimate charge—that nationalists were the potential bearers of fascism in Canada. Decent people, therefore, should have nothing to do with us.

In academic circles the situation was, if anything, worse. Some common sense about what was happening to this country, some identification with the national interest, these were the least compelling arguments in the academy. The overwhelming evidence of takeover—in the economy as well as in the cultural sphere, in defence as in foreign policy—was blandly dismissed with a dab of complacency and a touch of messianism about our destiny as an 'international nation'. Self-awareness was at a remarkable low among Canadian intellectuals as we moved through the decade from colony to hibernation.

I tried, through most of this period, to meet these issues squarely and formulate arguments for the 'defence'. Looking back on these essays, I am painfully conscious of their limitations, particularly the risk of becoming a mirror image of those ideas to which I was opposed. In the attempt to break out of the cocoon of a suffocating nineteenth-century liberalism in this country, these were only some faltering and difficult first steps.

The second part of this volume gathers together my ideas on an alternative perspective for the future. The new tasks of Canadian nationalism are first and foremost to relate to the changing landscape of the technological society, particularly its moral and political dilemmas. I relied mainly on the work of the late Karl Polanyi whom I knew first as a teacher and later as a friend and collaborator. The mark of his seminal volume, *The Great Transformation*, will be apparent in many of these essays. In 1956 we agreed to write a joint book to be called *Freedom and Technology*, following up the theme of *The Great Transformation* in a technological setting. The essay on Robert Owen, published here for the first time, emerged out of these conversations and was intended as an early chapter. The underlying ideas are Polanyi's, the research and writing are my own. The essay benefited greatly from his corrections of the various drafts that emerged. The book was shelved, however, when we turned to the completion of his manuscript *Dahomey and the Slave Trade* and was never written. Polanyi died in 1964 and when I turned more directly to Canadian issues, I found that the global framework of his ideas had an extraordinary relevance to the problems facing this country.

The influence of Polanyi's work in *Trade and Market in the Early Empires* will be discerned in the essays on "The Fur Trade" and "Economic Coexistence: Canada's Trade Relations With the Soviet Bloc." There is a common thread that links these explorations of two entirely different centuries and settings: the deliberate recognition of the political framework in which trade is carried on and its influence in shaping the institutions governing trade.

Some of these essays speak to the mood of the moment, particularly the pieces on the Teach-ins and on Claude Bissell. The latter half of the 1960's was a time of high excitement about the possibilities of creative institutional transformation, particularly at the university. Rear-guard actions in defence of the status quo were regarded with deep distrust and impatience. I suspect I would write a rather different appraisal today of Bissell and of the university—but that is a different matter.

Throughout the period, the University League for Social Reform was a small enclave of live discussion about the national issues of the day. *The Canadian Forum* likewise remained a centre of debate and dissent and I am grateful to have had the opportunity to participate in both. Together they account in their own way for the majority of the pieces in this book.

There are many other debts as well. I owe much to the inspiration of George Grant. Conversations over the years with Walter Gordon, Mel Watkins, Stephen Clarkson, Kari Levitt, Dave Godfrey and Stephen Hymer gave me the needed encouragement that we were on the right track. Peter Newman was a constant ally and friend from the very first. I leaned heavily on conversations with Denis Smith, William Neville, Viv Nelles, Jack McLeod, William Neilson, Jack Granatstein, Michael Cross, Douglas Myers and more recently, many of the members of the Committee for an Independent Canada across the country.

Perhaps the forty years in the desert are drawing to a close. My hope is that a new generation, less hemmed in by the old strictures of academe, will carry forward the task of building the intellectual and moral structure within which this country may survive and flourish.

A.R.
December 1972

The Precarious Homestead

Part 1
Concession Lines

The Precarious Society

1

Much will have to change in Canada if the country is to stay the same. The key to change, however, is the climate of public opinion. Change comes about more easily and is more effective if it grows out of the demands of an articulate public opinion; but in Canada, we have traditionally been conservative and reticent. Public debate on basic issues is, on the whole, diffident, halting and impoverished.

We may be inclined perhaps to persist in deeply rooted attitudes and to cherish reticence as a national virtue. Admittedly, reticence has its attractive side. We are, on the whole, less subject to the public hysteria which, in recent years in the United States, has produced tests and oaths of loyalty, elaborate passport restrictions, 'un-American activities', and sections of the legal code to support witch-hunts.

This is hardly a claim to moral superiority. Many different factors shape the climate of public opinion—religious and geographical factors as well as the public opinion of other countries. Canadian public opinion, for example, may on occasion enjoy a curious see-saw relationship with public opinion in the United States. The McCarthy era, a low point for the United States, was a high point for Canada. It stimulated in this country a renewed interest in civil liberties, a suspicion of cold-war hysteria in its various forms, and a calmer and more effective participation in international affairs.

This recent shift of the see-saw was in our favour, though there have been occasions when we were on the low end. Well over a century ago, in the Jeffersonian period after the American revolution, the United States was at a high point and stood for individual liberty and democracy. This reinforced, in turn, the opposite tendencies in Canada, namely, the anti-democratic and oligarchic forces that dominated the early history of this country. This occasional see-saw is a matter of our historical and geographical situation and contemporary political conditions; it serves as a self-protective device that entitles us neither to castigation nor to praise.

But this country does not take its shape from external light and shadow. The climate of public opinion is essentially the expression of the indigenous moral and spiritual condition of a country, and in Canada we are constrained and threatened by this condition. For I believe that what haunts our public life and gives rise to the reticence and conservatism is the silent spectre of the nation's *precarious* situation. This pervasive political intuition is grounded in the well-known circumstances of our national existence: the centrifugal forces of regionalism, the weak counterpoise to the American social and economic vortex, our high dependence on the shifting institutions and market forces of the international economy, the ambivalence toward 'the England within', and most of all, perhaps, the helpless paralysis induced by the seemingly insoluble quandary of Quebec's place in our national life. Each one of these has cast a continuing shadow over the country but has offered little prospect for a basic solution. Together they have produced a deeply cautious and taciturn climate of public opinion.

Perhaps we may elaborate on two of these circumstances and their effect on public opinion. In French-English relations in the past, the history of formal arm's-length cordiality masked a human indifference. This was as much, perhaps, as an apprehensive and uncertain country could then muster. As Pierre Trudeau told us: "Historically, French Canadians have not really believed in democracy for themselves; and English Canadians have not really wanted it for others." This moral gap could not be bridged and brought a paralysis of spirit on both sides in the absence of genuine community. It gravely retarded the emergence of this country as a human and moral force in the world and restricted the inner freedom and social imagination needed by the country to respond to its tasks.

The sense of precariousness was always reinforced by the proximity of the United States. The nominal equality of two sovereign states was contradicted by their vastly unequal economic, political, and military power. But what was to be done beyond the occasional self-protective movements of public opinion and the tariff wall?

If the problems appeared to be beyond basic solutions and the national equilibrium inherently precarious, the risks of change might then seem too great. In such a condition, it is not only a sound response but a matter of intuitive loyalty not to 'rock the boat'. Action or even frank and articulate public debate create additional risk and dubious consequences, and therefore are shunned.

But this passive consciousness of a fragile national existence has not only shaped the climate of our public opinion. It has also had more tangible effects in shaping our political and economic institutions and policies.

Political parties in this country have held power for unusually long periods of time under what C.B. Macpherson has called a "quasi-party system." In seeking and holding power, major parties have searched for a centre position to unite widely divergent interests and have therefore offered the country policies of a lowest-common-denominator variety. The aim has been to gloss over divisive issues in order to safeguard unity. Change was subordinated to stability both in terms of policies and in the infrequent alternation of ruling parties.

Similarly, class conflict in this country has been muted. The significant political victories of the left—indeed, of protest movements generally—have characteristically been at the provincial and local levels where the risk to a fragile national equilibrium could best be tolerated.

The strong reluctance of minority parties in this country to enter a coalition government reflects, in turn, an appreciation of this centripetal political response at the national level. Coalition governments in Europe do not present the same dangers to minority parties, namely, that these parties will be merged with a major party in the centralizing undertow of the country.

The emphasis of the political system has been, as Professor Macpherson puts it, on "the supposed fundamental oneness of the whole people." Put differently, our political system has been shaped as an institutional response to the precarious existence of the nation. The national coherence thus obtained, however, has often been at a high cost in terms of direct confrontation of public issues.

Harold Innis has effectively portrayed the centralizing tendencies of our economic life. The early phase of the fur trade consisted of sustaining fragile contacts over great distances. Competition proved disastrous, and centralized large companies emerged as a result, both in the period of French control and later under the English when the Hudson's Bay Company was dominant. After Confederation, active participation by the state resulted in the National Policy of building a *national* economy through railways, immigration, and land grants in Western Canada and protection of the manufactures of the central provinces through the tariff. However the results of this 'system of state planning' are to be judged, such an initiative was unusual for the late nineteenth and early twentieth centuries and was supported by the country as a response to the precarious material basis of the new state. This same underlying rationale has been invoked to justify the regional inequalities produced by the tariff.

Today, having conquered distance and established the national economy, we face the task of sustaining and improving one of the highest standards of living in the world. This task increases the burden of uncertainty and reinforces characteristic protectionist responses, as well as centralization through industrial concentration and governmental regulation and participation in the economy.

Thus the passive consciousness of the precarious circumstances of our national existence has had its effects. It produced a reticent climate of public opinion and characteristic institutional responses in the political and economic sphere that aimed above all at reinforcing the coherence of the nation. Essentially it was a strategy of minimum risk and maximum containment based on the assumption that the problems could in fact be contained.

However clear the reasons for the old strategy in the past, the awareness grows today that it has become obsolete. The pace of change can no longer be contained. Today, the issues that surround regional development and French-English relations, for example, can no longer be damped down. If for no other reason, we must shoulder the risk of change because it is the lesser risk. We must bypass the doctrinaire in a search for new legislative and administrative alternatives in the awareness that change must be more rapid and more effective than in the past if we are not to risk the country by default.

The task of humanizing and rationalizing a complex industrial society cannot be relinquished. But we may discover that the moral foundation of the welfare state—the upgrading of mutual concern and mutual responsibility—is not alien to the new political concern for *national* survival. Both may rest on a foundation that transcends liberal-individualist views of society.

But the old reticence does justice neither to the burden of our lives nor to the future of the country. Only a vigorous and articulate public opinion will bring forward the new standards, new commitments, and concrete reforms to release us from the growing precariousness of our condition and the paralysis of spirit that has gone with it.

September 1964

Innocents at Home

2

THE ECONOMIST'S QUANDARY

The economist has much to learn from the English butler. I have in mind the fine art of running the household without running the lives of the family. The efficiency of the economic process is important, but we might well pause before demands that we reshape our national existence around it.

In his collection of speeches and papers over a six-year period,* Professor Harry Johnson relentlessly pursues the arch-villain of Canadian nationalism which "has been diverting Canada into a narrow and garbage-cluttered cul-de-sac." His complaint is that nationalism seeks to impose restrictions on American investment in Canada and to maintain the high tariff wall, thus interfering with the operation of the free market for capital and for goods between the two countries. Interferences with the free market in the name of political objectives such as safeguarding national independence, are regarded as spurious since they inhibit economic efficiency. Efficiency is the key to everything and the proceeds will buy all our heart's desire, from slum clearance to bilingualism and independence:

> Independence, to my mind, and according to both the empirical evidence and the best tradition of the English novel, comes from the enjoyment of a high income; it is

The Canadian Quandary, Toronto: McGraw-Hill, 1963.

hard to see how a nation can be made more independent by lowering its citizens' standard of living and forcing them to earn their livings in occupations at which they are inefficient. If the public is to be taxed for the privilege of having a national identity—which is what the protectionists are really arguing for—there are far more worthy monuments to national independence than a second-rate manufacturing sector that could be constructed with the money—a decent social security system, a comprehensive public health programme, beautiful cities free of slums, a truly free and high quality educational system, a truly bilingual culture.

The old-new alchemy for our second-rate manufacturing sector is the abolition of the tariff and unlimited foreign ownership. If Professor Johnson is right, it does raise the question of what other national dross can similarly be turned to gold. For example, what of our second-rate defence establishment and our second-rate foreign service? The Americans might run our defence establishment at half of what it costs us at present—they might even do it free—and the English have a proven record of running our foreign service efficiently. Also the banks and the mass media could be made similarly efficient, while Canadians would pocket the proceeds and build monuments to their independence. No doubt we would need them. "More integration," Professor Johnson tells us, "means a richer and more prosperous Canada; and nobody is as independent as a man who can afford to pick up his own cheques."

Perhaps we would become richer as a consequence of more foreign ownership. But Professor Johnson gives us no clear idea as to what we should expect from his proposal of a "low or zero tariff." He assures us that we will become more "efficient," but should we then expect an expanded manufacturing sector, a truncated one, or no manufacturing sector at all? He offers no evidence to support his mollifying assertion that "there is little reason to think that such a trade policy would necessarily alter very greatly the amount of manufacturing activity in Canada." The fragmentary evidence that Professor Johnson does offer is scattered about the book and indicates that a different set of consequences is possible. First he refers to an unpublished paper by Professor J.H. Dales that indicates "the tariff makes it impossible to tell which of your industries are efficient and which are not." We are also told of another study by the same author on the question of why Canadian economic growth has lagged behind that of the United States. It appears that

> the increasing relative underdevelopment of Canada [is due] to the effects of the tariff, which has steered Canadian productive effort into secondary manufacturing, where not only is production comparatively inefficient, but its productivity has been rising no faster than American manufacturing productivity, and far less rapidly than has productivity in Canadian agriculture. The tariff, in short, has fostered the less dynamic sector of the economy at the expense of the more dynamic.

While we haven't any clear idea of which industries will survive a tariff cut and which will presumably not, we suspect that our second-rate manufacturing sector will decline and our dynamic agricultural sector increase. And how is the world likely to receive more Canadian agricultural output? Professor Johnson does give us an answer:

> opportunities for development on an agricultural basis are restricted by the policies of advanced countries that would rather protect their agriculture and save themselves a political problem than allow the law of comparative advantage to work itself out.

We are told further about "the uncertainty of agricultural protectionism and the resulting surpluses in the advanced countries," the upshot of which is "a complicated situation in which all countries' policies toward agriculture involve distortions from an internationally efficient allocation of resources."

This is the basis for Professor Johnson's proposal to turn Canadian commercial policy on its head and thereby provide us with both increased incomes and increased independence.

Turning to the political side of the issue, Professor Johnson would have us believe that the economic benefits of integration carry with them no political liabilities. The arguments hardly merit serious attention. For example, his simplistic explanation of our failure to recognize Communist China runs as follows: "the plain truth is that [such recognition is] . . .simply unpopular in Canada."

Then there is a variant of the old theme that laissez-faire brings freedom and intervention restricts it:

> But supposing that the development of closer economic ties with the United States might lead Canadians eventually to desire a political union with the United States, is this a valid reason for trying to prevent by government intervention now the formulation of these closer economic ties? . . .the present generation, whatever it decides for itself, has no right to try to limit the freedom of future generations by depriving them of the opportunity to choose.

Apart from the novelty of the suggestion that a state should pursue a policy geared to its own dissolution, it is difficult to see how a future generation in possession of its own economy would be less free than a generation whose economy is integrated. If the freedom to stay Canadian forms part of the choice, a generation in possession of its economy would be more free. It is a policy of intervention, it seems to me, which increases freedom, and laissez-faire which limits it.

Professor Johnson turns to the sovereignty of Parliament as his last bastion for laissez-faire, thereby clouding over the political aspect of the problem with the legal aspect:

> neither imports of American goods nor imports of American capital acquire voting rights in Canada, so Canadian independence as embodied in the sovereignty of Parliament can hardly be threatened that way.

American goods and American capital do, however, have voting rights in the United States. Independence, one thinks, is not frozen in some institutional sovereignty but has something to do with the political relationship of national sovereignties to each other. Has the U.S. State Department, for example, been slow to defend the interests of American periodicals now so strongly entrenched in this country?

The political innocence of the economic liberal is a source of wonder. Since 1950 in Canada, our total foreign obligations have been rising at a rate of some $1.3 billion a year. Americans now control two thirds of our extractive industries and three fifths of our manufacturing. Nevertheless, Professor Johnson feels that the economic benefits have no political consequences. If there is an issue at all, it is framed in purely economic terms, namely, does American capital commit economic misdemeanours in this country? If it turns out to be as 'efficient' as Canadian capital, only more so, then the question is settled. The political consequences vanish because somehow the nationality of the foreign capital has vanished. For those less innocent, the riddle is intriguing.

In the last analysis, it is the market mentality of the economic liberal which is at the core of his political outlook: the market is impersonal and its participants are anonymous buyers and sellers of the factors of production. These factors, even if they are foreign, have no nationality since the market recognizes only quantity and price and the only criterion for judgement is efficiency. Are American capitalists different from Canadian capitalists? Of course not. Are American workers different from Canadian workers? Is anyone in Canada different from anyone in the United States? Not as long as he is regarded merely as a factor of production on the market. But there is no reason to mistake an economic abstraction, useful in analysing market behaviour, for a political reality.

Needless to say, independence refers not to income, but to the power to make decisions. No national state concerned with its independence willingly shifts basic decision-making power in vital areas into foreign hands, however friendly and well-behaved these may be. In an interdependent world, such questions are matters of degree. Still, the loss of independence is readily apparent when decision-making power in foreign affairs and defence is shifted outside the country. Why is the loss of independence less apparent in foreign ownership of the economy? Partly because economic power is decentralized, but mainly because foreign ownership takes on a political façade in a market setting. Foreign capitalists are not 'foreign', they are 'efficient'.

From a purely political point of view, it is irrelevant whether U.S. capitalists are as 'efficient' as Canadian capitalists, just as it is irrelevant whether the Pentagon would be as 'efficient' in defending Canada as our own armed forces, or whether the English foreign service would be as 'efficient' as the Canadian External Affairs Department. A decrease in independence results from the loss of decision-making power in all three cases. The fact that we have legal sovereignty to alter or revoke the actions of foreign-owned firms is not unlike our power to abrogate defence treaties or to alter our foreign commitments. It does not nullify the political fact. The loss of decision-making power for the country is no less real if the shift occurs from Canadian citizens to U.S. citizens—as in foreign ownership—than the shift of power on an intergovernmental basis.

For those not mesmerized by the market, debate on public policy might centre on weighing real economic benefits against equally real political costs. No one can be indifferent to the problems of unemployment and lagging economic growth in this country, particularly if we have no development plans of our own. A likely outcome of such a debate is the conclusion that while there are political costs, some of these may be worth paying in the light of the expected benefits. But first, both benefits and costs would need to be scrutinized more closely. Yet we have done as little concrete study of the dynamics of Canadian-American political relations as the free traders have of the concrete consequences of the abolition of the tariff.

Once we begin to deal in realities and not fictions, either economic or political, we might be better able to translate a little of Professor Johnson's vaunted sovereignty into effective policy. It is fair neither to the Americans nor to ourselves to allow this capital in under laissez-faire conditions and then start fumbling with ineffective legislation when we begin to realize that incomes and independence are not the same thing.

The problems are complex, and it is naive to rely on simple formulas, least of all laissez-faire. It is true that the economic

history of this country has made the problems complex and
that part of our problem with foreign ownership, for example,
has been brought on by the high tariff.

The economic liberals have never forgiven the country for
having been conceived in original sin. The National Policy,
whether for good or ill, rejected laissez-faire and pivoted on
the tariff. The aim was to provide a material basis for
Confederation by subordinating the economic to the political.
There is nothing sacred about the mould in which we grew up
and some of the tariff provisions are badly outdated. But
neither are there magic formulas, especially those that run
counter to the entire history and structure of the country.
Professor Johnson knows this well enough:

> Imitative magic describes the process of looking at other
> countries with currently more successful records than one's
> own, discerning some obvious institutional differences
> that seem to account for their freedom from the problems
> that plague oneself, and recommending the transplantation
> of the relevant institution to one's own country regardless
> of how it came to be established, where it is or what makes
> it work.

A word on Professor Johnson's social philosophy as a whole.
The reader should not get the impression that this is the old
type of *sauve qui peut* economic liberalism. Professor
Johnson subscribes to the thesis of the affluent society—to
the point where he has 'rechristened' it the "opulent society."
In the opulent society we can well afford abundant social
welfare services as well as "town-planning, slum clearance
and imaginative public works"—but not, apparently, independence. The fruits in the one case come from bolstering and
manipulating the market—the sin in the second case is to
interfere with it.

For economic liberals, *The Canadian Quandary* will have a
superlative appeal, reminiscent of that best-seller *The Caine
Mutiny*. On the face of it, Professor Johnson titillates the
desire to be non-conformist. With a bravado and a flourish
he strikes out against the conventional economic wisdom in
Canada, the many years of maladministration in this country
and even against Canadian capitalists ("the small, smug mind

and large, larcenous hands of Bay Street.") Yet just as in the novel, all this out-spoken non-conformism is safe in the end. The economic liberal is deposited in the lap of an orthodoxy older even and more conventional than the National Policy.

It is a radical position, implacably hewing to the free market regardless of the political consequences—but a radicalism that is neither the radical right nor the radical left. On Canadian economic policy, Professor Johnson stands for the radical centre.

July 1964

THE POLITICAL ECONOMY OF
THE MULTINATIONAL CORPORATION

The multinational enterprise has created novel and un-expected problems that ramify into diverse areas of society and have challenged the traditional views of many disciplines.

While the multinational enterprise is recognized as being in essence an economic phenomenon, it clearly has political, legal and administrative consequences; government policies designed to deal with it must necessarily respond, to a greater or lesser extent, to the issues posed in these areas. General tools of analysis are still lacking, so that we tentatively venture this essay in political economy.

Canada, which has been in the forefront of the expansion of the multinational corporation (acting as a DEW line, or distant early warning system for the rest of the world) has been virtually the last to embark on a minimal and token regulatory policy which is now emerging after a decade of debate in this country.

Perhaps, more than in any other country, the Canadian debate has focused on the theoretical issues, both economic and political. In this paper an attempt is made to recapitulate briefly some aspects of this debate, indicating from the outset the *ex parte* stance I have pursued, namely, that there is a sensible and legitimate case to be made for Canadian national-ism and for a regulatory policy in the light of the global expansion of the multinational corporation.

The position of the liberal economists, spearheaded by

Professor Harry Johnson, has been that foreign firms were in essence no different from domestic firms—they maximized profits and obeyed the laws of competitive enterprise in a world of free markets. All firms danced, in effect, to the same refrain. "Are Canadian capitalists different from American capitalists?" became the classic question.

Viewed in this traditional economic framework, political and legal differences of foreign firms were obscured and the way was paved for an uncritical acceptance of the multinational corporation (M.N.C.) as the chief engine of growth, progress and international division of labour. Classical doctrines of the law of comparative advantage were invoked, and all opposition was dubbed protectionist, yet another instance of irrational opposition to the incontrovertible doctrines of free trade and free capital movements. Those, for example, concerned with the issue of national independence were accused of sacrificing the general economic welfare to the traditional vested interests of an entrenched middle class.

Nation-states, acting in the economic sphere, seemed inclined, in this view, to do the opposite of what reason demanded—imposing tariffs and setting up restrictions on capital flows. By seemingly preventing the achievement of a global vision of unhampered laissez-faire, nation states were relegated to the nether world of archaic and recidivist institutions, blocking, for no good reason, our emergence into the 'modern age'.

This entire perspective has now been challenged from many sides, and we have begun to appreciate how badly we have misread what was happening. As the global thrust of the M.N.C. emerged in clearer outline, and as its actual features became apparent, a quite different assessment began to emerge. It may best be designated by Professor Kari Levitt's phrase, the new mercantilism,[1] harking back as it did to the global trading corporations of the seventeenth and eighteenth centuries, the islands of colonial power operating in an enclave of their own jurisdiction with a thrust that was as much political—the imperial outpost of the mother country—as it was economic.

The new mercantilism has as its primary asset not trade

but technology. The internal relations between parent and subsidiary, and between subsidiaries themselves in different countries are characterized by administrative arrangements falling outside the normal supply-demand nexus of partners trading at arm's length. Thus internal transfer prices rather than market prices characterize these transactions and today, a significant and growing portion of world trade conducted under the auspices of the multinational corporation falls outside the traditional market framework. Local conditions —e.g., tax advantages to be taken up either by the parent or subsidiary—will determine the prices at which parts and components move. This administrative discretion of these global oligopolies affects the terms of trade of a country, and includes the ability to switch export orders between countries and to alter transfer payments internal to the corporation. In the past year, moreover, we have seen how multinational corporations can influence exchange rates by swiftly moving large funds between countries.

In the legal sphere the extraterritorial extension of the law of the home country has been amply detailed by the Watkins Report[2] in the case of American corporations operating in Canada. The Foreign Assets Control Regulations (Trading With the Enemy Act), the anti-trust provisions of the Sherman Act and the Clayton Act, the balance of payments guidelines, and so forth, form a network of law and administration which claims primary jurisdiction over American corporations abroad. It is not the economic significance of these extraterritorial laws which has aroused concern everywhere, but their political and legal significance—the fact, for example, that the American government, operating in its own benign fashion, reserves the right to primary jurisdiction over $40 billion of assets in Canada.

Extraterritoriality was the first of the difficulties that came to the fore in Canada and commanded immediate attention. This uncomfortable legal fact was inclined to be dismissed by some as a pinprick, a minor nuisance in a plethora of economic benefits. The debate, moreover, on the economic costs of these extraterritorial restrictions was never resolved. For example, how could one measure the effects of a situation where Canada was largely excluded from the network of commercial contacts for manufactured goods organized by the state-trading corporations of communist countries? What sensible buyer or supplier from these countries would wish to be involved in the long-drawn-out ambiguities of obtaining special exemptions for Canadian subsidiaries of U.S. corporations dispensed on a case-by-case basis by the U.S. Treasury Department? When the contacts for commerce dried up, many were prone to suggest that there was no evidence of potential sales to be made. The economic problem faded into a hypothetical and inconclusive debate.

In reality, what had been revealed was the tip of the iceberg. The American government claims primary jurisdiction over these Canadian subsidiaries, as stated above, even though this jurisdiction is only exercised occasionally. But this was just the top level of control. Beneath it lay the more comprehensive network of parent-subsidiary relations. The benefits to be derived from this new type of division of labour on a global basis necessarily required the global controls and planning of the head office. While several different patterns can be distinguished here, these controls were generally exercised in the form of highly centralized research and development laboratories, a strict division of marketing zones for each of the subsidiaries, managerial rotation among different countries, and an overall co-ordination and forward planning of the entire enterprise. There were monopoly profits from specific patents and technologies, but the maximizing of global returns necessarily meant the exercise of global control over subsidiaries. This was inherent in such a transnational exercise in the division of labour.

The protectionist course on which the United States embarked after August 15, 1971 has highlighted the vulnerability of countries such as Canada that have assumed that global economic integration through the aegis of the multinational corporation was an unmitigated advantage. Under the strain of a major balance of payments crisis, which has not been adequately resolved, the United States has decided to use those instruments that were at hand to shift the burdens of this crisis onto other countries. The subsidiaries of its multinational corporations have become a prime agent for such a solution. Under the legislation promoting the Domestic International Sales Corporation (D.I.S.C.) the postponement of taxes has been offered as an incentive to greater domestic production for export in lieu of manufacturing abroad.

American multinational corporations are ideally placed to take advantage of these incentives. Administrative control over their subsidiaries permits a switch in production from subsidiary plants in other countries to plants in the United States. A country such as Canada is faced with the choice of seeing domestic employment decline or of foregoing tax revenue in order to offer equivalent incentives. The costs of either submitting to such American measures or resisting them are high. But the increased vulnerability of host countries with M.N.C.'s is increasingly apparent. Only a supreme optimist would venture to predict that more such crises, either economic or political in scope, will not recur in the next decade.

The iceberg beneath the surface therefore is precisely this great web of decision-making exercised through both managerial and governmental personnel in the home country of the M.N.C. in response to both normal objectives and to national crises. For those concerned with the issue of national independence, this shift in the locus of decision-making outside the borders of the host country is indeed the central issue. Independence, of course, is more than a rhetorical phrase invoked on ceremonial and state occasions. It refers in practice to the ability of citizens of a country to take those decisions that affect their daily lives and to retain control of the levers of power in relation to their own future. Otherwise, they become the instruments of other countries' policies. The relevant category here is citizenship rather than class, the category that unites the members of a nation state in a common experience or destiny which transcends internal class divisions.

At issue is the apparatus of decision-making traditionally hidden beneath the surface of the market system. The pre-

vailing orthodoxy of liberal economists has sidetracked the
need to peer beneath this surface. It still basks in the heritage
of Adam Smith which glossed over the political structure of
economic life through the doctrine of the convergence of
private and public interests inherent in the operation of
market institutions. The butcher and baker, it may be recalled,
by pursuing their own self-interest, thereby serve the interest
of society as a whole. These are one and the same. The
constraint of competition in the market guarantees a harmonious result. The economy is never defined nor is its scope
delimited either regionally or nationally. In practice, the
economy is viewed as the nexus of the market system, which
is potentially at least, global in scope. Add further the fact
that traditionally the economy takes precedence as the
primary institutional framework in a market society (as Karl
Polanyi pointed out in *The Great Transformation*)[3] and one
can see why no problems in regard to national independence
can emerge even theoretically. Both the political and geographical dimensions of the economy are lost. Thus, when
a liberal economist views the global march of the multinational corporation, he sees it as an extension or simulation
of the global market nexus, which is the dream of orthodox
economic analysis; progress, equity and harmony are destined
to follow in its wake. In the real world, there is no reason to
assume that the global interests of the multinational corporation will necessarily coincide with the interests of a particular
nation-state. Moreover the pressures put on the M.N.C. by its
home government may be designed, as we have seen, to
subordinate or even damage the interests of the host country.

One side of this debate, I maintain, has become the victim
of its own abstractions, glossing over the complex realities
of the multinational corporation, particularly the political
implications for the survival of indigenous societies.

I plead here for a basic shift in perspective, setting actual
societies and their broadest goals in the forefront and treating
the economy as a component part of the whole. In the light
of this perspective, nationalism in Canada should appear less
mysterious and partisan a movement than it has appeared
to some in the past. Indeed, I have argued that nationalism

is, in general, not a movement at all but a countermovement. It is a response to the strains in the social structure, a form of political mobilization responding to the threat of erosion or disintegration of the basic institutions of the society.[4]

This introspective concern with the integrity of the social structure or with national identity is, admittedly, artificial. The task of a healthy society is to *live*, not to brood about its survival. But that, indeed, is the point. Nationalism is the symptom of distress, not a cause. The root cause, seen from a political vantage point, is the draining away of power and the possibility of self-determination. When crucial decisions are made outside the nation-state, nationalism represents the effort to restore this decision-making power and to safeguard the enduring institutions of a society. In an interdependent world, this is necessarily a matter of degree; still the degree is crucial. Nation states are subject to increasing demands today in the achievement of domestic goals—education, welfare, redistribution of income, ecological control and so forth. It makes little sense to have them abdicate—or have their citizens abdicate—their crucial powers of decision or the setting of their own priorities, in the name of some reputedly harmonious process of international integration. This global harmony, in recent decades, has been distinctly conspicuous by its absence.

Thus far, basic theoretical questions have been discussed because it is the sharp disagreement about these questions that has paralysed the formation of effective policies till now. Some have decried the presence of too much nationalism in Canada, others have argued that there was too little. My own position on this matter should be obvious. To warn a country that it is in danger of becoming too nationalist when 58.1 per cent of its manufacturing is already in foreign hands, as well as great stretches of its natural resources, is about as gratuitous as warning St. Francis of Assisi not to become a possessive individualist.

Policies of regulation and control that have been invoked in an unselfconscious way in countries such as Japan, Mexico and France are still the subject of fearful anxiety in Canada. Canadians seem to feel dependent on foreign capital to

sustain their economic growth and to solve their unemployment problem (currently about six per cent.) They fail to
realize that they already have about one third of the total of
American investment throughout the world and that this has
made no substantial inroad on their unemployment, which is
higher than that of any industrialized country. Nor does the
record of economic growth particularly reflect the spectacular
amount of foreign investment. Japan has clearly done better
on both counts while having a fairly stringent set of controls
and restrictions on foreign investment. My intention is not to
suggest fanciful correlations between economic growth and
employment on the one hand, and foreign investment policy
on the other, but to suggest that we can become, as have
other countries, far less dependent on foreign investment than
we have been in the past without endangering our economy.

Different approaches have been suggested in Canada. The
Watkins Report[5], the Wahn Report[6] and the Gray Report[7]
are in the mainstream. They suggest the creation of a special
agency or government department to deal directly with
M.N.C.'s on issues such as their patent and licence agreements,
marketing restrictions, investment and employment policies,
pricing agreements, dividend and royalty policies, and so
forth. There are also suggestions in the Wahn Report for
fostering a greater degree of Canadian ownership (aiming at a
general level of fifty-one per cent). The Gray Report offers a
policy to prevent further takeovers of Canadian companies
while the Watkins Report advocates the use of the Canada
Development Corporation to mobilize capital and entrepreneurship for large resource projects, as well as to assist in
the rationalization of industries with too many firms.

Unfortunately, all three Reports have been repudiated by
the Canadian Government over the past four years and a very
weak policy limited to screening takeovers by foreign firms
has now been proposed. (In 1969, takeovers accounted for
only twenty per cent of the growth of foreign-controlled
corporations in Canada and in 1968 takeovers were only five
per cent of the total.)

Further to the left on the spectrum, the Waffle Group of
the N.D.P. has proposed a policy of nationalization of industry

to regain control of the economy due to the effective absence of a Canadian business class to take the lead. Unfortunately, in my view, neither the federal nor the provincial governments in Canada at present possess a burgeoning cadre of managerial expertise to fill the gap, as can be witnessed in the recent fiascoes of such government-sponsored ventures as Churchill Forest Industries in Manitoba, the Parsons and Whittemore pulp mills in Saskatchewan and Gulf Garden Foods, in Prince Edward Island. We may be as weak or weaker within our governments as we are within private industry. In the circumstances we must pool our available talent in both the public and private sectors for a common effort.

The main thrust of Canadian policy in my view should centre on regulation of the multinational corporation. The objectives of such a regulatory policy, which we have referred to earlier, extend beyond the traditional and limited aim of regulatory agencies—namely to control the financial abuse of monopoly powers where an industry is not subject to the discipline of competition. Instead, the aim should be to restore national control over a much wider range of functions, from research and development policy through to assuring the presence of Canadian personnel at the operating and management levels. The objective of this regulation should be to restore Canadian priorities on a broad front.

The primary emphasis, then, is not on titles to property but on putting an increasing number of the functions of ownership under national control. The separation of functions or property rights from titles is not a new idea. Traditional regulation of various industries has been with us for a long time. Once we specify clearly the goals and objectives of our society, appropriate functions may be subsumed to meet these objectives.[8]

Within the next decade, I venture to suggest, neither the M.N.C. nor the nation state will disappear from the scene. What we should attempt to achieve is some *modus vivendi* between the two. The new technology which the multinational corporation brings with it must be deployed and controlled within the social framework and social values of the societies in which it appears.

Complacency about uncontrolled technological change is no longer warranted anywhere, neither in rich nor in poor countries. Our environment is in jeopardy, our cities are becoming unliveable, both the national and international distribution of technological benefits are being questioned, and the bureaucratic structures necessary to make the whole system operative are losing their legitimacy in the eyes of a growing number of people everywhere. The call for democratic control is being heard in neighbourhoods, in schools and universities, in industry and even in the church.

The underlying message of the new politics is democratic participation. The new nationalism that has been evoked by the M.N.C. draws its strength from the same source. Its voice should be heeded in Canada before its tones become shrill and its demands desperate.

Although there are as many different varieties of nationalism as there are social philosophies, the mainstream in Canada—for example the Committee for an Independent Canada—speaks for the national interest, for national survival, not for a class interest.

A great deal of nonsense has been written on the subject by people who should know better, but who have become victims of their own antiquated dogmas, that nationalism is merely the protectionist armour for an incompetent middle class.

It takes only the briefest acquaintance with the realities of the Canadian scene to appreciate that the middle class in this country has been the spearhead of the great sell-out. No other business class in an advanced industrial society has presided so gracefully over its own liquidation. No other university establishment in an advanced country has flooded its ranks with so many non-Canadians to the point where the preservation of a Canadian intellectual tradition, or a social science addressed to contemporary Canadian problems, is now in grave doubt. No other trade union movement in the world, is as dependent on direction from abroad. Had the middle class put its weight solidly behind Canadian nationalism, this erosion of national control would have been substantially impeded.

The most elementary facts are overridden by the dogma of the economic liberals. For example, a nationalist programme designed to block further takeovers of Canadian business by foreign corporations, will *lower* the market value of Canadian-owned companies. Does such a programme bear any resemblance to middle-class protectionism?

The protectionist argument of entrenched vested interest which is still upheld today by Professor Johnson and others as an argument against nationalism, is the strongest example of a tradition of intellectual colonialism in this country. Arguments emanating from the nineteenth century debate on free trade in England are misapplied to serve the interests of a continentalist establishment and the unimpeded spread of the new mercantilism. While the world of the free market society is fading away everywhere, it remains firmly entrenched in our minds.

But the winds are now blowing from a different direction in Canada and in many other countries. What is being 'protected' is the search for genuine independence among nation states who are now challenging the global spread of the M.N.C. The confrontation, and it is to be hoped, the accommodation of the two, is high on the agenda of the 1970's.

August 1971

NOTES

1. Kari Levitt, *Silent Surrender*, Toronto: Macmillan, 1970.

2. Canada, Task Force on the Structure of Canadian Industry, *Foreign Ownership and the Structure of Canadian Industry*, Report, Ottawa: Queen's Printer, 1968.

3. Karl Polanyi, *The Great Transformation*, Boston: Beacon Press, 1957.

4. This theme is elaborated in my paper "The Twentieth Century Prospect: Nationalism in a Technological Society," in *Nationalism in Canada*, P. Russell (ed.), Toronto: McGraw-Hill, 1966. See below, 203-17.

5. Canada, Task Force on the Structure of Canadian Industry, *op. cit.*

6. Canada, House of Commons Standing Committee on External Affairs and National Defence, Second Session, Twenty-eighth Parliament, 1969-70, Proceedings No. 33.

7. Canada, *Foreign Direct Investment in Canada*, Ottawa: Information Canada, 1972. All three Reports are discussed below, 37-57.

8. "Functional Socialism" (below, 58-68) elaborates this theme.

One Forest
—Two Flags

3

Several of us stood huddled against the snow and cold at the bus stop in Windsor. The first session of the annual Seminar on Canadian-American Relations at the University of Windsor had just ended and we were on our way back to the large and stodgy Norton Palmer hotel. The bus was slow in coming and we stared at the brilliantly lit skyscrapers of Detroit across the river and at the magnificent arc of the Ambassador bridge. I pondered the vagueness of both of these 'facts' and longed to escape into the concreteness of a theory.

"Somehow you can sense the difference the very moment you cross over from Detroit to Windsor," I mused aloud.

My colleague, an inveterate opponent of the tariff, replied skeptically, "You sure can—it's poorer."

In a nutshell, that may be what conferences on Canadian-American relations often come down to in the end. In any case, this report on the proceedings in Windsor in December and at Columbia University in April 1964 will spare the reader the long way round and will be neither comprehensive nor impartial.

The opening session at the University of Windsor on the flow of communication between the two countries dealt largely with the grievance that news and information seemed to flow overwhelmingly from south to north. But none of the panel felt that much could be done to right the balance.

The newsworthiness of the two countries was vastly different. Yet it was surprising to learn that the Canadian Press wire service sends about 20,000 words a day of Canadian news to the A.P. service; but little of it can be used since it is written initially for Canadians and "lacks an American accent"—a problem which apparently had either been solved or did not exist with news flowing the other way. Louis Lyons, a long-standing American journalist, doubted that more news coverage of Canada by resident American reporters was possible under the limits of the free enterprise system.

Professor Robin Winks of Yale University thought that some confusion in communication was due to the fact that the values and ideology of Canadians were not clearly defined and thus Americans were not sure what Canadians stood for. The value systems of the two countries were different, he told the audience, since Canada had achieved her independence by evolution and the United States by revolution. "I'm a nationalist," he remarked and suggested that Canadians should be nationalists as well.

The next day was spent in praising both world-wide and bilateral free trade by economists from Canada and the United States. It seemed difficult for the listener to understand why a programme possessed of so many virtues was so difficult to attain. Were the difficulties 'economic' or 'political'? J.H. Latimer of the Department of Trade and Commerce reviewed Canada's position in the current G.A.T.T. negotiations at Geneva which centred (hopefully) on a reduction of fifty per cent in the tariff schedules of all member nations (the Kennedy Round). Tariff schedules in the world are already low for raw materials and are much higher for manufactured goods. Since the bulk of Canada's exports consists of raw materials and semi-processed goods and the bulk of her imports are manufactured goods, the tariff concessions we were likely to obtain for our exports in these negotiations, might be substantially less than those we would be required to grant to other countries. Over half of our exports to the United States, for example, and twenty-nine per cent of our exports to the E.E.C. already enter free of duty. Thus Mr. Latimer's conclusion:

I do not wish to detract from the total importance to Canada of a successful negotiation. I do suggest, however, that it would be wrong to ignore these elements in considering Canada's approach to the Kennedy round of trade negotiations and what there might be in it for us.

The Canadian proposal in these negotiations, tabled on November 16, is reported to offer tariff concessions by Canada equivalent in value to those that Canada expects to receive in these negotiations, presumably very little.

Professor R.J. Wonnacott reviewed the preliminary results of a study that has been under way at the University of Western Ontario of the consequences that would result from removing all trade barriers between Canada and the United States. He indicated that "a substantial reorganization and rationalization of Canadian industry is implied," following which there would be a relative expansion of manufacturing industry in Canada with "upward pressures on the Canadian wage and exchange rate. . .until prices and costs in the two countries are brought into line." The possible result might be an increase in Canadian national income of ten to twenty per cent. Such a scheme would require a treaty on the part of both countries not to raise tariffs against the other nor "would we be quite so free to devalue the Canadian dollar." The substantial risks in such a venture would fall on the Canadian economy, Professor Wonnacott remarked during the discussion, but this was a measure of the fact that we had more to gain.

The general interest of the American speakers, however, was in multilateral or world-wide reductions of tariffs rather than bilateral reductions with Canada. The inference, at least to this listener, seemed to be that, for the United States, a free trade agreement with Canada would be difficult for political reasons since it would imply discrimination, for example, against South American and European countries. Besides, the benefits to Americans of an additional Canadian market of nineteen million people was marginal and was only the equivalent of six years of population growth at home. Thus it did not seem that Canadians could be optimistic that new policies would emerge from either the multilateral negotiations at Geneva or from bilateral negotiations with the United States for a free trade area.

Yet there was no absence of optimism. One American economist, in discussing the possibility of free trade between Canada and the U.S. in products such as lumber, mentioned that already some Americans referred to "one forest under two flags."

The significant innovation in the field of Canadian—U.S. trade was not discussed at the Conference. Press reports had indicated that a new plan to abolish tariffs on automobiles in both countries would replace the existing scheme of tariff rebates. Instead of the 'sink or swim' approach of the free market on an economy-wide basis, the transition was being prepared on an industry basis by advance consultation of interested parties—the governments, corporations and trade unions of both countries. Guarantees were being obtained on the expansion of Canadian production and the preservation of employment in the industry. The plan made economic sense by providing for greater specialization in Canadian plants and the political cost was less since the industry was almost entirely American-owned in any case. Perhaps in this ad hoc fashion an unexpected and important new pattern for removing trade barriers was being established.

In the session on the National Policy a lasting contribution to Canadian scholarship was made by J.H. Dales. The conclusions of his paper "Effects of the Canadian Tariff on Canadian Economic Development" draw on the empirical and theoretical results of his recent research (cf. *Queen's Quarterly*, Autumn 1964 and *C.J.E.P.S.*, November 1964). He has shifted the entire discussion between the opponents and defenders of the National Policy to new ground where a proper debate can be joined on concrete issues. Economic liberals have traditionally attacked the Canadian tariff, and the larger strategy of nation-building based on it, as the purest economic nonsense which has only succeeded in making the country poorer by inhibiting specialization in the products the country could produce most efficiently. Their charges of 'irrationality' have occasionally seemed to imply that a free trade policy flows out of the logical structure of human consciousness itself. Defenders of the National Policy, unable to find any logical flaws in the economics, but distrusting it nevertheless on political grounds, have retreated to a position of political idealism and of protection as the better part of valour. The polar positions taken in this debate, have contributed to the existence in this country of two intellectual establishments—and 'the two cultures' could find no common ground where either economic or political research of interest to both could be pursued.

The traditional attack on the evils of protection has been based on the (unpublicized) assumptions that men, capital and knowledge don't cross borders, that only goods move in the world. If these assumptions are relaxed in favour of a closer approximation to the real world, particularly the Canadian case, it becomes clear that "the trade model yields the conclusion that a protectionist policy does increase a country's population and does increase its National Income." This results from the profit opportunities created by the tariff in the protected sector which creates, in turn, additional employment and thus stimulates immigration. But equally important is the conclusion "that a tariff reduces a country's National Income per capita," due to the encouragement given to less efficient industry. Thus Professor Dales presents the issue as follows:

> the choice between protectionism and free trade is a choice between a larger National Income with a lower Standard of Living on the one hand and a lower National Income with a higher Standard of Living on the other. I confront you with this choice. It is a hard choice, both in the sense that it has to be made, and in the sense that reasonable men may differ about how it should be made.

There is no doubt, however, about Professor Dales's own choice. Since "the economic ethic is an ethic of proportion not an ethic of size," the choice is given: "I opt for a high Standard of Living because I am an economist." As Professor Dales implies, this is not a cross which everyone must bear. I suspect that most people would avoid either the one pole or the other and take a position on the spectrum somewhere between the two.

As a result of Professor Dales's research, much of the previous debate is obsolete. The new questions that are raised lead in many directions. For example, we may be in a better position to answer the question of how the economic process spreads spatially or geographically, particularly in a newly developing country. It may turn out that Sir John A. Macdonald's implicit option for an 'ethic of size' rather than 'proportion' may have been bad economics (old style) and good economic development. Such an appraisal need not make us prisoners of the past but may, for instance, throw some light on the formulation of a rational immigration policy.

The political implications of Professor Dales's work also deserve to be explored. Professor Jacob Viner has pointed out that the lesser "size" of Canada has had a significant influence on "the outcome of economic bargaining and of economic diplomacy" in relations with the United States and in the formation of "prevailing Canadian attitudes and opinions toward economic, political and even cultural relations with the United States." The Canadian-American Committee has touched on the same issue. It claims that the great difference in size of the two economies results in a situation where "certain American actions might prove to be a serious infringement on the sovereignty of the smaller Canadian economy, whereas similar actions on the part of Canada might have little, if any, effect on American sovereignty.[1] It thus becomes possible to give a partial answer to the rather pointed question of the free traders as to "how a country may be made more independent by being made poorer." Answer: by being made larger.

What I am trying to suggest is that the discipline of economics is not as stringent a taskmaster as we had been led to believe. Professor Dales's paper, as well as the new automobile plan, indicate that the range of 'rational' economic policies vis-a-vis the United States is broader than we had suspected, and that these policies imply, moreover, different kinds of political consequences. If this conclusion is correct, it may give the 'two cultures' the necessary freedom to move off their polar positions of 'efficiency' on the one side and 'independence' on the other to find some optimum combination of economic and political objectives.

Both polar positions have been bypassed by the actual progress of events in Canadian-American relations. Irrevocable forces moving toward integration in many areas are being met by a groundswell of resistance legitimately concerned with the future of national independence.

Some of the essays in *The United States and Canada*[2] (the result of a similar conference) express the nature of the resistance fairly clearly. James Eayrs captures the spirit of the protest in this precise rebuttal:

> President Johnson, with the best intentions in the world, observed in his first official reference to the Canadian-American relationship that "Canada is such a close neighbor and such a good neighbor that we always have plenty of problems there. They are kind of like problems in the hometown." They are kind of not like that at all. They are the problems not of neighbours but of friendly foreign powers.

Professor Eayrs himself tackles 'the hard issues' between the two countries. But there is a difficulty. The hard issues are divided into two groups: those which are real—"those which arise from some ascertainable fact: a diversion of a river, an expropriation of an industry, an incarceration of a citizen" and those which are spurious—"which arise from the misapprehension of reality." The real hard issues are: the defence of the continent—Norad, the Bomarc bases, sharing of arms production and strategic raw materials; the sharing of resources such as hydroelectric power; American control of the Canadian trade union movement as evidenced by the S.I.U. affair and the intervention of George Meany, the president of the A.F.L.-C.I.O. and Willard Wirtz, the U.S. Secretary of Labor. The spurious hard issues (those resting on a soft bottom) are the concerns with the movement of capital and goods and the flow of culture across the borders. Professor Eayrs then attempts to blend political realism and economic liberalism—to keep one foot in *raison d'état* and the other in *raison de marché*. His prescription is a general one, namely, that "good neighbours make good fences," that "the two nations of North America are of the states-system, not beyond and above it."

The division of the hard problems into the real and the spurious is, Professor Eayrs concedes, arbitrary; he knows that some people in Ottawa might readily disagree. But perhaps his division might be subjected to the test of internal consistency. To take the hydro-electric power problem, the exposition of its political aspects is brilliant:

> Falling water is to twentieth-century North American diplomacy what fisheries were to the nineteenth century's. Hydro-electricity is not just an ordinary resource of nature. It provides communities with the means of existence; and if withdrawn may cause the death of those communities. This being the case, international sales of hydro-electric power could safely take place only under conditions of perfect confidence and trust, in the expectation of assured sources of supply and renewal of contracts in perpetuity. Even when, as between Canada and the United States, such conditions were satisfied more fully than as between most other neighbouring countries, there was always a risk in the sale of power. The future being inscrutable, the rate of economic growth notoriously difficult to predict, it was always to be borne in mind that a government which, in all good faith, has sanctioned the export of surplus power to the other country, would discover in ten or twenty years time that it needed it for its own development. How then repatriate it without an act of war?

If I understand Professor Eayrs rightly, the political problem posed by hydro-electricity arises out of the vital dependence of citizens of one state on decision-making power located outside its borders. The political problem posed by foreign capital is, it seems to me, analogous but less severe and matters of degree fall well within the purview of the 'art of the possible'. Foreign-owned manufacturing facilities may not involve issues of life and death and are not easily 'repatriated', but they do involve matters of livelihood and the interdependence of sectors of an industrial economy. While the issues that may arise may not be matters for war, they are legitimate matters of concern for national states. For example, during a cyclical downturn, the choice may arise for an American company to reduce employment either in the main plant in the United States or in the branch plant in Canada. The political consequences of such a decision are hardly 'spurious'. The sovereignty of Parliament may be absolute within the state where the foreign capital is invested, but this hardly dispenses with the political difficulties that the exercise of such sovereignty may create between states. Isn't "the expropriation of an industry," for example, on Professor Eayrs's real hard list?

Jacob Viner's dilemma is similar. He regrets the "survival in both countries of strong elements of mercantilist thought." The concern of Canadians about their high dependence on trade with the United States and about the level of American ownership of Canadian industry is an undoubted political fact in the relations of the two countries, but "why the phenomenon appeared at precisely the time it did is, however, a complete mystery to me." Professor Viner recommends that trade be reduced and presumes that capital inflows will be restricted. He concludes that "if things should work out this way, they would reduce the economic stimulants to the 'Canadian-American Problem,' and probably at an economic cost to Canada not excessive for the sentimental gain."

The most perceptive essay in the volume is that of Douglas LePan. Much of it is anecdotal, lyrical and poetic but the organizing intuitions are profound. We are given clues to the puzzling forces that underly some of the preceding expressions of mystery and ambivalence in the earlier papers. Professor LePan views Canadian-American relations in the general context not of the mercantilist past, but of the modern crisis of the nation-state, a crisis that has at its roots the protection of society against vast technological change and against the creation of immense foci of power in the world, including the power to destroy. He reminds us, at the start, of John Kennedy's view:

> For 186 years this doctrine of national independence has shaken the globe—and it remains the most powerful force anywhere in the world today.

"It is as powerful," LePan continues, "on the northern doorstep of the United States as anywhere else." National independence then is viewed "as a kind of protection, whether illusory or not, against forces that would otherwise seem too much. . .In a world of rapid change and alienation, and nightmare not far beyond the horizon, nationalism can be a comforting thing." Again, "When the nature of power has been transformed so radically, it is only natural that there should be a similar escalation in the anxieties felt about it."

On specific issues, such as foreign ownership:

> The nagging suspicion remains that Canada's independence is being sapped and undermined as the ownership and control of many of its most important industries falls increasingly into American hands. This suspicion can be supported, it can be controverted, it can be argued over. But what is more important, in my opinion, than any of the arguments is the fact that the deep and baffling unease in Canada over this issue is fed by the expectation, so widely shared throughout the world nowadays, that national independence, if it is to be real and satisfying, should be able to find expression in economic as well as in other terms. And that expectation, together with the developments in the Canadian economy that run counter to it, provides another reason why relations between the two countries are likely to become, if anything, even more sensitive and troublesome than they have been in the recent past.

The concern with national independence is neither a 'mystery' nor a 'misapprehension of reality'. On balance I agree with Douglas LePan. The central issue in Canadian-American relations turns on safeguarding the viability and political integrity of the nation-state in a situation of close and growing interdependence.

It is a close-up of a world-wide problem. In a complex industrial society, the nation-state takes on significant new functions on both the domestic and international scene. The bourgeois nation-state of the nineteenth century stood for private property and the enforcement of contract. In our own day it is giving way to the nation-state committed on the domestic scene to full employment, to increased equality and social welfare, to the mediation of the disruptive effects of technological change and to the fostering of the cultural values of the nation. On the international scene the nation-state becomes increasingly committed to foreign aid, to the tasks of peace-keeping and to other forms of international co-operation.

The internal stresses generated by a technological civilization are substantial. Nationalism is not a movement but a counter-movement, responding in various ways to the points and degree of stress. Its implicit premise is that existence is not individualist but collective. The weakness of present-day liberalism is that it views our present situation as simply an attempt to graft the twentieth-century welfare state onto nineteenth-century individualism. But the interdependence of persons in a complex industrial society has made such a position obsolete. The spontaneous counter-movement to protect the centres of power in such a society is a consequence of their crucial importance for our lives, particularly for the fulfillment of the varied objectives we have assigned to the nation-state.

The international community, moreover, is a community of nations not of persons. Utopian illusions about abjuring nationalism in the name of a sentimental internationalism or a graceful individualism, will shatter on the remnants of the conservative forces of the old nation-state, or on our growing commitment to the tasks assigned to the new. Liberals who choose to contract out of the issue of nationalism may discover, however, that the frustration of the nationalist attempt to protect the modern nation-state may present this country with even worse prospects than more Diefenbakerism.

January 1965

NOTES

1. *Statement* (May 1962) 6.

2. Edited by John Sloan Dickey for the American Assembly of Columbia University, Englewood Cliffs: Prentice Hall, 1964.

Journeys of the Magi

4

THE WATKINS REPORT

For most of the post-war period Canada has harboured the
DEW line (Distant Early Warning), a radar network designed
to warn the United States of a bomber attack from beyond
its shores. Now that this network has become obsolete and
been abandoned, Canada's role may be reversed. She now
stands as a DEW line for the rest of the world, revealing in
high definition what may be expected from the global
penetration of the American corporation. The aggregate
production of these corporations in countries outside of the
United States already stands at well over $100,000 million
annually, forming the third largest economy in the world.
Only the domestic production of the United States and of
the Soviet Union exceeds this figure.

Nowhere has foreign investment, with its accompanying
benefits and costs, been higher than in Canada. At the end
of 1964, the total value of long-term foreign investment in
Canada stood at $27,000 million. About sixty per cent of
this investment was direct investment, i.e., was under the
control of non-residents. Americans own about eighty per
cent of this direct investment and residents of the United
Kingdom about twelve per cent. In particular industries, the
extent of foreign (mainly American) control is spectacular:

ninety-seven per cent in automobiles and parts, and in rubber products; seventy-eight per cent in chemical products and seventy-seven per cent in electrical apparatus.

Rumblings of discontent and political unease have accompanied this Americanization of the Canadian economy, but have been matched by equally vociferous responses on the Canadian political scene not to look at gift horses too closely when the obvious benefits were piling up at such a visible rate: jobs, tax revenues, new technological processes, higher standards of living—all kept pouring out of the American cornucopia. Were the objectors to foreign investment exhibiting more than a spirit of provincial ingratitude? Or were its supporters hiding behind façades of internationalist sentiment while fostering an increasingly dangerous Canadian dependence on the United States? Was it, in Mr. Harold Wilson's phrase, a new industrial helotry, or were we fumbling incompetently before the wave of the future?

So little was known in any precise way of the economic and political consequences of this investment, and so much debate was being carried on from polar positions of black and white, that the Canadian government decided in February 1967 to appoint a Task Force to study the entire question. A group of eight academic economists from across the country devoted themselves to the subject for a year and issued, in February 1968, the report entitled *Foreign Ownership and the Structure of Canadian Industry*,[1] known in brief as the Watkins Report, after Professor Melville H. Watkins, of the University of Toronto, Head of the Task Force.

The underlying rationale and proposals of this Report give a clearer focus to the concerns with foreign investment as now seen in Canada and may be of interest to other countries. Britain has not been free of sporadic outbursts of concern in the past and has commissioned a similar study. M. Servan-Schreiber in his book *Le Défi Américain* has now rung the alarm bells in France. Other countries such as Mexico and Japan are re-evaluating the strong stands they had previously taken and Japan also has a Task Force at work. In the circumstances, Canadian perspectives and Canadian solutions may offer a lead to this new problem of global dimensions as American investment abroad continues to grow.

The Multinational Corporation

An appraisal of the mixed blessing which foreign investment provides turns largely on weighing economic benefits against political costs, the latter obviously more difficult to measure than the former, but nonetheless real. Speaking generally, a broad theoretical scheme may be set out within which we may consider the Canadian case in more specific terms.

The main protagonists in the arena are the so-called multi-national corporation and the nation state. Mr. George Ball, formerly of the U.S. State Department and now U.S. Ambassador to the United Nations, suggests in *Fortune* (June 1967) that:

> while the structure of the multi-national corporation is a modern concept, designed to meet the requirements of a modern age, the nation-state is a very old-fashioned idea and badly adapted to serve the needs of our presently complex world.

Neither of the protagonists, however, exists in a pure image. The *multinationality* of the international corporation (its role as a good corporate citizen of the host country) is compromised by the legal obligations and directives of its home country and its corporate parent. The political tension which it engenders within the nation-state arises because of the overlapping and conflicting jurisdictions to which it is subjected.

However 'old-fashioned' the nation-state may be, it has been increasingly saddled with new economic responsibilities for achieving full employment, growth, modernization and higher standards of social welfare. It is also an increasingly active partner to international projects of co-operation. Can we continually require more from the nation-state and at the same time restrict its power of decision? This is the issue which is raised by foreign investment through a shift in the locus of control outside the borders of the nation-state to the board rooms of the parent corporation, and also to the government departments of its home country.

None of this would be a problem if a further pure image

prevailed—namely, the world of competitive free markets of classical political economy. In such a world, the day-to-day discipline of the market would reconcile and order all economic interests in the harmonious way Adam Smith has described. The fact of the matter is that in Canada (as elsewhere) much of the foreign investment is embodied in large corporations where the world of competition has given way to the special discretionary powers of oligopoly. In the modern economy, corporations have widespread autonomy in making decisions in their own interests. The public significance of these decisions is substantial and a harmonious outcome is by no means assured. From the early days of anti-trust legislation, it has been appreciated that only the power of the state stands as an effective supervisory and countervailing force to ensure that the economic policies and decisions of large corporations (both foreign and domestic) conform to the public interest. When the large corporations are *foreign* oligopolists, an additional set of problems remains to be dealt with by the state.

On the economic side, the multinational corporation looks to global horizons within which profits are maximized. With its plants and facilities in many countries, arrangements for research and development, the location of production facilities, marketing agreements, licence and management fees, and pricing policies for components and final products, bear no necessary relation to the national economic interest of a particular host country. The wide discretion which exists in the division of labour among the plants of such a corporation in many countries may damage the interests of individual countries concerned to the benefit of the parent corporation or of other countries.

Higher Costs in Canada

An approximate measurement of the net economic benefits of foreign investment reveals that it has been responsible for about one-fifth of the increase in *per capita* real income which has taken place in Canada. These benefits might have been considerably higher but for the fact that American subsidiaries have higher unit production costs than their parent company.

They often attempt to reproduce most of the products of the parent firm while remaining much smaller in size. Short production runs, lack of competition and the effects of both the Canadian and American tariff have created a relatively inefficient industrial structure in Canada. This has, in turn, reduced considerably the economic benefits from foreign investment.

On the political side, the scope of the legal and administrative directives that may be issued by the home country to its multinational corporations is revealing. A review of the present areas of control by the American government over its subsidiaries abroad illustrates the underlying principle involved—namely, that the American government operates on the assumption that these subsidiaries are a proper area of its own jurisdiction. Specific policies are created in an ad hoc fashion to meet new American objectives and crises as they arise, although the present scope of controlling legislation is still limited.

American laws and directives in regard to subsidiaries fall into three main areas: control of exports, control of mergers, and balance-of-payments policy. (Other areas such as securities and exchange regulations will be ignored here.)

Under the Export Control Act of 1949, the Office of Export Control of the United States Department of Commerce controls the export from the United States of all commodities and all technical data. These regulations also apply to the re-export from third countries of all goods containing American components or goods manufactured through the use of American technical data. Communist destinations, of course, face the severest controls. While Canada enjoys a special position under these regulations through an 'open border' arrangement, this is so only because of assurances given by Canadian authorities that American regulations will, in general, be observed for American goods and technology. The presence of a large number of American subsidiaries in Canada substantially increases the flow of American components and technical data into the country. This binds subsequent Canadian exports dependent on these components and technical data to American foreign policy objectives, in spite of the fact that official Canadian trade policy with Communist countries is not itself restrictive (apart from strategic goods).

No Trade with Cuba

Under the well-known United States Trading with the Enemy Act, Foreign Assets Control Regulations as well as Cuban Assets Control Regulations specifically apply to exports of foreign affiliates and subsidiaries controlled by Americans abroad, even when they make no use of American components or technology. The curious feature of the Cuban Assets Control Regulations is that they do contain a legal exemption for American subsidiaries to trade with Cuba in cases where United States dollars and United States transport are not involved in the transaction. But this exemption has been nullified in practice through a request by American government officials for 'voluntary compliance' with the regulations. Through the use of such an informal administrative technique, it does appear that American subsidiary companies have voluntarily complied and do not trade with Cuba.

Under the Sherman Act and under section 7 of the Clayton Act, combinations and takeovers involving American firms both within and outside the United States are subject to scrutiny and prosecution. by the United States Department of Justice. This intrusion of American anti-trust law has been subject to substantial criticism in other countries besides Canada.

Numerous examples could be cited where these American regulations have operated contrary to national policy in Canada. The crux of the issue, however, lies neither in the economic cost of exports which have been forgone, nor whether American anti-trust law has had 'good' or 'bad' effects on the Canadian industrial structure. The central issue is the intrusion of American jurisdiction in Canada through the agency of the American subsidiary. The effectiveness of such regulations (as with any set of regulations) is hardly to be measured by the number of 'cases' involved—that is, in violations, near-violations or prosecutions—but rather by the way in which they sanction day-to-day behaviour. There is no reason to believe that these laws are being violated by American subsidiaries. An elaborate administrative apparatus encompassing several American government departments ensures effective enforcement and severe penalties in case of violation.

The United States balance-of-payments difficulties were met initially by voluntary guidelines issued to American subsidiaries suggesting behaviour to bolster the American balance of payments. When the American balance-of-payments position deteriorated further, these voluntary guidelines became mandatory in January 1968 and the original administrative machinery for surveillance was turned to the purpose of regulation and control on new investment and retained earnings of subsidiaries.

As the pressure mounted on the Canadian dollar, owing in part to the behaviour of U.S. subsidiaries, Canada entreated the United States for exemption, and such exemption was granted on condition that Canada give assurances that these regulations would be observed in dealings American subsidiaries might have with third countries. Once more, as in the case of the 'open border' arrangement, exemption from American controls was bought at the price of conformity with American policies.

It is clear why Mr. George Ball, in his recent volume *The Discipline of Power*, was able to offer Canadians the following pessimistic prognosis:

> Sooner or later, commercial imperatives will bring about free movement of all goods back and forth across our long border. When that occurs, or even before it does, it will become unmistakably clear that countries with economies so inextricably intertwined must also have free movement of the other vital factors of production—capital, services, labour. The result will inevitably be substantial economic integration, which will require for its full realization a progressively expanding area of common political decision.

The Watkins Report

The proposals of the Watkins Report are not directed to restricting the inflow of American investment, but rather to increasing its economic benefits and reducing its political costs. For the present, access to new American technology is regarded as indispensable.

On the political side, the most intractable and most sensitive of the issues in the past has been extraterritoriality. Diplomatic representations and negotiations between Canada and the United States have so far not produced general solutions to the problem.

The report entitled "Canada and the United States, Principles for Partnership" issued under joint Canadian and American auspices in June 1965 (the Merchant-Heeney Report) recommended that American subsidiaries in Canada be exempted from American extraterritorial legislation. The investigations of the Task Force, however, revealed that there was no early prospect for such an exemption to be implemented by the American government. Such a general exemption would have been the best solution to the problem. Alternatively, concerted international action might be considered; but with this prospect still in the distant future, the Task Force had to turn to second-best solutions. In the case of export controls, it recommended the creation of a Government Export Trade Agency to purchase goods from American subsidiaries on behalf of the trading corporations of communist countries after such an agency had established that there were no Canadian-owned companies available to supply these goods and that only American law inhibited the export of these goods by such a subsidiary.

Should such an agency be established it would, in my view, very likely not have to be used. The problem with Canada's efforts in the past to solve these issues has been the sole reliance on 'quiet diplomacy', the tradition of goodwill and private discussions between the two countries. Thus Canada has traditionally brought few solid counters to the negotiating table and has neglected to avail itself of relevant legal instruments to cope with the intrusion of foreign law. American diplomats in these negotiations would point helplessly to their laws, which in effect tied their hands, while Canadian diplomats had no parallel backing of their position on their own Statute Books. The creation of effective legal and administrative instruments to countermand American extra-territoriality would move this issue to the conference table in a new framework for negotiation.

The same may be said of the proposal to block American anti-trust legislation in Canada. The Task Force recommended that legislation be enacted to prohibit compliance in Canada with foreign anti-trust decrees (modelled on The Netherlands Economic Competition Act of 1956). Such a conflicting legal obligation may deter American courts from extending their jurisdiction abroad.

A Special Agency

The more general political issue, the shift in decision-making power outside of the country by virtue of foreign control, cannot be completely countermanded if foreign investment is to continue. But it can be counter-balanced by the creation of an effective Canadian government presence and scrutiny of the activities of foreign-owned corporations.

The Task Force recommended that a special agency be created to co-ordinate policies with respect to multinational corporations, now dealt with separately by a number of government departments and agencies. Its functions would include the collection of substantially more detailed information than is available at present; it would review licensing agreements with the aim of reducing restriction to a minimum; it would examine market-sharing and international commodity agreements; and it would review taxation procedures to prevent hidden tax evasion. As mentioned earlier, these are the characteristic areas for wide discretion by foreign oligopolists.

Some parallel measures were also recommended to deal with domestic large corporations, particularly in the area of disclosure of financial and performance data. The relative inefficiency of the Canadian industrial structure, however, requires other broad measures such as a reduction of the tariff and the rationalization of industry through the encouragement of selective mergers under government auspices. The Task Force recommended the creation of a Canada Development Corporation to aid in the financing of industrial rationalization programmes. By retaining a certain equity in these schemes this corporation would thereby provide a Canadian presence, particularly in industries with a high degree of foreign control.[2]

It was intended that the Canada Development Corporation should become a focal point for the mobilization of entrepreneurial and management skills as well as for Canadian capital. Larger projects could be undertaken both in resource development and in secondary industry.

Tax incentives were also recommended by the Task Force to encourage wholly-owned American subsidiaries to offer their shares to Canadians. This would facilitate financial disclosure (such wholly-owned subsidiaries are not required at present to publish their financial statements); it would extend the range of investment choices for Canadian investors; and it would broaden the capital market in Canada. The presence of even a minority interest of Canadian shareholders would loosen the close control of the parent firm over its wholly-owned subsidiary and provide a further concrete basis for supervision by the Canadian government in the name of the Canadian shareholders and the broader national interest.

Finally, it was recommended that the American balance-of-payments guidelines and controls to subsidiaries be countervailed by Canadian guidelines made operative by the necessary surveillance machinery.

These are the major proposals of the Watkins Report. They were offered on the assumption that much could be done to increase the economic benefits and reduce the political costs of foreign investment. At the same time an active programme of economic development and rationalization would be required in the domestic economy if the present level of domestic ownership was not to be further reduced.

Even if all these proposals were implemented, they would form a relatively moderate set of controls on foreign investment compared to those of many other countries. Some of the proposals on extraterritoriality might even be welcomed by American subsidiaries who are today caught in the difficult position of owing allegiance to two masters. In any case, they might help to render genuine some of the present claims of these corporations to multinationality.

The Question of Power

Mr. Ball is not alone in his pessimism about the future possibilities of Canadian independence. General de Gaulle's
adventurous diplomacy with the province of Quebec also
rests on the assumption that Canada as a whole has capitulated
and become a helpless pawn of the United States.

Such opinions are reinforced not only by the massive
amount of American investment in this country but also
by the hitherto *carte blanche* policies of the Canadian government. The former Minister of Trade and Commerce, Mr.
Robert Winters, could conceive of no more effective policy
than issuing a piece of coloured cardboard to American
subsidiaries, containing a list of principles of good corporate
behaviour. This 'scout's honour' approach to the problem was
met in some quarters with the derision which it deserved.

But the deep division and confusion of Canadian public
opinion on this question has itself inhibited more effective
policies. Defining the central issues that surround foreign
investment has proved an elusive and often frustrating task.
In the name of an objective empiricism, some insisted that
the main dimensions of this economic problem must necessarily be judged on economic criteria. In practice, these
criteria turned out to be linked to the theory of markets of
liberal economics. Such a frame of reference has no room
within it for non-economic factors, including such vital
political issues as national independence (the power to make
decisions in the national interest).

Buried beneath discussions of economic performance,
efficiency and export policies of foreign-owned firms is an
issue almost invisible to liberal western societies, namely, the
issue of power in the economy. Crude but illuminating
analogies can be drawn with sensitive national issues such as
defence. Here the loss of decision-making power by virtue of
foreign control would instantly be recognised to be a vital
concern in its own right, quite apart from other criteria such
as efficiency and economic cost. Whatever balance is struck
in the end among diverse economic and political considerations relating to domestic and foreign control, no one regards
foreign control of defence as a matter of indifference. In an

uncertain world, the loss of decision-making power in this area of vital national interest is instantly discernible and generally regarded as a high cost.

The new world of the multinational corporation focuses on the crucial factor of the future—the new technology. Control over this technology, its disposition, the distribution of its benefits, its social consequences, becomes an increasingly vital national interest in its own right. Loss of even partial control over this technology can hardly be a matter of indifference. That is why the grass-roots but often inarticulate unease over foreign control is to be taken seriously. The economy is the home of the new technology and the appropriate agency of control today (whatever the speculations about a distant future) is the nation-state, still the major locus of power in our society. The fine nexus of co-ordination of interdependent technological systems, the elements of uncertainty about these new and very significant processes, the safeguards required—all of these questions converge on one issue, the locus of power in the economy.

But the political heritage of liberal thought—Lord Acton and all the rest—has relegated the issue of power to a netherworld of shadowy suspicion. Economists have contributed to this intellectual vanishing act by continual assurances of the justice, efficiency and benevolence of market institutions. Foreign capitalists do not differ from domestic ones; all are profit maximizers and dance to the same refrain. Notions of the 'mixed economy' are merely a variant on the main theme and have hardly come to grips with the issue. But the new world of the multinational corporation has shattered the built-in harmonies of Adam Smith.

Few other countries exhibit at the present time the wide range of problems posed by American investment in Canada nor benefit from it to as great a degree. The Canadian case is unusual in many respects because of the special relationship of the two countries. But other countries have also begun to discover that geographic distances and indigenous cultural traditions will begin to count for much less in the future as a safeguard of independence. The global expansion of the American corporation will be impeded only temporarily by the present U.S. balance-of-payments difficulties.

Neither the nation-state nor the multinational corporation will quietly remove itself from the scene. If we are to aim for a *modus vivendi* rather than a costly political fracas, then the points at issue must be defined clearly and new instruments created that relate to the nature of the problems which are posed. Diffuse waves of unease and xenophobic slogans will carry the day unless issues are clearly identified and effective policies formulated that span both the economic and the political dimensions of the problem.

The Watkins Report is a major step in that direction in Canada. The Report stands midway between those who argue that the entire problem is imaginary and those who argue that it is already too late. Even if the pessimists are right, Canada may still be able to exit with a measure of dignity.

July 1968

NOTES

1. Ottawa: The Queen's Printer. It was the original intention of the Canadian government to issue a White Paper on the subject, but it has only published the Task Force Report without endorsement.

2. One example of what is intended can be provided by the refrigerator industry in Canada. Seven of the nine firms in the industry are American-controlled, virtually duplicating the number of firms in the United States ("the miniature replica effect"). Most plants in Canada produce 40,000 to 60,000 refrigerators per year when the most efficient level of output would be about 200,000 units per year. Ideally, therefore, the Canadian market should be supplied by about two large firms in order to achieve the lowest unit cost. Rationalization of the industry would proceed on a voluntary basis, providing, of course, that American anti-trust legislation is countermanded for these American subsidiaries.

THE WAHN REPORT

One of the jokes in Czechoslovakia these days runs as follows:

Q: "Why is Czechoslovakia the most internationalist of all countries?"

A: "It is does not interfere in anyone's internal affairs, not even its own."

Without exaggerating the analogy with Canada, some wry thoughts are prompted by the skeptical and indifferent re-action of the Press to the Wahn Report on foreign ownership. A national schizophrenia develops apace. On August 15th for example, the Toronto *Globe and Mail* warned against the export of nine trillion cubic feet of natural gas to the United States under its new banner that "Canadians feel a new na-tionalism." All well and good. The very next day it (pre-sumably a different editorial writer) warned against the pro-posals of the Wahn Report because they would involve too much bureaucracy—"just about the biggest bureaucracy this country has yet conceived." What can one say about a position that is keen to preserve our control over natural resources and hesitant about the fate of our industry and technology?

It was fashionable at one point to think of Canada as the most advanced of the underdeveloped countries. Whatever truth there is in the notion may be more political than eco-nomic. The strange deficiency in this country's makeup—what is conspicuously absent if one thinks about it—is the instinct for national survival. What is second nature to every other country, is the weakest and most fledgling element of our national existence.

Think of the 1960's, for example, when so much of our energy and national ambition was shunted off into a dis-embodied and misplaced idealism. Certain phrases were symbolic, such as that Canada should become an 'international nation'. Again, a moment that remains vividly in my mind from a meeting of the Learned Societies in 1964, was an impassioned talk by a professor of economics at Carleton University. In the strongest warning he could give against nationalism he intoned: "Those who have not learned the lessons of the twentieth century, are condemned to repeat them."

Keep in mind what was happening at the time: great stretches of our natural resources were being alienated by the Americans, Canadian companies were being bought up left and right, the top of the 'Vertical Mosaic' was beginning to come apart, as our financial scions sold out to the multi-national corporations and gave up. And what were we solemnly warned against? The possibility that we would become another Nazi Germany, and the sea of totalitarian repression would overwhelm us if we manifested any response at all in the protection of our own interests.

In retrospect, this whole tinselled idealism is amusing but sad: the overdeveloped panacea of lowering the tariff, the ethereal goals of world federalism, the simplistic Keynesian formulas to cure both inflation and unemployment (ignoring how closely dependent we were on the American economy), peacemaking as our ordained calling in the world. . . . So went our best academic minds, many of them shaped by a common experience: Graduate School in Chicago or M.I.T.; admittedly, a genuine fondness and concern for this country but a *trained incapacity* to respond to what was happening. The innocence and irrelevance of that generation's outlook only becomes apparent as we grope laboriously back to some national reference points that relate to the real world and to the Canadian situation as it is.

We realize now, as we begin to shake off all these cobwebs, that we have sold out the country in the grip of some powerful myths about being desperately short of capital (the second richest country in the world!). Thus we have put ourselves in a position where the outflows of dividends and related payments to American owners now *exceed* the capital inflows, and it will all get worse. We wonder today if there is a road back at all. We talk anxiously about economic growth as we strain toward our three per cent growth rate—and are outpaced four-fold in the rate of growth by Japan which has, paradoxically, one of the best developed systems of control of foreign capital.

These are the residual elements of the national mood amidst which the Wahn Report descends.

The Wahn Report *(The Eleventh Report of the Standing Committee on External Affairs and National Defence Respecting Canada-U.S. Relations)* retraces substantially the itinerary laid out by the Watkins Report. The main recommendations that are reaffirmed include a central government agency (the Canadian Ownership and Control Bureau) to co-ordinate and supervise all government activities concerning foreign corporations, measures to bring about greater Canadian equity participation in foreign firms (a long-term and qualified goal of fifty-one per cent), stringent laws to countervail American extraterritorial jurisdiction over U.S. subsidiaries in Canada, and the Canada Development Corporation. There are also some important new proposals which highlight in retrospect, the omissions of the Watkins Report: Future takeovers of Canadian business could not take place without the consent of the Canadian Ownership and Control Bureau and "key sectors" of the economy would be identified "where no further takeovers would be allowed."

The Wahn Report improves on the Watkins Report on the issue of extraterritoriality. The latter report recommended a government export trade agency to insure that export orders from communist countries are filled where American subsidiaries are enjoined from trading by the U.S. Trading with the Enemy Act. The Wahn Report proposes a simpler solution, namely, that such subsidiaries be made subject to existing public utility regulations applicable to railroads and telephone companies; that is, they be required to sell to all credit-worthy customers to the extent that products are available. This would be supervised by the Canadian Ownership and Control Bureau and would avoid the creation of an additional agency.

Thus we have another demonstration that the seemingly insoluble issue of American extraterritorial jurisdiction in this country (as we thought of it) *is* capable of solution. Admittedly this problem would best be solved at the diplomatic level, if the Americans were to withdraw once and for all their claims to control over their subsidiaries abroad. But Canadian diplomats could now come to the bargaining table with a package of domestic legislation on the books to back them up. Our pious pleading in the past for administrative exemptions on an ad hoc basis was a testament only to our impoverished imagination and to our acquiescence in satellitic status. To wrap up the package, the Wahn Committee recommends that any company that continues to be subject to American extraterritorial control be taken over by a federal government trustee for the duration of this foreign jurisdiction. At last the message is coming through loud and clear.

The Wahn Report is significant as a grassroots move by M.P.'s that has won wide acceptance by representatives of all parties. The Report is larger in scope than indicated by most press comments—the abolition of *Time Magazine*'s tax privileges, the creation of greater autonomy for Canadian trade unions, the brief but important emphasis on cultural factors—all speak of an awakening consciousness of this country's major dilemma.

The Report sets a standard against which subsequent proposals will be judged, particularly those which Mr. Gray is preparing for the Cabinet, and which should form the basis of a foreign investment code later this fall.

This is probably the last chance we will have for an all-party endorsation of a foreign investment programme. In a country already sharply divided on the issue, the government can only expect *more* dissension rather than less if it fails to move. More radical solutions than the Wahn report will undoubtedly receive greater impetus if all we get is more foot-dragging by the government in the fall.

This extended failure to interfere in our own internal affairs is best summed up in George Bain's sardonic statement:

"If there is one thing that worries Canadians more than economic domination, it is that someone, sometime, will try to do something about it."

September 1970

THE GRAY REPORT

The ship of state floats aimlessly toward the next election on a sea of unalleviated mediocrity. The sails are hoisted, and on the rigging we see all the trappings of flow charts, 'priorities', cabinet committees, budgeting of the P.M.'s time, computer analysis, and a gaggle of experts stumbling over each other in the halls of the East Block. Meanwhile in Quebec, we are reaping the bitter harvest of the War Measures Act as French Canadians polarize around militant groups. In the area of foreign ownership, a travesty of a policy has been offered that will block further progress for the lifetime of this government. Having removed the state from the bedrooms of the nation as its single achievement, the government has now applied this prohibitive injunction to the board rooms as well.

Whatever time the Prime Minister's entourage, the Supergroup, could spare from their diagrams and visions of 'efficiency', they have devoted to the neglect of the issues that will determine the survival of this country. The old consensus politics in its drabbest and most unimaginative form has come into its own once more. On three occasions in the past four years, a Liberal government has produced a decent draft of a foreign ownership policy and in each case these policies have been repudiated. The Watkins Report, the Wahn Report and now the Gray Report are the tributes that impotence pays to conscience and the will to survive. The root of the government's paralysis is consensus politics at its lowest and most demeaning level; the Spirit of Kingsmere is alive and well and living in the senior echelons of the Liberal cabinet.

Credit where credit is due. The Governor General's award for spineless accommodation must go, by virtue of seniority, to Mitchell Sharp. Not everyone will remember that Mr. Sharp led the fight in the Pearson cabinet to prevent the tabling of the Watkins Report. The decision to publish it (with a disclaimer) was arrived at by the slimmest of margins. It was one factor of which we were fully cognizant when the *Canadian Forum* editors decided to bring out the abbreviated version of the Gray Report. Meantime Mr. Sharp has distinguished himself as a benefactor of the New York firm, Business International, in attempting to arrange a meeting of the Cabinet with an international lobby for the multinational corporations in April. At $600 a head, American executives were to be given the opportunity to lobby the Cabinet in favour of muting any action to control American subsidiaries in this country. The meeting was cancelled when the Press reported the details, but Elliot Haynes needn't have bothered with his string-pulling in high places. The multinational corporations could not have asked for a better policy than the one the government provided. Mitchell Sharp must be drawing some satisfaction from his double role as Minister of External Affairs both for the multinational corporations and for this country.

Mr. Pepin's agile calisthenics as he 'took over' Mr. Herb Gray at the press conference suggested that the government could take no stronger stand on foreign control because of the opposition of the 'provinces'. The reactions of the provinces were at best mixed and not monolithic as interpreted by the government. Ontario and Saskatchewan claimed that the government's policy did not go far enough. Alberta, in turn, had beaten everyone to the draw by actually implementing the main principles of the Gray Report in the case of the Syncrude consortium extracting oil from the tar sands. Lougheed insists that shares in the company be made available to Canadian investors, that more purchasing and processing by the company be done in Canada, and that there be Canadian directors and managers in the company. Lougheed's objection is clearly not to the principles of the Gray Report but to the absence of a voice for the province in its implementation. Claude Ryan and Claude Lemelin argued similarly for a screening process in Quebec adapted to that province's own priorities—something which would have made a foreign investment programme more palatable to all the provinces had the machinery been organized to take their legitimate interests into account. Other proposals to stimulate provincial development had also been offered in the original draft of the Gray Report such as an expanded Industrial Development Bank. All of these proposals were ignored by the government. The strong popular support across the country for a full screening agency indicated by recent Gallup polls was also dismissed. The least common denominator was invoked in classic Liberal fashion to justify the ideological premises on foreign investment long held by the Prime Minister, Mitchell Sharp, Jean-Luc Pepin and Bud Drury. None of this was convincing.

Timidity combined with the absence of a Canadian development strategy have once again confirmed the present government's dogmatic commitment to maintain open season in the Canadian economy for everyone else's economic priorities but our own.

The full, 523-page report recalls the familiar tale about the "dangers of excessive concentration on natural resource extraction" and the "few jobs" it generates. It tells us about the "truncated firms," the subsidiaries of foreign corporations that may have "less opportunity for innovation and entrepreneurship, fewer export sales, fewer supporting services, less training of Canadian personnel in various skills, less specialized product development aimed at Canadian needs or tastes" and so on.

We are told about several ways in which foreign direct investment weakens domestic control of the Canadian economy and that multinational enterprises "are less responsive to macroeconomic tools such as monetary and fiscal policy." We are told also that direct U.S. investment has a "deficit impact on the Canadian balance of payments after a period of ten years," and that "new capital inflows tend to force up the exchange rate and make Canadian industry less competitive."

In spite of the sentimental attachment of many economists to the 'free market' to look after everything, there can hardly be an excuse any longer for doing nothing. The 'free market' is a vanishing institution in the age of the multinational corporation with its globally oriented administrative decisions. (The auto pact that governs over twenty per cent of our foreign trade is a case in point.) The report warns us quite properly that "governments cannot rely on the 'invisible hand' to give their country an equitable share of world growth and distribution of wealth."

Beyond the descriptions of the problem there are some careful and conservative proposals in the report for dealing with global corporations that are in a position to put their own and their home countries' priorities above the national interests of this country.

The case rests, not on the actual demonstration of misdemeanours by foreign corporations, but on an 'internal audit' function, which is at least as necessary in looking after a national economy as it is in every bank and major business establishment in the country.

The full scope of the review agency envisaged in the report extends to all foreign investment in this country and not just to the paltry issue of takeovers, as the government proposes.

(In 1969 takeovers accounted for only twenty per cent of the growth of foreign-controlled corporations and in 1968 takeovers were only five per cent of the total.)

The most serious criticism of the government's emasculated policy is offered in the report itself:

> If the review agency blocked the takeover of a Canadian firm because the foreigner would not add anything of significance to its operations in terms of technology, managerial efficiency, markets, etc., there would be nothing to stop this particular foreign direct investor from setting up a company in Canada and perhaps managing to drive the Canadian out of business.

We can only face the long-run political consequences of the government's neglect with the deepest pessimism. If our main premise is correct, the increasing loss of control over our new technology, the continued distortion of priorities in emphasizing natural resource exploitation and the growing dependence of this country on research and development and managerial expertise, will increase the sense of powerlessness and the erosion of our autonomy in vital areas. Many Canadians may continue to face such a prospect with only slightly troubled equanimity. Others, a small group, will react very differently.

In the same week in which the Gray Report appeared, a book on Canadian education was published containing the following passage:

> . . .since no improvement has been achieved in three years of struggle on this particular issue (i.e. foreign professors) and ten years of struggle on the issue in its largest sense,— that is why, paradoxically, for those who are most seriously concerned with Canadian survival, the possibility of revolution—violent and/or other—must be before them as never before in Canadian history.

The author may be correct. Unless the next election produces some unexpected results, the Trudeau government may come to realize during the next few years that it has sowed in English Canada the early seeds of the F.L.C.

May 1972

Functional Socialism

5

A Canadian edition of Professor Adler-Karlsson's book, *Functional Socialism,* [1] is of more than passing interest in this country. Indeed, it could be a major event. Canadians have looked to Swedish developments in recent years partly because our two countries have been close competitors in the race for the second highest standard of living in the world. Our resource-oriented economies and our high level of industrial development are very similar. Beyond the impressive statistics however, there are also the common traditions of peaceful political change and the rapid evolution of comprehensive social welfare policies. In international affairs we are both middle-rank countries, and many Canadians envy Sweden's successful neutralist role in the Cold War. Yet intellectual interchange between the two countries has fallen far short of what it should have been.

Professor Adler-Karlsson's book is a valuable one for Canadians, but not only for the reasons cited above. He has unwittingly given us a theoretical key to an overwhelming problem faced in this country, though one which Sweden hardly knows at all—foreign domination of the economy. This is not a problem in which Professor Adler-Karlsson is disinterested, but it is not the problem to which his theory of functional socialism addressed itself in the first instance. Nevertheless, his ideas are bound to create a flash of recognition in Canadian readers.

Canadians have become profoundly troubled by the erosion of our national independence. Two thirds of our manufacturing and great stretches of our natural resources are now under foreign control, and every day we seem to uncover fresh constraints which this imposes on our ability to formulate our own economic policies. In the manufacturing sector, to cite one example, we have become a miniature replica of the American economy; the result is that there are often too many firms to serve our much smaller market efficiently. But the rationalization of industry through mergers of these small firms is impeded by the grip which American anti-trust law retains on American-owned subsidiaries.

In other realms of economic policy we have seen, in the past decade, how closely both our monetary policy and the rate of inflation have been tied to those of the Americans, by virtue of the continuing integration of the economies of the two countries. It has been costly to us in many ways, such as the substantial outflow of dividends.

I leave aside the overwhelming cultural dependence, the significant military dependence and the constraints on foreign policy which the American connection has imposed. At this late date we do not need to be persuaded of the facts; we need some way to keep from being mesmerized by them.

Professor Adler-Karlsson's approach of *functional socialism* has important implications for all Canadians—whatever point they occupy on the political spectrum, and whether they are socialists or not. He presents us with a Swedish method for dealing with this external control which provides, at the least, a common basis of discussion for all those interested in reclaiming our economy and regaining our independence.

Over and above its significance for the issue of independence, this theory offers an important approach to domestic reform in other areas which are of particular significance to those on the left. It is to these two groups, then, that my own comments are addressed: first to all those who care about the survival of Canada, and secondly to those whose approach is on the left.

It is estimated that, at market prices, the amount of American long-term investment in Canada exceeds forty billion dollars. Confronted with this enormous sum, many Canadians retreat into despair: we are not in a position financially to reverse the tide, they conclude, nor in fact to do anything significant about the issue. 'Buying back', whether with public funds, private funds, or a combination of both, seems a hopeless task.

There are many significant steps, however, in my view, that can and should be taken towards restoring financial control. We should, through legislation and incentives, open the stock of wholly-owned U.S. subsidiaries to Canadian investors, to the extent that our capital market can absorb these shares. The Canada Development Corporation can also play a significant role in mobilizing both public and private capital.

Nevertheless, these proposals seem, to an increasing number of Canadians, to be a prescription of too little too late. It is for this reason that we are being urged to nationalize the multinational corporations, to take over title to their Canadian holdings. And it is at this critical point that Professor Adler-Karlsson's theory becomes relevant, since it is essentially a theory which separates *titles* to property from the *functions* or powers of this property. In practice, this provides an approach to restoring an increasing level of Canadian control and advancing further on the road to self-determination, without having to scare up forty billion dollars on the one hand, nor persuade ourselves to nationalize I.B.M. on the other.

The theory is quite straightforward and illuminates the close commitment western societies have traditionally had to the concept of private property, and even more to that large cluster of property rights (in Adler-Karlsson's term, the *functions*) which come with ownership or title. In the case of a factory or corporation, for example, the title to property includes the right to set wages, hours, and conditions of work (subject of course to whatever rights trade unions succeed in bargaining away), to set prices of components and final products, to determine the timing and extent of economic expansion, to invest or take over other companies, to distribute profits and dividends, to send sums abroad, and even to pollute the environment.

But these rights can be subsumed individually and in groups by society at large, leaving the titles themselves unchanged.

The separation of titles and property rights comes as a somewhat startling departure from the traditional way we have thought about these matters (though not from our actual practice). Liberal philosophers from Locke onwards have built their theories on the recognition of property rights as a *package*, and have designed around it particular concepts of freedom and a free society. Indeed socialist philosophers made the same assumptions, even though they drew opposite conclusions. Marx, for example, based his entire sociology of capitalist institutions on the indivisibility of the cluster of rights traditionally associated with ownership of the means of production. It was a correct assumption in terms of the realities of a nineteenth-century bourgeois society, and he drew the logical conclusions—namely, since the property rights flowed from the title, only expropriation of titles would restore these rights to society.

Today, in most Western countries, property rights are no longer considered inviolable and democratic practices have been extended to subsume (through legislation, regulation, taxation and collective bargaining) successive functions or rights previously considered the prerogative of owners of property. Indeed, most advances that have been made in the past century in the realm of greater democracy, equality and social welfare have necessarily either abridged or subsumed the classical rights of property.

Professor Adler-Karlsson's conclusions from the Scandinavian experience do not rule out nationalization of industry where a clear and specific case can be made, but they rest in the end on a faith in an evolving democratic process—that greater control of those functions which are required to meet ongoing social and political objectives can be acquired by legislation. He states:

Let us formally socialize those sectors where particularly good reasons demand such an action. But for the rest, let us continue the rather successful course, that of socialization of the most essential functions of ownership.

This simple proposal provides Canadians with a common framework for discussing foreign control of our economy—a framework within which all shades of political opinion may participate. It is crucial to appreciate why this is so.

Professor Adler-Karlsson is not proposing a new or wild-eyed approach to the problems of ownership. On the contrary, he is drawing our attention to *exactly what we are already doing*. The effect is liberating. As long as the debate over ownership is polarized into two camps, with each side accusing its opponents of 'socialism' or 'capitalism', it is unlikely (at least in an affluent country) that very much will change. But quite apart from that, neither side is talking about the characteristics of the immediate world which they inhabit.

For it is not a question of principle *whether* any of the functions of ownership should be brought under public control. A great many already are. The only question is *which* functions of ownership should be under public control. When that is realized, the slogans fall away and the serious, difficult business of deciding what kind of country we want can begin; national debate can re-enter the world in which the participants live. It is even possible that national action can begin.

Let us set aside the debate, then, about nationalization versus free enterprise. If we are to have a Foreign Investment Control Agency, what precisely should it control? Which of the decisions now made in board-rooms in New York, Chicago and Washington are vital to Canadian interests? By what new laws and administrative procedures should these decisions be taken over and made by Canadians? Will existing foreign subsidiaries be allowed to expand and take over additional Canadian firms? Will they be allowed to set any level of royalties, management fees or dividends they wish, to be paid to the parent company? Are there 'key industries' whose decisions are more vital to us and which should, consequently, be stripped of more of their property rights? Should any be nationalized outright?

Conservatives, liberals, social democrats and socialists—all who are concerned with the national interest and with restoring decision-making powers to Canadians—share a common concern in these specific and topical questions, and acquire thereby a common basis for debating immediate policy issues. By speaking in terms of functions, we can begin a debate in which Canadians might even discover that they substantially agree. In the process, both 'buying back' and nationalization of foreign investment cease to appear as the only way of doing something meaningful toward restoring Canadian independence.

Professor Adler-Karlsson, obviously, does not recommend which functions of foreign ownership Canadians should socialize, since foreign ownership is not his immediate problem. But he sketches a position from which we can begin that debate in earnest among ourselves.

This approach may interest liberal and conservative Canadians, but is it an acceptable position for the left? Does it water down the doctrine of socialism too far? Some Canadian socialists have argued that nationalization can help solve both the problem of Canadian independence and the problems of life in a capitalist system—that the resolution of both sets of problems coincides. I wish to argue against this position: the struggle for Canadian independence must come first because we will lose it forever if we wait until a majority of Canadians are prepared to nationalize I.B.M. and Inco; furthermore, many of the domestic problems which nationalization is intended to solve cannot be touched by that means. In expanding on this case, there are certain theoretical questions which need to be raised, particularly those which concern the left.

Over the past few years, voices from the right and the left have begun to carry a strangely similar ring as they discuss ownership. In the 1960's Professor Harry Johnson led the crusade against Canadian nationalism and against the growing concern about the inflow of foreign investment. "Are Canadian capitalists different from American capitalists?" he asked. His answer, rooted entirely in the liberal market mentality, was: No! All capitalists have their own typical rules of behaviour as laid down by the free market; it is illusory to imagine that their nationality makes any difference to anything. What the world is about is free markets, so that *foreign* investment is by definition a specious problem.

On the left one often hears a remarkably similar question, in relation to regaining control of the Canadian economy. "Is there any point in replacing American capitalists with Canadian capitalists?" "Why the struggle for independence if it is not for the sake of creating a socialist society?" "Is the exercise worth it?" Thus the Waffle group of the N.D.P. argues ambiguously for "nationalization of the leading sectors of the Canadian economy," both as a means to independence and also as a primary objective in itself. There is an unresolved tension in this approach.

The nation disappears from the market model of society. But, curiously enough, it also seems to play at best a tenuous role in the socialist view of society as primarily a struggle of classes.

A nationalist position, however, would argue that the whole should take precedence over the struggle of its parts. I believe that an independent capitalist Canada is preferable to a dependent capitalist Canada, particularly if it has begun to learn that the functions of capital ownership can be brought under public control. I believe that we must first remove the American vise on our economic development and restore the levers of control to this country, if we wish at a second stage to opt out of the American way of life. The reason for these priorities is simple: if we do not regain Canada in the next few years, there will be no Canada left to regain. Yet there is no doubt that this priority poses a serious dilemma for those interested in social change.

There is an important sense in which nationalism is inherently a conservative force; that is, it attempts to conserve and protect existing social institutions from outside penetration, in the name of the autonomy and self-determination of that society. This is at least one reason why nationalism has reawakened in the past decades, as new empires began their world-wide march. It is perhaps the most persuasive reason for nationalism today.

This is an obvious point in the realm of our cultural, social and political institutions. The conservative nature of nationalism becomes more controversial to the left, however, when we realize that in the economy, nationalism creates a serious tension with the indigenous forces working for social change. These forces are suspicious of a preservation of the *status quo* in the name of national independence.

The positions taken by different countries (more precisely, by their 'national liberation' movements) vary substantially on this issue, and the question is in the end a matter of political judgement related to the strategy and tactics of 'national liberation' in any given country. (The evidence from the third world runs both ways, but both the Algerian movement and the Chinese adopted a 'united front' approach which included the local bourgeoisie.)

In the Canadian case the nationalist movement, despite recent stirrings, is on the whole weak; it must, in my view, mobilize all classes and segments of society in order to be successful. An attempt to link the restoration of autonomous control to wholesale nationalization is bound to disrupt this effort and create strong internal opposition. To seek to nationalize the 'commanding heights' of the economy, for example in banking and finance, is to take on the opposition of the strongest remaining sector of the Canadian bourgeoisie. If there were world enough, and time. . . .

My own notion of the proper strategy is a two-stage approach: the first is restoration of effective national control on the basis of a non-partisan approach supported by all groups concerned with our independence. At the second stage, we will be able to move much more effectively towards social change on the basis of indigenous and democratic forces—with real though limited successes under their belts—which aim to alter the miniature replica of the U.S.-style business structure we now have.

There is no doubt that this business structure is unsatisfactory. Concerning the domestic issues which it creates, the left should consider the implications of Professor Adler-Karlsson's argument in the area he originally intended, namely the strategy and objectives of social change. The failures and difficulties of relying primarily on nationalization of industry are apparent everywhere, from the post-war experiences of the English Labour government to the critical economic problems of eastern Europe today. It is often conceded that nationalizing industry alone may produce nothing more than a new bureaucratic overlay, often termed 'state capitalism'.

In this sphere, the displacement of many functions should not be from the corporation to the state at all, but from the corporation to its members. The critical issue is the devolution of control, the attempt to institute greater democracy at the workplace and in the community. This is a problem which is equally present in the public and the private sectors of our society. The fact, for example, that the public school system, the C.B.C., various public utilities or the C.N.R. are already nationalized, obviously provides no assurance that these social objectives are being, or will be realized. Nor would further nationalization of manufacturing industries offer any similar guarantee of democratic control.

Some may argue, however, that the present proposals seem to amount to nothing more than government regulation of industry—a procedure that has often proved disappointing in the past, particularly where regulatory boards themselves became the captives of the industry being regulated. Are the present proposals open to the same objections as those against nationalization?

Let us recall that the *traditional* basis for regulation was usually a very limited one, namely the control of monopoly powers where an industry was not subject to the discipline of competition. Regulation has therefore centred on control of prices, and to a lesser extent on the contraction or expansion of services as in the case of public utilities and transportation. Its aim was to protect the public interest by simulating the results that a competitive industry would have produced in order to guard against financial exploitation of the public.

The questions raised by foreign ownership however and the objective of national independence centre on a much wider range of functions—research and development policy, patent and licensing agreements, expansion and further takeovers of new companies by existing foreign-owned firms, Canadian personnel at the operating and management levels and so on. The aim is not simply to simulate or restore the operations of a competitive economy, but to safeguard the national interest, and substantially restore Canadian control on a very broad front.

Much of this will necessarily be done by government agencies of one kind or another. But beyond that the main issue veers away from *both* nationalization and government regulation. It centres instead on subsuming control or property rights for democratic decision-making.

In the field of industry, the immediate objective falls directly within the scope of Professor Adler-Karlsson's analysis. Traditional and so-called 'inviolable' property rights must be successively brought within the scope of workers' control to achieve greater democracy at the work place. This would be accomplished through the extension of collective bargaining to the various sections of the 'management rights' clauses of the industrial labour agreement. In other areas of community life, the upsurge in popular activities centring on greater control of the neighbourhood and the municipality, the schools, the universities, the media and the transport system are now a growing feature of most urban communities in Canada.

At the national and local levels then, the thrusts of our politics converge. The primary issue in both cases is not titles to property but democratic control of functions or rights. We must specify in detail what functions we wish to bring under democratic control and deploy our best energies to achieving these directly. If, as is sometimes argued by social-ists, we cannot muster political support for such popular control under present conditions of private ownership, can we indeed hope to muster support instead for outright national-ization, an infinitely more difficult political task?

The battle for democratic control is not a matter for complacency, and the resilience of our democratic system will be tested to its limits against strong opposition, both domestic and foreign. My hope is that in the next decade the battle for both national and community control will not be shunted down the wrong alley. What political strength we have for this battle should be deployed in the most effective way. Fervency in the pursuit of the classical socialist objective of nationalization runs the risk of compounding our failure to achieve an independent Canada. The prerequisite to realizing whatever kind of Canada we may wish for the future is the restoration and safeguarding of our independent powers of decision. Those who add needless risks to this task assume a grave responsibility.

July 1970

1. *Reclaiming the Canadian Economy: A Swedish Approach through Functional Socialism*, Toronto: Anansi, 1970.

The Search for Independence

6

FRACTURED NATIONALISM

Canada has become the land of the *cri de coeur*. Across the political spectrum and on the most varied occasions the listener will pick up the cries of the heart, now as a manifesto, now as a personal credo, occasionally as an editorial outburst. The cries are worth listening to and pondering, for the barely ruffled political waters conceal some deeper currents running beneath the surface.

The Waffle

The most important *cri de coeur* last month was "For an Independent Socialist Canada" (The Watkins Manifesto). The title was the message: Canadian independence from the American empire could only be achieved by socialism. The Manifesto was a measure of the growing impatience of a segment of the left in the N.D.P. including Watkins, Laxer, Laurier Lapierre, Charles Taylor and Cy Gonick; time was running out as the American economic takeover moved ahead, and no effective action was to be seen on the horizon.

The document was addressed to members of the N.D.P. with the aim of creating a 'left grouping' within the party. We will know more about the fate of the Manifesto and its adherents at the end of this month when the N.D.P.'s national convention takes place. Our concern for the moment is with the national significance of the document rather than the party verdict of the N.D.P.

A surprisingly large number of subjects are touched upon in the Manifesto apart from the issue of independence: the extension of workers' control in industry, regional disparities, Quebec ("two nations, one struggle"), the extension of public services and the erosion of the Canadian business class. The hysterical tirade of the daily press from coast to coast against the Manifesto, failed either to take note of some of the genuine merits of the document or to argue the issues as presented. (George Bain's column in *The Globe and Mail*, September 6, and Dalton Camp in *The Telegram*, September 8, are the two exceptions.)

I write as a critic of the document and as one who is unable to endorse its major formulations however urgent and well-intentioned the cry for Canadian independence. My reservations centre first on the kind of socialism which is proposed— namely, full-scale nationalization:

> Capitalism must be replaced by socialism, by national planning of investment and by the public ownership of the means of production in the interests of the Canadian people as a whole.

This has a ring about it that is more fundamentalist than radical. We are back to the socialism of the Regina Manifesto but attempting to apply it to a different problem than was originally intended. The early 1930's witnessed the collapse of Canadian capitalism with massive unemployment and hunger as the main issues. In the days preceding Keynes and prior to the economic stimulus of military spending, the nationalization of industry appeared to be the only solution to the creation of jobs and the restoration of production. Economic independence was not an issue at the time and there is not a word in the Regina Manifesto about foreign control of the economy.

Admittedly, there are additional problems that are inherent in a capitalist economy. The distortion of priorities (as between the public and private sectors) is a problem common to 'corporate capitalism' regardless of its nationality, as the authors of the Manifesto indicate. It is not clear however, why this distortion requires the same solution as was advocated for the depression of the 1930's. Some discrimination in technique is required, related to the problem at hand. This applies as well to the problem of economic independence.

Toward the end of the Manifesto the authors do qualify their position:

> . . .extensive public control over investment and nationalization of the commanding heights of the economy, such as key resource industries, finance and credit, and industries strategic to planning our economy.

It seems to me that all of this requires rethinking. There is the question of financing the massive nationalization which the authors contemplate; the cost of buying out the Americans as a start, boggles the mind. How to retain access to the stream of new technology generated by the multi-national corporation is a second question. It is odd, moreover, that the authors of the Manifesto hardly take note of the trends in socialist thinking in the West in the last two decades that provide for alternatives to nationalization. One broad stream of socialist thought distinguishes between *titles* to property and property *rights* or *functions* that attach to the titles. In the industrial sphere for example, titles to property include the right to set wages and working hours, to allocate capital, to establish new investment, to set prices on the product, to distribute dividends, to invest abroad, etc. Individually and together these powers can be modified, controlled or subsumed altogether by legislation and regulation. It is not necessary for the government to acquire the *titles* to property in order to exercise these functions on behalf of the public interest. They are powers equally available for the control of foreign and domestic corporations. Such an approach requires that objectives be spelled out in specific terms, and appropriate regulatory functions selected to meet these objectives. Different controls for example, may be needed for 'distortion' than are needed for 'independence'. Future takeovers that are not in the national interest may be blocked by such devices as the proposed monopolies commission recently suggested by the Economic Council (although needless to say, this was hardly the Council's intention). The expansion of the public sector and the establishment of development corporations offer a further range of possibilities.

The fact that the present Liberal government shows not the least inclination to exercise these prerogatives, is no reason to dust off the battering ram of wholesale nationalization. But I doubt that any of this is new to the authors of the Manifesto. Why then take the road back to nationalization? Is there a hidden political rationale which governs this unexpected economic logic?

My second reservation about the Manifesto is its reaction to the United States, which is placed at the forefront of the argument. When the Manifesto characterizes America as "militarism abroad and racism at home," it utters an obvious truth but neither a comprehensive nor necessarily an enduring one. The phrase comes out of the handbooks of the American left, and the present reality is obvious for the world to see. But we should remember the implicit message of the American left: 'there is another America out of which we have sprung and to which we shall return'. With apologies to H. Rap Brown, both violence *and* Staughton Lynd are as American as cherry pie. Is the raison d'être of Canadian independence to be based on the permanent victory of violence and the permanent failure of the American left? If by chance America were to change course and become a social democracy, would the authors of the Manifesto logically be required to go continentalist? A Manifesto which pivots on a reaction to America at a low point in its history is, in my view, not an enduring basis on which to construct the edifice of Canadian independence.

The political significance of the Manifesto, however, does not lie entirely in the strength or weakness of its substantive formulations. Its stated objective is to create a new and coherent political grouping on the Canadian left, more radically committed to the issue of Canadian independence. But how is such a group to be crystallized out of the scatter of diverse elements in the N.D.P. and out of a party platform that has 'everything'? The political genesis of such a group can only be accomplished by a signalling process based on symbols that would render an unambiguous message to the sympathetic listener. It is in the end, a sign of the weakness of the Canadian left, that the only two such unambiguous signals are on the one hand, classical and outdated—the Regina Manifesto—and on the other, external and derivative—America as 'militarism abroad and racism at home'. The authors of the Manifesto gave prior importance to the clarity of the signal over the substance of the text. From a purely political standpoint, they may have been correct, for the crystallization of this political grouping has now begun to move swiftly. (I do not mean to imply incidentally, that the centre and the right in Canada could be rallied by symbols that are less cliché-ridden. The opposite is probably true.)

The national importance of such a new grouping goes beyond the number of adherents it will manage to secure. It is a fringe development, but a movement on the fringe is itself of substantial significance. It may be the clearest indicator of what is happening in the less articulate median, a bellwether of the silent centre. We should read it as an early warning.

It is no coincidence that the Manifesto comes at a time when the Prime Minister has abnegated any direct action on the issues surrounding Canadian independence. The limits of the government's aspirations are defined by the Prime Minister's declaration of the ten to fifteen per cent by which Canada can be independent. The Watkins Manifesto is now the major reaction to this position. A brief review of the Canadian political scene reveals the backdrop against which the movement for left-wing solutions to independence is evolving.

Trudeau: Reason over Passion

When John Porter published *The Vertical Mosaic* in 1965, it was already to be read as history. The Upper Canada College—Rosedale—Bay Street axis had passed its apogee and we were living amidst the decline of this country's political and economic élite. The great takeover by American business was both a symptom of this decline and hastened the process further. Apart from the industrial performance of this élite, which was second rate when judged by American standards, its very will to survive had definitely eroded.

No obvious class or grouping was available to replace it and only a nascent populism, sporadically erupting on the provincial fringes could fill the gap. First Diefenbaker and later Trudeau found the key to tap this pent-up populist undercurrent. The Diefenbaker fiasco need not be recapitulated here. The important question today is the shape which Trudeau will give to the populist upsurge which brought him to power. Populism is in its essence a vaguely defined political movement, deriving in this country from a mixture of agrarian and urban grass roots elements, united in their resentment against a declining establishment. Such a movement coheres well with Trudeau's slogan of "participatory democracy," but is remarkably open-ended on specific commitments and policies.

The only determination of concrete policy in the situation is the cast of mind that the Prime Minister brings to bear, his own vision of the rightness of things and the tasks to be accomplished. The Prime Minister's anti-nationalism is well known, but not so apparent is the classical liberalism out of which this derives and how that shapes his basic outlook. A man of many sides claiming a pragmatic approach to politics, he is the most deeply ideological of Canadian prime ministers. This surfaces rarely, but when it does in an unguarded moment of candour, the statement may be a revelation (even after the P.R. types have rushed in to set the statement 'in context'.) The most famous of his personal *cris de coeur* is the query to western farmers, "Why should I sell your wheat?" It is the perfect embodiment of the ethos of the market economy—it expresses the P.M.'s personal sense of the rightness of things economic. It is worth reflecting on how deepseated a commitment it would require to wash out, even momentarily, seventy-five years of the history of the Canadian west—the wheat pools, the battle around the Winnipeg grain exchange and finally the Canadian Wheat Board itself!

The new policy toward Canadian Indians provides a second case. The attempt to have Canadian Indians 'sink or swim' in five years, is reminiscent only of the Poor Law Reform Act of 1834—the pivotal legislation for the creation of a free labour market in England's emergent laissez-faire economy. To be told further, as we have been, that one section of Canadian society cannot form treaties with another section, is to wash out in an instant, another two hundred years of Canadian history. The valuable civil rights legislation of the last session of Parliament, in itself a great achievement, rounds out the picture. The cast of mind is unmistakably that of classical liberalism. Despite the P.M.'s personal motto—*la raison avant la passion*—he himself expresses the triumph of ideological passion, not only over reason but over history as well. This stance is his personal privilege, but in the circumstances it is also the country's burden. No ideological determinism need be invoked to appreciate that his anti-nationalist obsession is part of a coherent and unshakable philosophy of atomistic individualism and that little support can be expected from the present government in the battle for Canadian independence. In spite of all this, can the P.M. maintain the support of a populist electorate without taking a stand on the issues of independence? I doubt it. New issues and new incidents crop up continuously. Trade with China is on the immediate horizon and some brisk winds have been blowing from the north.

The Manhattan and Other Icons

As our final example we turn to the *cris de coeur* of Canadian newspapers that accompanied the voyage of the United States tanker *Manhattan* through our Arctic waters. It was a remarkable spectacle. The Toronto *Telegram* demanded hysterically that *The Manhattan* fly the Canadian flag. *The Globe and Mail* proclaimed that she "ploughs through Arctic ice to what might well be history—and a nasty precedent." The message was echoed from coast to coast, some newspapers printing two or three editorials on the subject in the same issue. The peculiar shape of the concern for Canadian independence was suddenly revealed—a classic territorialism. The newspapers it seemed, rose to the defence of every ice pack, inlet and practically every ocean wave that touched our shores. The very newspapers which offered only a blithe unconcern or hesitant commentary on the loss of control over our economy and technology, became militant to the point of hysteria when the fate of the polar region was at stake. It was incredible to see into what peculiar channels the independence issue had been shunted and where it had burst forth. Seemingly, only territoriality and extra-territoriality have become the active issues in the minds of the Canadian public.

How much of this sentiment grows out of the unease and confusion that has let the major issues thus far go by default? For the issues that matter in the twentieth century are the control of technology, communications, and decision-making power, and these centre on economic life.

The Prime Minister tried to calm down the popular eruption by invoking (not unexpectedly) the dangers of 'ultra-nationalism', and promising a statement at the opening of Parliament. To the layman it appeared that the legal position of our Arctic claims was not at all assured. A variety of international precedents and criteria might be invoked. If the issue then shifted from the legal sphere to the diplomatic, to negotiations with the United States, that was hardly the area of Canada's greatest strength. This country seemed to be on the high road once more to its traditional solution of 'quiet diplomacy', and that was hardly reassuring to public opinion.

Mr. Sharp attempted to deal with the public outcry by a statement on September 18 which moved in two directions at once. On the international plane he welcomed "vessels of all flags" to use the Arctic route, glossing over the substantive issues such as whether the limits of Canadian sovereignty were to be defined by the three mile limit around the Arctic islands or not, as the Americans had contended last June. For purely domestic consumption he injected the military factor into the situation, referring to the Prime Minister's statement on defence policy last April 3 which promised "an effective multipurpose maritime coastal shield." When the Minister of Defence announced the following day that our aircraft carrier, *The Bonaventure* was to be taken out of service, leaving us with thirty aging Argus aircraft for the task and little more planned, one defence analyst commented: "given that Canada has 7000 miles of coastline to protect, the [original] objective is in any case unattainable." The addition of Arctic surveillance to an already 'unattainable' task, turns Mr. Sharp's statement into a purely symbolic gesture.

It is the nature of the symbol, however which is of interest for the moment—territory and coastline. No doubt it was reassuring, even though we were without the adequate means in the twentieth century to achieve the objective. This statement had simply followed the note which the P.M. had struck last April when justifying our partial withdrawal from Nato. One might have expected at that time some reference to the international political situation, the changed climate of the cold war, how circumstances had altered the reasoning behind Canada's initial sponsorship of Nato, or possibly what a 'middle power' might achieve by loosening its ties with military alliances. None of these were deemed appropriate for public consumption. Vestigial symbols alone were offered. The P.M.'s statement referred simply to "the surveillance of our own territory and coast lines in the interest of our own sovereignty."

It was an act of homage to the national icon but little else. The gap between the symbolic and the substantive issue was at least half a century greater than the one on the Canadian left to which we referred earlier.

Thus we have the *cris de coeur* in Canada of the politics of independence, marking a debate that is incoherent, outbursts that are sporadic, issues that are out of focus, and an inadequate political vocabulary in which all this is expressed. Politics outside of the electoral system has become highly volatile, and even the Prime Minister may be unable to defuse the situation. If he persists in his non-recognition of the issue of independence, he can only succeed in the long run in making his government irrelevant, however successful his short-term tactics. The political tides will turn elsewhere. That is the real significance of the Manifesto. For however incoherent in its expression, this country has a rage to live.

October 1969

CLEARING THE SMOG

That issues of great importance to our future were dimly perceived and often consciously blotted out was one of the characteristics of the 1960's. I think of the whole decade as one of low visibility. But as a new mood of self-awareness spreads across the country, we are beginning to ask why the obvious eluded us for so long, why we lived so long with incoherence.

This new mood is typified in Joe Greene's recent Denver speech, and even more surprisingly, in the editorial columns of *The Globe and Mail*. I refer to its endorsement of the 'new nationalism'. We are reassured that it is the 'positive' kind, carefully dissociating itself from everything Walter Gordon has been saying for over a decade, and Mel Watkins more recently. I find this disclaimer rather fanciful and contrived, and the reasons for it open to question.

There are, of course, as many varieties of nationalists as there are social philosophies (start with Donald Creighton, if you will). But I suspect that the label 'new' nationalism is designed to avoid that encounter with our troubled conscience that is necessary if we are ever to come to terms with the 1960's. The whole issue comes to a head in the public response to the political career of Walter Gordon. Already it has become fashionable to put a fine gloss on this unsettling decade by referring to Walter Gordon as being ten years ahead of his time. The policies he proposed are, in fact, coming to the fore again.

Beneath Walter Gordon's stand-offish style and his clouded political career, there still remains at an intuitive level, I believe, the soundest political instinct of any of our public figures. It is an old truism, of course, that Canadian survival involves a social bulwark against the many forms of American influence, however benevolent. But Gordon has intuitively perceived the import of the new political landscape. In a society increasingly bound together by a proliferating hydro-electric grid (now more and more tied to the American network), computer technology directing industrial operations from coast to coast, increasing and relentless moves to industrial automation, and startling advances in science and communication, we are becoming a closely meshed, inter-dependent society in ways undreamed of when 'inter-dependence' was only a benevolent rhetorical catchword. The real question we must face up to is why the country turned its back on him and on the issues he was raising. What kind of blinkers were we wearing?

In *Gordon to Watkins to You*, Dave Godfrey, who is a writer, critic and novelist, reconstructs the foreign ownership debate largely through a series of documents. This feels less like a book and more like the sound track of a television programme with Godfrey acting as host. Major events of the 1960's are played back: the Mercantile Bank affair, the U.S. guidelines, the Watkins Report, the recent N.D.P. convention and its debate between Mel Watkins and David Lewis. Inter-views, press clippings, transcripts of debates, testimony to parliamentary committees, American extraterritorial laws, all move by in a rapid and compelling sequence. These are inter-spersed with some commentary by Godfrey and some valuable biographical sections on Walter Gordon and Mel Watkins as well as several articles by Watkins.

The political architecture of the era comes clearly into focus. But the question remains as to why, at the time, did we stumble through all these things with so little sense of their national significance? Why the confusion, the ambiva-lence and the low visibility? While there was (and still is), room for a substantial debate on policy toward foreign owner-ship, most of the country was hardly convinced that loss of control over our economy (and over the new technology which finds its home in the economy) was a problem.

Let me comment only on two groups who did their share in contributing to the political smog. I start with some of my academic colleagues, particularly the economists. Chief among these was Professor Harry Johnson. Canadian nationalism, he said, "has been diverting Canada into a narrow and garbage-cluttered *cul-de-sac*." Dave Godfrey captures this particular scenario of the 1960's in a perfect thumbnail sketch:

> Lecturing and speaking almost constantly, he mesmerized the entire profession of Canadian economists with the self-assured flourish of his style, the intellectual thrust of his

free trade and free market arguments. He presented a
messianic vision of global proportions based on nothing
more than Ricardo's simple arithmetic about the law of
comparative advantage. Any other policy was considered
pure boondocks economics.

I remember some of those economics meetings of the
1960's very well. Economists hung on his every word and
when Johnson finished speaking there was nothing left but to
cheer the latest rash of takeovers of Canadian companies.
After all, they were being made more 'efficient'. Did anything
else matter? Would anyone in the audience dare to challenge
this high road to 'progress', and to the never-never land of
'internationalism'? Free market economics had been turned
into a religion and this faith overrode considerations of both
common sense and the national interest.

Other social scientists and even some of the historians
weren't much help either. Their contribution to the intellectual smog centred mainly on telling us that the real danger in
this country was too much nationalism. Keep in mind that
three fifths of our manufacturing had been taken over, along
with great stretches of our natural resources; prime time on
TV was being flooded with *I Love Lucy*, *The Beverly Hill-
billies* and the rest; *Time* and *Reader's Digest* got their special
tax exemption, Canadian publications and publishers teetered
on the financial brink (and still do); American professors
flowed into the universities—and what did many of our
liberal social scientists have to say about our national
dilemma? Above all, they kept repeating, don't go berserk on
nationalism! As current social commentary, that takes a
little doing. Sort of like warning the Canadian Indians against
the dangers of an affluent society.

But academics aren't alone. The business community also
has to come to terms with the 1960's and the Great Sellout.
Godfrey presents us with a list that covers twenty pages of
small type of Canadian companies taken over between 1963
and 1969. It was an unprecedented event in the annals of
advanced industrial societies. Never before had a business
community opted for quiet suicide. And all it could think of
in the process, was lambasting any proposal for a Canada

Development Corporation (designed to do what they them-selves were neglecting) and railing against Walter Gordon.

Mel Watkins emerged out of the vacuum left by the de-parture of Gordon from the political scene. He has already, in his own way, entered the imagination of the country. The great paradox is that the very brief existence of the Waffle Group in the N.D.P. has already done more to break the log-jam in the Liberal Party on the independence issue than any other single factor. Of course the ineptness of American policy has also helped matters along.

Largely through the default of other groups, the battle for Canadian independence in the 1970's opens up as a dialogue on the left—somewhere between the left wing of the Liberal Party and the left wing of the N.D.P.

There are real issues to be sorted out and concrete policies to be formulated. Alastair Gillespie and Mel Watkins close the volume by offering two alternative programmes. Both seek to regain control of the economy in several ways including placing restrictions on future takeovers. Gillespie advocates the development of Canadian multinational corporations; Watkins is for an independent, socialist Canada.

There are, it seems to me, a lot of questions to be asked about both formulas. But they won't be answered by turning Watkins into *persona non grata* while we continue to avoid the issue itself. What we don't need is a repetition of the 1960's with Watkins replacing Gordon. On the independence front will the visibility in the 1970's be much better?

June 1970

Homesteading on Bay Street

7

CONSPICUOUS ABSENCE: REGIONAL DEVELOPMENT

There are few tasks in Canada that have ranked as high on our list of priorities as regional development. Few, in turn, have remained so elusive and difficult to achieve. Again and again we return to the underlying problem of the 'have-not' areas of this country—whether the issue is unemployment, foreign investment, national unity or any number of other problems. And invariably we are brought up short before this intractable dilemma which is reminiscent only of the stubborn physical features of our landscape.

Heroic efforts in the past have been launched with great fanfare, only to be followed by an uneasy silence. The plans and strategies are dissipated against the cruel realities; one after another of these projects goes awry amidst reports of inept management, endless delay, misuse of public funds and, more recently, a monumental swindle. New government agencies are launched and one acronym follows another into a state of suspended animation—A.D.A., A.R.D.A. and F.R.E.D. act as funnels for public funds with only token results; the total benefits, it appears, are less than the actual costs, i.e., we might have done better just giving the money away to the local inhabitants. Worse, one of our most recent projects, Churchill Forest Industries in Manitoba, is unveiled as a grotesque horror story and a scandal of international proportions.

Our impatience with this sad sequence of events tempts us perhaps to overlook the successful achievements in natural resource exploration and the development of increased energy capacity. But we must return in the end to the fact that the gap between the developed and the impoverished regions of this country continues to grow and that we are puzzled completely as to how we shall eventually right the balance. The hit-and-miss character of the whole approach to regional development seems more entrenched than ever.

The book, *Forced Growth,*[1] is a good place to begin a reassessment of the problem. For the first time, we can have a close look at the experience of the most important projects in five of our 'have-not' provinces. These compelling case studies present an excellent factual account of what transpired in the inter-relations of government and business. The narrative is unencumbered by a prejudgement of the issues or any set conclusions which the author forces on his data.

If our response to this book is merely to confirm the initial prejudices that each of us brings to this subject, then we shall be doing ourselves a disservice. Some may be tempted to reiterate that government has no place in the economy and that its intervention is once again shown to be wasteful and mistaken. Others in turn, may be tempted to conclude once more that private entrepreneurs, particularly foreign investors, are out to press their advantage for all they can get—so why not have the government run the entire show, particularly since so much public money is already involved?

Both of these stances are inadequate in themselves if we wish to go beyond scoring a few traditional debating points. We would do better to draw up an interim balance sheet based on what we can learn from these development projects. The dominant impression must surely be that our provincial governments appear vulnerable, if not helpless, before the magnitude and complexity of these projects. Surprisingly enough, it is not primarily a question of finding the money. The projects discussed here encompass almost $400 million of public funds; the citizens of these poorer provinces are being forced to pay exorbitant amounts of money for their new job opportunities. The bottleneck appears rather to be the absence of expertise, judgment, experience and reliable advice on which these governments can draw. They are hardly a match for the sophisticated and experienced multinational corporations which are often called upon to be their partners. Given the present level of technical and administrative competence, it seems highly premature to propose that governments take over the whole area of regional development on their own.

Relying entirely on private enterprise (domestic or foreign) to go forward in its own good time appears to be no solution either. New industries tend to locate, wherever possible, around existing urban concentrations. New resource projects are guided by criteria that bear no necessary relation to employment needs. Creating employment opportunities in depressed regions is not an uppermost concern of either domestic or foreign entrepreneurs. But it is, and must remain, a concern of governments, federal and provincial. They must assume full responsibility for a strategy of development and begin to explore in a realistic way the means at hand to execute it.

The story of the new pulp mills in Saskatchewan built by the American firm Parsons & Whittemore illustrates one basic dilemma of development. Why, the reader might ask, with so much Canadian expertise in the pulp and paper industry, was it necessary to go to a foreign firm to undertake the project? The question can be asked with even greater urgency after the fiasco of Churchill Forest Industries in Manitoba.

In both cases, but particularly in Saskatchewan, the provincial governments must be credited with a persistent and sincere attempt to find a Canadian company to undertake the project among the half-dozen large pulp and paper companies. This search met with no success. In Saskatchewan, Parsons & Whittemore was a last resort. The Manitoba case is somewhat more ambiguous.

But we can in both cases raise some classic questions: Is Canadian business too conservative? Is there some inherent attitude that shuns more speculative ventures? Is it a matter of indifference to an urgent national task, some lack of patriotism, some ideological barrier to involvement with government at any level? Are Americans, in turn, inherently more venturesome?

This issue, arising from the episodes that are recounted in this book, is central to the future of this country. It needs a close and realistic analysis and more extensive discussion. I would venture to suggest some preliminary thoughts on this matter in the hope that the discussion will be taken up by others.

I am inclined to distrust an analysis of business operations that rests on intangible psychological elements such as 'character' and 'attitude.' Much more pertinent to such an analysis is an exploration of the 'rules of the game' under which business operates. The key to the dilemma may lie in a realization that large Canadian corporations abide, implicitly and explicitly, by certain rules that guide their behaviour. These may include a preference for certain modes of traditional financing, certain acceptable levels of risk in relation to expected normal returns on their investment, and a certain level of independence and internal control of decision-making which cannot easily accommodate a governmental partner. Put differently, normal commercial ventures imply a quite different economic setting and different rules of the game from development ventures sponsored by government. Canadian business may not feel at home with the ground rules, different modes of financing, and higher levels of risk which are inherent in developing the poorer regions of this country. The aim of government—to create employment opportunities—may not coincide with their own general aims of an orderly and controlled expansion of their operations geared to normal profit opportunities and unencumbered by novel administrative relations to government agencies.

If this is so, it only deepens the paradox. Why should foreign, particularly American, firms feel entirely at home in this setting and operate quite easily under a different set of 'rules of the game'? The answer lies in recognizing the character of the multinational corporation, particularly of the kind represented by Parsons & Whittemore, whose experience lies primarily in establishing new ventures in developing areas around the world. They are equipped to assess the unusual risks involved in the financial, managerial and economic side of the operation and to cope with these problems accordingly.

Their talents, however, do not come cheaply and we must appreciate fully the price we pay for foreign investment. As Woodrow Lloyd, the former leader of the N.D.P. opposition in the Saskatchewan legislature summed up the matter, Saskatchewan had assumed eighty per cent of the risk of the project in return for thirty per cent of the equity. Additional commissions and fees for supplying the machinery and looking after the sales of the product make the returns to Parsons & Whittemore even greater.

At the present time, it appears that the Saskatchewan project will be successful even though at an exorbitant cost for each new job created. The opposite is the case in Prince Edward Island's frozen fish plant, Manitoba's venture at The Pas, and Nova Scotia's heavy water plant. They are all unqualified disasters. Even when Newfoundland's successful Churchill Falls project is taken into account, it appears that the state of regional development in this country is in a highly precarious condition. Only chance considerations seem to lay down the fine line between qualified successes and unqualified failures. If future projects carry with them no greater chances of success, we would be better off to suspend our operations in regional development and find some other way to help the unemployed.

But this is not meant as a serious suggestion at the present time. We are at the point of *reculer pour mieux sauter*—a point where we must assess our errors and weaknesses in order to launch a new and more effective effort.

Home-grown expertise and technology available to government are the first items on the agenda. A federal control agency for dealing with foreign investment (which has been much discussed in the Watkins Report and the Wahn Report) must include a capability of assessing the terms on which new ventures are being offered. This expertise must be available to provincial governments to assist in negotiating optimum terms or suggesting alternative companies that might provide a better package. The costs of new foreign investment, where it is absolutely necessary, must be reduced.

New federal-provincial development corporations for specific projects should be organized with an eye to licensing new technology rather than ceding majority equity control to foreign corporations. Where the expertise is not available in Canada, management consultants should be imported for a limited period, keeping in mind the pitfalls of consulting as exemplified by the ambiguous role of Arthur D. Little in Manitoba.

The role of Canadian corporations in future regional development is a crucial question that must be made the subject of an open national discussion. As suggested here, the key to greater participation lies in a recognition of the different "rules of the game" which are involved. On what terms will business participate? How are the financial risks and the corresponding returns to be assessed? What new modes of financing can be provided, perhaps under the aegis and participation of the Canada Development Corporation? What corresponding changes are necessary in the tax structure? Whatever remains of the Canadian business structure has a heavy responsibility for this country's future. If it chooses to opt out indefinitely, Canadian business will either be replaced by foreign firms or displaced by Crown corporations.

The regaining of control over the Canadian economy and the support of regional development are, in many ways, complementary questions. No major effort at repatriation can succeed or will be tolerated politically, unless we make some effective progress in regional development. These two issues point to a common objective: a renewed effort to create improved management and technical skills in Canada available to both government and to Canadian business.

Mr. Mathias's book has shown us graphically how helpless and dependent we have become and how costly it is to be hooked on foreign investment. I am sure we can do better.

But first, let us explore further that elusive image which Canadian business has of itself; this seems to me to be the key to its inadequate role.

February 1971

1. By Philip Mathias, Toronto: James Lewis and Samuel, 1971.

CANADIAN BUSINESS AND THE ETERNAL NO

Among the first and most important problems in designing an industrial strategy for Canada is the present unsatisfactory relationship between government and business in this country. Successive pieces of important legislation have recently come to grief on the shoals of persistent and effective opposition by the business community. We need only refer to the strong lobby mounted against reform of the tax system which succeeded in emasculating virtually all the important features of the Carter Commission proposals, the quiet death of income security for Canadians, the furious assault upon Mr. Basford's rather mild Competition Act, the gathering attack upon the technological change clauses of the new Canada Labour Code, and the rough reception given the initial announcement of the screening mechanism in the Herb Gray Report. On all fronts the government's record is one of retreat before the vocal and effective business lobby. There is a strong likelihood that the business community would also respond to the formulation of an industrial strategy for Canada in the same way—with its seemingly eternal no.

Some observers see in this pattern the simple reactionary instincts of an inbred, embattled business sector, reluctant to yield any of its power or privileges. But in our view the problem is more complex and elusive. Behind the rhetoric and self-interest of the business response to these government proposals, we detect, if not a clearly articulated line of argument, at least a consistent mood of beleaguered indignation. There are the continual references to a struggle in which business is engaged and to a viability that must be preserved; the modest proposals of the government mentioned above, seem to constitute for business, an invasion of a sanctuary where the state has no right of trespass. We sense in all this some larger ideological conception lurking in the background to which these rights and wrongs seem to relate.

One can hardly lay the major blame for this falling out with the government. This is no mere problem of bad public relations. Neither is it an indifference to the sensibilities or strategic importance of the business sector in the national economy. No recent government to our recollection, has tried so hard to keep open its lines of communication with the business community. The number of dinners served to our business leaders at 24 Sussex Drive, the flood of memoranda solicited from the business community all to be given careful consideration, the notable deference of the Prime Minister and members of his Cabinet to the business sector—including the budget of October 14, 1971 awarding business a seven per cent reduction in its income tax payments compared to a three per cent reduction for everyone else in order to "restore business confidence"—all of these efforts appear to have been to no avail. Even the extraordinary descent recently of thirty-six of Canada's most important business leaders upon Ottawa for an earnest working lunch with the Prime Minister failed to allay the widespread anxiety. This it would seem, is plainly an 'anti-business' government and the businessmen will not hear a word to the contrary.

According to the president of the Canadian Bankers Association (the general manager of the Bank of Montreal and no wild-eyed western oilman to be sure), "irrelevant policies" are responsible for the loss of business confidence in the Trudeau government. In the midst of an economic crisis when jobs must be created, the government thinks only of inhibiting, controlling, restricting and regulating enterprise. "More specifically," he continued, "confidence is being damaged by a welter of legislation. . ." which would "so engulf Canadian corporations with regulations and prohibitions that they are unable to compete in international markets. Foreign companies will gain such advantages that they will be able to send cheaper and superior goods to Canada." He singled out as being especially objectionable the tax bill, which no one understood but which everyone nevertheless agreed would reduce investment, and the "incredible" technological change clause of the labour code which, he claimed, has no parallel in the world and "absolutely guarantees the spread of economic disruption and inflation." Whatever could have inspired the government to sponsor such abominable legislation, especially at a time when businessmen should be concentrating their energies on putting the economy back on its feet, he concluded, was beyond mortal comprehension.

It takes only a modicum of detachment from the scene to recognize how absurd is this charge of an 'anti-business' government. Indeed, a good case can be made for the opposite position: that a good deal of public interest has already been compromised by the present attitude of the government towards the business community. After a decade of debate for example, we are hardly nearer a rational system of taxation and for that the businessmen themselves must bear the responsibility. They told us at first that Mr. Carter's "a dollar is a dollar" formula was far too simple a proposition upon which to build a tax structure for an industrial society. After a massive business lobby went into high gear, the government caved in, humiliated, and permitted business virtually to rewrite the tax bill, allowing all the requisite exemptions and particular exceptions. These same outraged businessmen now tell us that the resulting bill is far too complicated; it cannot be understood and should, therefore, have been thrown out!

A similar fate no doubt awaits the Competition Act. We recall that the complaint against the old Combines Investigation Act was that it lumped together in court businessmen with common criminals. It also left the question of 'undueness' in the restraint of trade to the vagaries of the legal system when what was involved was an economic question. Nevertheless, to the new proposal of a public regulatory body fully equipped to examine the economic implications of mergers and inter-company agreements, the businessmen complain of the lack of due process, fulminate against arbitrary bureaucracies, and demand the right of appeal. To them, apparently, competition is a matter for the businessman and his friends to decide by themselves. What could courts or councils possibly know about it?

In regard to the labour code, the government put forward the humane and sensible proposition that industry and labour should get together to plan for technological changes affecting the work force, even if these occur in mid-contract. Once more, the business community recoiled in horror. According to the Chamber of Commerce, admitting unions to the decision-making process as it affects technological change would be "tantamount to legalizing Luddite-like conduct aimed at arbitrarily stopping progress and promoting featherbedding."

In short, after having gone substantially out of its way to establish harmonious relations with business on all these matters, the government has received only strong abuse for its efforts.

In the pursuit of a new industrial strategy designed to repatriate the economy without sacrificing primary objectives such as efficiency and full employment, we now discover that perhaps the most serious obstruction is to be found in this complex interface between government and business. While hardly getting anything worthwhile done, and in spite of its own best efforts, government has been rubbing business the wrong way. Inadvertently it has provoked the business community to militance, a mood in which business refuses to take any direction whatever in the area of the massive changes that will be needed if we are even to agree in principle on such an industrial strategy.

This mood of standoffish irritation appears in sharp contrast to the classical rhetoric and folklore of Canadian economic history. We all recall the iconic status of Sir John A. Macdonald's National Policy, the governmental framework of tariffs, railways, immigration and land settlement within which the new confederation grew. The intimate relationship of government and business represented by the National Policy was, we were told, founded on a pragmatic interaction devoid of the ideological presumptions that prevailed on such matters in the United States. Thereafter we moved with ease and without crises of conscience into such projects as the nationalization of hydro-electricity in Ontario and elsewhere, into the creation of the C.N.R., the C.B.C., Air Canada, Polymer, the modern crown corporations and now most recently, the Canada Development Corporation. This all flowed apparently from the hand-in-glove operation of governmental financing of the C.P.R. and the subsequent close interlocking of business, political, intellectual and civil service elites at the top of the Vertical Mosaic. Canadians,

unlike their American neighbours, possessed no profound
ideological aversions to state intervention in the economy; we
were more open minded and practical concerning the tasks
that needed to be done.

We have reached the point however when it is no longer
possible to continue to ignore the evidence that points
massively in quite a different direction. If Canadian business
has been notoriously unenthusiastic in rallying behind a
policy to stem the foreign takeover of this country, if it must
be dragged kicking and screaming into a new economic
framework designed precisely to safeguard the last vestiges
of an autonomous business sector, if it cannot even be rallied
by the instinct of self-preservation, then it is apparent that
there are distinct and hidden peculiarities about this business
community, particularly the way in which it views its own
situation. What compels us to embark upon an examination
of the special cast of mind characteristic of the Canadian
business community is the present crossroads we have reached
on the issue of an industrial strategy. Only fragmentary bits
of evidence are available to provide an outline of the image
that this community has of itself. Our initial exploration must
necessarily remain speculative and preliminary, but it is
hardly a subject that can be avoided much longer. If Canadian
business is to be saved despite itself, we must at least
understand its mentality.

Homesteading On Bay Street

Symbols and self-images are in many respects as important
components of the businessman's reality as profits and costs.
Through symbols, businessmen rationalize their conduct, link
their behaviour to the value system or objectives of the community as a whole, legitimize and sanction their vested
interests. We would argue that it is in this realm of symbols
and self-images rather than profits and losses that recent
government legislation confronts, confounds and agitates the
business mind. The cost, in real terms, of tax reform, social
security, the competition tribunal, the screening mechanism
and the labour code may not be great, but the psychic costs
of submission in each case may be very great indeed. The

truculence of the business community during the first phase of discussions concerning the Canada Development Corporation and the expressions of outrage and indignation produced during the debate on tax reform and the capital gains tax seemed to suggest a depth of righteous commitment to some hidden principles and values that went far beyond a simple reluctance to pay more taxes or the desire to defend vested financial interests. The shrill pitch of business protest left the impression that an established frame of mind, an entrenched set of self-images and symbols, existed within the business community of which these protests were only the surface manifestations.

In some ways this entire frame of mind is curiously reminiscent of pioneer days—what might be termed the *homestead mentality*. Briefly and arbitrarily reconstructed, the early settler faces the overwhelming difficulties of clearing his plot in the wilderness, cutting down his trees and hauling out the stumps. After having completed the task and built his log cabin, he has indisputably earned the total proprietary rights to his land. Anyone who would dare to trespass upon that territory—whether an individual or a representative of the government—could only do so at his own peril. Belligerence and grave suspicions greet the invader of this autonomous enclave newly fenced with natural rights. Politically this is a self-contained structure with only minimal connection to the larger society. The homesteader may become suspicious of his neighbours and increasingly disinclined to innovate or enter complex schemes of co-operation and improvement. His fences are the actual and symbolic limits of his political jurisdiction; his inclination is to keep them well mended and continue to stay behind them.

The National Policy, with its high tariff, symbolically recreated on a national scale, a frame of mind to echo and reinforce this ongoing mood and outlook which Canadian business carried over from a pioneer birth. Within that framework, government might be welcomed now and then to offer some direct assistance—to keep the tariff wall in good repair or provide another railway—but would be fiercely resisted if it threatened natural rights and prerogatives. On other matters, the esprit de corps of the homesteaders was at a minimum; for example, the systematic sellout of neighbouring homesteads could hardly produce a collective and focused response. Seeing the state only as a potential violator of a sacred, territorial integrity, the homesteading businessman failed to see state programmes as potential devices of protection and help. His political horizons were too narrow.

The truculent posture of the Canadian business community when confronted by reformist social and economic legislation is, we would argue, still rooted in the proprietary imperatives of a homesteading mentality. These reforms challenge the self-images, the symbols, of the business community more than its financial well-being. Competition tribunals, screening mechanisms and labour codes demand that the business community share its power more than its profits. Behind the circumlocutions of the tax debate and the grumpy assertions of failing confidence in the government, the businessmen know exactly what they want but they cannot come right out and say it. They want to be left alone in their exclusive possession of the Canadian economy.

The business community correctly interprets the screening mechanism of the Herb Gray Report as a rudimentary form of economic planning for the foreign sector. And the competition tribunal can be seen as the domestic counterpart of the screening agency. The labour code insists that business share with organized labour the responsibility of accommodating human needs in the process of technological change. At the symbolic level the businessman sees himself being hemmed in; the 'they' are threatening to control the 'we'. The paranoid homesteader reverts to his basic symbols and reiterates his eternal no.

But two related factors operate to discredit partially the effort. In the first place, the society at large no longer wholeheartedly subscribes to these business symbols—they divide rather than unite the society. Secondly, the relatively unsatisfactory performance of the Canadian business community (according to any number of indices) has helped to create a new and conscious distinction between the economy and business.

The Canadian businessman is at present in a situation somewhat analogous to that faced by the farming community some fifty years ago. At that time the once dominant farmer discovered that the agrarian myth was no longer heard in an increasingly urban and industrial society. The myth system of the farmer no longer served as the ideology of the whole community, but only one part of it.

In a similar way the symbols appealed to by the business community have begun to disintegrate in the process of social change. We are all aware of these classic figures: in mining, in marketing and in manufacturing. Typically we encounter the symbolic representative of an industry engaged in a search—the solitary, independent prospector searching for the mother lode, the salesman for the first trusting buyer, and the inventor for the final technical breakthrough. Faith, stamina, and a transcending will denied lesser men, eventually triumph bringing the mine/innovation/market into production. Along the way the symbol also serves to justify the task and, by asserting the elementary dignity of the calling, relates this private activity to the general welfare. A secular righteousness pervades this business symbolism, as well as a certain exclusiveness, a we-they dimension. For every sturdy farmer, inventor, salesman, producer and prospector there exists an army of laggards, layabouts, second-handers, hangers-on, carpers and welfare bums pressing in upon him. It is the purpose of the symbol, while sanctioning the role, to create a dichotomy between the worthy 'we' and the burdensome 'they'. At this point the symbol becomes protective and defensive. For the reward of self-sufficiency amid adversity is exclusive possession.

Instead of integrating business ambitions with the goals of the community at large, these obsolescent business symbols have now come increasingly to represent the visible interests of only one group. The old traditions upon which businessmen are taking their stand have simply broken down in the face of a whole series of national economic and social problems.

In recent years we have witnessed a growing tendency to make a distinction between business and the economy. This differentiation has been prompted more by technocrats operating within the ideology of liberal capitalism than by critics on the outside. One hardly needs to be a nationalist or a socialist to be profoundly disappointed with the performance of the Canadian business community. A host of federal and regional economic councils that have sprung up over the past decade or so, have consistently measured the shortfall of business against the needs and potential capacity of the economy. Surveying the performance of Canadian industry over the past five years, the Economic Council of Canada recently reported that Canada experienced the lowest productivity per capita increases among seven industrial nations. Similarly, the Science Council, in a review of the relative decline of the technologically based secondary sector, was moved to comment gloomily:

> If these trends continue—and there are no signs in the last four years of their improvement, or even of their arrest— Canada's economy in this decade will increasingly become dependent on the resource and service industries. Resource industries offer limited opportunities for employment; furthermore, much of their profit does not remain in Canada. The funnelling of funds out of the country is likely to stunt the growth of our service industries, which are unlikely in any case to use the very people in whom our most substantial educational investments have been made. Our participation in international trade will become less and less significant and we will become—once again—mainly suppliers of raw materials to the North American continent.[1]

Together the Science Council and the Economic Council have helped Canadians conceive the needs and social purpose of their economy independent of the interests of the business community presently in possession of it. It is readily apparent that there are important national objectives that are currently in jeopardy—not the least of which is the provision of employment to a rapidly growing labour force. The business community's demand to be left alone to get on with the job, in view of its past performance, is no longer very convincing. We are beginning to see with a clarity previously denied us that the economy is too important to be left in the hands of the businessman.

Towards an Industrial Strategy

But here we confront an ideological impasse. How can the industrial strategy being urgently recommended by the Science and Economic Councils, the Gray Report, and even the *Financial Post* be so constructed that it will meet with the necessary approval of the Canadian business community? Now that there is a manifest need for a new National Policy, how can Canadian business and government be brought together into a genuine partnership to plan strategies of development?

Alarmed business lobbyists have detected a mysterious spirit abroad in Ottawa working itself out in the legislation of what were thought to be fragmented and dispersed government departments. Piece by piece a master plan seems to be taking shape. The competition tribunal, the screening mechanism and the Canada Development Corporation are parts of the same whole. It is not so much the competition tribunal itself to which the business community takes exception as to the clearly stated goal of "the social control of the economy" which it is intended to serve.[2]

But the businessmen mistake the machinery of economic planning for the plan. The process of economic planning has yet to begin. An industrial development strategy will, of course, form a key element of any national economic and social plan—the two cannot be separated. But how are we to avoid direct confrontation between the homesteaders and the planners? It is imperative that the two forces be brought into harmony. Looking out across the myriad of homesteads, many of them now already sold to strangers, it is apparent that it is in the interest of the community at large and the business community in particular that the homesteads be rezoned. The question is how can that be done without another paralysing collision?

We would begin that process of accommodation by suggesting that the present 'crisis of confidence' in the business community is essentially symbolic in character. Planning challenges the symbols of enterprise more than the present procedures of business itself. The outmoded symbolism upon which business rests must be raised to the level of general awareness and it must be shown how inadequate it is when judged against present needs. We might do worse for example, than to replace the homestead mentality by the pragmatic relations of government and business originally envisaged by the National Policy.

Not that a return to any mythology of the past can be adequate to meet the urgent issues of the moment. We must create an atmosphere however, whereby the *process* that leads to a new industrial strategy can be discussed on its merits. We would argue as well that businessmen will not be convinced of the need for planning unless they are assured an important role in the planning process. No group can be expected to respond favourably to a design drawn up without consultation and imposed from above.

Our modest proposal is to begin the decentralization of economic planning and the participation of business in it, through the creation of Industry Councils for each sector of the economy. Businessmen themselves would be brought together to state their own long-range goals for their particular industries, including the survival of a Canadian business sector, and to consider strategies of improving productivity, employment and export performance. In our minds such councils would initiate the process of business thinking in national terms once again, and at that stage the co-ordination of public and private planning would be at least theoretically possible.

While the Canadian economy and Canadian business are no longer to be viewed as identical, each is still closely dependent on the other for its survival. Is Canadian business prepared at the eleventh hour to give up its eternal no?

NOTES

1. Economic Council of Canada, *Performance in Perspective*, 1971. Ottawa, 1971, 13-14; Science Council of Canada, Report No. 15,

Innovation in a Cold Climate: The Dilemma of Canadian Manufacturing 22.

2. Economic Council of Canada, *Interim Report on Competition Policy.* Ottawa, 1969, 5-27.

With Viv Nelles
January 1972

LAST CHANCE

Bay Street showed less than buoyant enthusiasm when the announcement of the Canada Development Corporation was finally made. One report described the reaction as "nervous resignation to the inevitable." A mild reaction, one might say, compared to the vehement objections bordering on apoplexy that one had come to expect when the subject of the C.D.C. had been raised up till now in financial circles.

Which leads us to ask some long overdue questions about the attitude of the financial community as the national concern mounts to do something at last about an eroding Canadian independence. Recall as well, that a recent Gallup poll reported that eighty-three per cent of the Canadian population was in favour of the C.D.C.

Some may regard this concern with the financial community as artificial and obsolete. Canadian business, they argue, has sold out completely and is now too deeply committed to the foreign-owned sector of the economy to support any independent Canadian initiatives to stem the tide. But the fact remains that the financial community is a protected sector and is still fairly intact.

Very little discussion has actually taken place of what is expected from Bay Street if the C.D.C. is to operate successfully. Instead, the image that has grown up in the press about the C.D.C., shows granny digging into her sock to buy a $5 share, or more generally, a grass-roots 'people's capitalism'. No doubt there will be a groundswell of small investors coming forward for patriotic as well as financial motives. And this will be an important political factor, for the public will maintain its pressure for the C.D.C. to do something significant with its money, particularly in the development of natural resources.

But some simple arithmetic will indicate that the C.D.C. cannot reach its proposed capitalization of $2 billion— 400,000,000 shares at $5 each—by relying on the man in the street, even allowing for the ten per cent participation by the government.

All of this suggests some questions about how the financial community proposes to respond to this project—the investment houses, the stock exchange, the pension funds, the mutual funds, and so on.

The government has already gone out of its way to accommodate the financial community by various assurances, including the independence of the Corporation from government control, the use of strictly commercial criteria for investment decisions as well as the notion that the Corporation will not become a buyer of last resort for foundering Canadian enterprises.

It is time to have some positive reactions in turn from the financial community that go beyond the economic sophistry of free market logic—"if it's worth doing we'll do it ourselves and don't need the C.D.C., and if it's not worth doing, then the C.D.C. shouldn't bother" or "we have a responsibility to provide the best returns for our shareholders" etc. Events have moved far beyond that stage.

What we need in the first instance are experienced senior people from the business community to take on the responsibility of directors, and with that an attitude of positive support for the project. Non-co-operation in providing personnel and later, in providing funds may sabotage the entire enterprise. An attitude of irritated indifference will not do.

As we read the emerging public mood, there will be very little patience left for a business community that already bears the responsibility for the great sellout and still persists in regarding the future integration of the Canadian and American economies as a virtue.

New types of development corporations are in the offing

both at the federal and provincial levels in addition to the
C.D.C. and their essential message is that the Canadian
business community—or what remains of it—must begin to
pull its weight in stemming the tide of American control and
creating new Canadian ventures.

It should be obvious to somebody down there that this is
the last roll call. There are other ways to regain control of the
economy. If Bay Street remains conspicuous by its absence
at this late date, then it will be writing its own maudlin
epitaph in less than a decade.

February 1971

La Survivance

8

THE B & B REPORT

What happens when the all-too-familiar items of daily life—the soup tins, cereal boxes and soap wrappers—are mounted on a canvas and nailed firmly in place? Pop art forces us to take a second look at the familiar items in a new setting, but, in the words of one critic, "is it art?"

The Preliminary Report of the Royal Commission on Bilingualism and Biculturalism leaves one with a strong feeling of *déjà lu*. The Commission met—incredible as it may seem—some 12,000 Canadians across the country and put together a national 'portrait' out of the remarks it has heard. They are all too familiar. In Halifax someone states "I suggest there is little or no motivation for people in Nova Scotia to learn French...," while in Rimouski: "In an environment where only French is normally spoken, a child has no motivation to learn the other language." And so it goes.

But is it art?

The intention of the Commission to start its work at the grass roots level seems courageous and democratic, and a refreshing departure from the way Royal Commissions generally operate. But after twenty-three regional meetings and 12,000 personal encounters, the Preliminary Report offers us neither recommendations nor a general diagnosis of what it terms "the greatest crisis in [Canadian] history." "Our inquiry is not far enough advanced," the Commission tell us, "to enable us to establish exactly its underlying causes and its extent."

Then why the Report?

> ...the feeling of the Commission is that at this point the danger of a clear and frank statement is less than the danger of silence; this type of disease cannot be cured by keeping it hidden indefinitely from the patient.

But if one merely offers a patient who is gravely ill a list of his symptoms, can one hope to produce anything more than annoyance and frustration? Does this have the suggestion about it of *épater le bourgeois*?

Undoubtedly the Commission appraised the risks of such a report with care, and it decided that the major risk was "that we would reach our conclusions before a part of Canadian opinion had really grasped the problems."

What the Commission may not have posed is the paradox of why, after years of newspaper headlines and articles about the crisis, the problems still have not been 'grasped'. After all the crisis is not about Viet Nam or Cyprus and did not begin yesterday. Countries are not in the habit of 'ignoring' their own deepest crises for superficial reasons. There have been enough vivid and spontaneous storms in this country on less vital issues to refute any assumption that the problem lies in some intrinsic lethargy or indifference of Canadian public opinion.

If there is a solution to this important paradox, it may have something to do with the moral and political functions of 'not knowing'. To grasp a crisis of this order may be more than a matter of information flows. To 'know' is to face the challenge of responding to such knowledge. And if this challenge calls into question basic beliefs and the entire structure of national life which is built on them, then this knowledge cannot easily be assimilated or even 'known'. The temptation is then to retreat into protective myths or stereotypes and to blur issues. (In recent times we have discovered that the Germans didn't 'know', and that the French didn't 'know' about Algeria. These dramatic cases are certainly not comparable, but we may have something to learn from them.)

The most widespread of these protective myths in English Canada is that of a 'quaint old Quebec', e.g., in Kingston the view that "Quebec has emphasized a rather peasant-like culture—one which amuses rather than educates." The political function of such a myth is to place Quebec, and all the disturbing questions she raises, beyond the pale. It is a declaration of the absence of genuine community and the suspension of the moral obligations which community involves.

It may be naive for the commission to assume that exposure of these myths through factual refutation is sufficient. Myths are the building blocks of a total structure of values and outlook on the political process and the national environment. The building blocks cannot be selectively picked off one at a time. No one will abandon one structure until he is offered a second which is habitable and which he can accept.

This is my basic objection to the Preliminary Report. If we were not to be given recommendations at this early stage, we should have been given a much more substantial and systematic analysis of 'underlying causes' and some indication of the shape of things to come from the Commission. The abandonment of old positions, which the Commission seeks, is contingent on knowing where we are generally heading and why. Otherwise puzzlement and defensive reactions set in. (One commentator has already remarked that the English Commissioners don't really speak for English Canada.)

If it is correct to suggest that the underlying causes of the crisis have something to do with basic political values, then it is clear that some evidence, at any rate, was at hand for the formulation of a basic diagnosis. There are also some suggestions of this kind by the Commissioners.

The most useful remarks in this regard may be those of a Quebec lawyer:

When they speak of equality, English Canadians mean equality of individual civil rights, that is, of persons considered individually, while when we French Canadians speak of equality we do not mean civil rights at all, we mean collective national rights, we mean the rights of the French Canadian nation to develop in accordance with its own characteristics. . . .

His view of the English Canadian outlook is partly confirmed by the remarks made by someone in Kingston:

Canada, I don't think for many of us has very much meaning, nor has 'the Canadian'; but *a Canadian*—the individual—has his rights and his obligations. Canada and Quebec are abstractions; 'an English-speaking' or 'French-speaking' Canadian is real, concrete. Their freedom is of supreme importance.

The Commission adds that:

Most important, however, was the inference in this majoritarian view—so often apparent to the Commission—that Canada is one state within which majority rule and individual liberty are central tenets.

Our crisis, in short, may have something to do with the confrontation of the two different sets of political values. If 'freedom' and 'equality' for example, turn out to mean quite different things to the 'founding races', can they find a *modus vivendi* and continue to share the same society?

Some scepticism about this type of diagnosis is justified. After all, the ebb and flow of daily life runs on concrete and routine matters. Are we imputing too much theoretical and political sophistication to the man-in-the-street? What kind of concrete examples do arise where political values make a difference? One example which springs to mind is the not-so-hypothetical case of vice-presidencies in the C.N.R. If there are two candidates with roughly similar qualifications for a vacant position, and one is appointed *because* he happens to be a French Canadian, it might meet the criterion of equality as seen by French Canada, but would be an abridgement of equality as English Canadians conceive of the term.

One of our most eminent observers of French Canada, Ramsay Cook, has recently posed the dilemma in similar terms. (cf. *International Journal*, Winter, 1964-65.) It is a "basic difference in public philosophy," Cook claims, "which divides Canadians."

> Because they are a conquered people and a minority French Canadians have always been chiefly concerned with group rights. . .The English Canadian, as is equally befitting his majority position, is far more concerned with that characteristic North American middle class ideal: equality of opportunity. . .The English Canadian has, therefore, tended to look upon privileges asked for or granted to groups as inherently undesirable, indeed, undemocratic.

The Commission will have to take up the crisis on many different levels: the cultural, the economic and the constitutional among others. But a basic investigation of the underlying realm of political values and the political process as conceived by the two groups, may be crucial.

And here, the relevance of the Acton formula, advocated by Ramsay Cook, will become apparent. Lord Acton maintained: "The co-existence of several nations under the same State is a test, as well as the best security of its freedom." But before proceeding through the Acton gateway, we would have to ask what Acton meant by "freedom." "A people averse to the institution of private property," Acton tells us in the same essay, "is without the first element of freedom." This does not appear to be what French Canada, or possibly even English Canada has in mind. A further notion of Acton's central concern is given in a passage that just precedes the one quoted above:

> diversity in the same State is a firm barrier against the intrusion of the government beyond the political sphere which is common to all into the social department which escapes legislation and is ruled by spontaneous laws. This sort of interference is characteristic of an absolute government.

It is important to note that Acton's intention was to safeguard 'English liberty'. He was a nineteenth-century spokesman mesmerized by the fear of the State. It is hard to see what *L'Etat de Québec* will find in the original Lord Acton. But if we are to adopt his formula for our own purposes, we must begin by inquiring whether different meanings are now being attached to the term 'freedom'.

The task of the Commission is to work out "an equal partnership between the two founding races." The pleasant, rhetorical ring of the phrases is deceptive. It soon becomes apparent that this is a radical task. If the Commission is to discover an opting-in formula somewhere on the spectrum between co-operative federalism and co-operative separatism, it will have to be as radical as the task requires.

April 1965

EVERY COUNT BUT THE CRUCIAL ONE: TRUDEAU AND THE CONSTITUTION

Amidst an atmosphere of excitement and intense expectation, the Constitutional Conference in February opened under Lester Pearson's injunction that "what is at stake is no less than Canada's survival as a nation." It was a rare occasion when rhetoric and reality coincided.

A new mood quickly settled in. While Ontario and New Brunswick led the other provinces in their willingness to accept the B. and B. recommendations on bilingualism, all provinces except Alberta and British Columbia indicated a spirit of accommodation that would have been unimaginable even a year ago. Much of the credit must go to the Confederation of Tomorrow Conference held the previous autumn in Toronto.

But if the Conference took only preliminary steps for the actual revision of the Constitution, the climate of mutual confidence it established provided an important basis for the success of the coming detailed negotiations. The decision in the end was for a 'continuing conference' to operate for the next two or three years through some eight committees to deal with such diverse topics as constitutional amending procedures, economic disparities, and division of powers for a 'made-in-Canada' constitution.

The least successful proposal was Pierre Elliott Trudeau's attempt to build a Charter of Human Rights into the Constitution. Not only did the provinces feel uneasy about a potential invasion of their jurisdiction, but the sense of a brilliant but diversionary ploy haunted the proceedings. English and French language rights, highly relevant to the Conference, were lumped with the traditional freedoms of speech, association, equal protection of the law and freedom from discrimination. But individual freedoms were not what most people regarded as the theme or the purpose of the Conference. The emergent redistribution of powers remained the central issue, and language and education rights were regarded as a first step in that direction.

All the positive momentum of the Conference will be needed to pass beyond the issue of the language and education rights for French Canadians, to the second stage, a new division of powers. Premier Johnson's vision is of a two-tier constitution operating simultaneously at different levels, namely a 'ten-partner' Canada and a 'two-partner' Canada. Johnson's immediate claim was for power for Quebec in three fields: social security, foreign relations and communications including radio and television. In foreign relations for example, he reassured the Conference that Quebec "has never questioned the federal government's jurisdiction," but he insisted on Quebec's right to make international agreements in areas of provincial concern. Johnson made a reasonable and convincing case for Quebec's legitimate interest in these areas leaving other semantic and ideological questions such as 'special status' to the future committee negotiations. All three objectives have already begun to be implemented in Quebec.

Even though there were seats for ten provinces and the federal government, two nations, in effect, confronted each other at the table. Implicit in Quebec's moderate and effective participation in the Conference was the desire to build a place for itself within a Canadian federal system. As long as these constitutional negotiations continue to be taken seriously, they are the best pledge of Quebec's basic intent. But Johnson's formula, *"égalité ou indépendance"* keeps the final option visible.

Three major areas can thus be discerned in the spectrum of Quebec demands. We are barely embarked on the first, the demands for linguistic and educational opportunities for French Canadians across the country. Major differences centre on the second area, which Premier Johnson sums up as the recognition of French-Canadian nationhood "in the sociological sense." If we are to find an accommodation here and avoid moving into the third stage, already tenanted by René Lévesque and Pierre Bourgault, then the Johnson approach will have to be explored in detail, especially the term *'égalité'*. If the proper partners to the negotiations are indeed two nations, then we shall be negotiating the granting of some equal powers to a numerically unequal group.

That this runs counter to English Canada's conception of equality as equality of individuals (or, in a federal system, the equality of provinces) is the nub of the issue. For the argument runs that Quebec members of Parliament can hardly expect to exercise their powers for determining policy in English Canada at the same time that Quebec reserves the right to self-determination on these same issues at home.

It is a dilemma which Trudeau and others have not ceased to point out. If all provinces receive the same rights as Quebec, this would preserve the traditional notion of equality in a federal system. Decentralization might take place, we are told, on some pragmatic criterion—according to which issues are best decided by Ottawa and which by the provinces. Otherwise we face the seemingly insuperable conundrum of Quebec members of Parliament deciding issues for English Canada where they have no proper jurisdiction. Can there be more *égalité* for Quebec than for the other provinces?

It is difficult to imagine that this logical conundrum is beyond the wit of man to resolve. A radically different use of the Senate, for example, is one possibility. More to the point is the fact that this conundrum is being regarded as logically (and forever) insoluble, thus creating the basis of a hard line toward Quebec and inhibiting the creation of new and perhaps unprecedented constitutional relations.

This may well be an occasion to cite parables about motes and beams. Quebec is too often accused in English Canada of an intransigence that grows out of a nationalist ideology.

And *"les modes idéologiques,"* Trudeau tells us, *"étaient le véritable ennemi de la liberté."* But the liberal-individualist notions of equality and freedom as we find them articulated in English Canada (and in Trudeau) are no less ideological, and produce inflexible postures as well, if they go unrecognized.

For all his claims to pragmatism, Trudeau is the most deeply ideological of any Canadian politician today. This is illustrated in his recent volume, *Le Fédéralisme et La Société Canadienne Française.* The book is, on the whole, an inspiring and vigorous account of a great intellectual and political career in social reform. But we are also told of *"une tyrannie de la masse: elle s'appelle la Terreur"*; that *"l'idée même d'Etat-nation est absurde"*; John Stuart Mill and Lord Acton command the front benches with 'Reason' and 'The People' (denationalized). It seems vaguely, in its intellectual under-pinnings, *à la recherche d'un siècle perdu.*

Because the Constitutional Conference and the Liberal leadership race ran so closely together, much of the lime-light was on Trudeau. For many years he has held the view that a new constitution was not necessary, that the existing one offered whatever flexibility was needed for the exercise of provincial powers. He failed, at least in this round, in the strategy to defuse Quebec's demands with the offer of a Bill of Rights. But how could a true pragmatist have neglected the fact that Johnson's key demands were already a virtual reality? What battle was Trudeau actually fighting? In retro-spect, the achievements of the conference seem to have come about more in spite of Trudeau than because of him.

If the Constitutional Conference has bought us some time—perhaps three years—and a new climate for an accom-modation with Quebec, it would be a national disaster to have these dissipated by the forthright and intemperate exercise of Trudeau's ideological convictions on the evils of nation-alism. Already his exchanges with Johnson are becoming serious and may poison the climate of reconciliation. Claude Ryan's apprehension goes to the heart of the matter: with Trudeau as Prime Minister, his "hard line toward Quebec, if it were maintained, could only lead to a rupture of the federation" (*Le Devoir,* Feb. 17, 1968).

For an impatient generation that has waited far too long for the end of 'brokerage politics' and wallpaper solutions in this country, the choice of the new prime minister will be a very difficult one. On every count but the crucial one, Trudeau would be ideal—the most attractive political figure of his generation. The mystifying term 'charisma' which is so often invoked, refers to his ability to tap the latent populism always rumbling just beneath the surface of Canadian politics. It would be a pity if the survival of the country in the end, could only be assured with an old-time politician and the moth-eaten political style of the past.

If we are ever to possess the blessed land wherein Lord Acton dwells—"the coexistence of several nations under the same State. . .," then I suspect it will be only because we have managed to keep our respective ideologies and counter-ideologies in check. Pragmatists might devote their intellectual and political energies to staking out the ground that is truly common and for the creation of new political institutions. That may be what 'coexistence' is really about.

March 1968

LES JUIFS MONTREALAIS

J'avoue être intimidé par l'ampleur du sujet. Il suscite tant de questions. A propos du passé, certes! Mais surtout à propos de l'avenir, toujours incertain. Faut-il pour autant renoncer à dégager les perspectives inhérentes à ce problème et cesser d'élaborer des principes moraux aussi bien que politiques appropriés? Je ne le crois pas.

Je n'ai ici qu'une prétention: soulever les questions qui m'apparaissent les plus significatives. Ce qui, somme toute, constitue une approche toute subjective: celle d'un Juif montréalais conscient d'être à la fois observateur et objet de son observation. Vous me pardonnerez donc si j'écris à partir de ma propre expérience.

Qui a oublié ce roman de Hugh Maclennan où l'on trouve une description poignante des deux solitudes de notre pays? Mais, à vrai dire, plusieurs Canadiens n'appartiennent ni à l'une ni à l'autre de ces communautés. Ils vivent entre les deux et forment une troisième solitude.

Celle-ci fera l'objet de mon propos, c'est-à-dire la communauté juive de Montréal, celle que j'ai connue, avant les événements qui ont produit le Québec nouveau, celle qui se perpétue aujourd'hui avec ses valeurs et aussi ses préjugés, alors que la situation a changé du tout au tout.

Je me permets de faire d'abord appel à une allégorie que j'emprunte aux temps les plus lointains de notre passé canadien. Historien en économique, j'ai trouvé dans les archives et les vieux documents que je suis appelé à consulter un fait mystérieux qui me hante souvent. J'évoque ici l'existence d'une tribu d'Indiens établie sur les rives du lac Ontario, près de la rivière Niagara, entre deux tribus ennemies qui se faisaient inlassablement la guerre, celle des Hurons, postée au nord du lac Ontario, et celle des Iroquois, installée au sud du lac Eriée. On l'appelait la Nation Neutre. Songeons au caractère vraiment exceptionnel de cette neutralité dans le contexte indien. Pour les historiens, cette attitude demeure une énigme. J'ai beaucoup réfléchi à cette nation en songeant à la communauté juive.

Les Neutres étaient une nation riche. Voyons la description qu'en donne le père Jérôme Lalemant en 1640 dans *Les Relations des Jésuites:*

Ils ont le bled d'Inde, les faizoles et les citrouilles en esgale abondance. La pesche pareillement y semble esgale, pour l'abondance de poisson, dont quelques espèces se trouvent en un lieu, qui ne sont point en l'autre. Ceux de la Nation Neutre l'emportent de beaucoup pour la chasse des Cerfs, des Vaches et des Chats sauvages, des loups, des bestes noires, des Castors et autres animaux, dont les peaux et les chairs sont précieuses. L'abondance de chair y a esté grand cette année pour les neiges extraordinaires qui sont survenues, qui ont facilité la chasse. . . .Ils ont aussi quantité de coqs d'Inde sauvages, qui vont par troupes dans les champs et dans les bois.

(*Les Relations des Jésuites*, vol. 21, p. 194-196)

Cette prospérité allait de pair avec la paix dont témoigne cet autre extrait:

> Nos Français qui les premiers ont esté ici, ont surnommé cette Nation, la Nation Neutre, et non sans raison. Car ce pais estant le passage ordinaire par terre de quelque Nation d'Iroquois et des Hurons ennemis jurez; ils se conservent en paix également avec les deux. Voire mesme autresfois les Hurons et les Iroquois se rencontrans en mesme cabane ou mesme bourg de cette Nation, les uns et les autres estoient en asseurance tant qu'ils ne sortoient à la campagne; mais depuis quelque temps la furie des uns contre les autres est si grande qu'en quelque lieu que ce soit, il n'y a pas d'asseurance pour le plus foible. . . . (p. 192)

L'histoire de la tribu pacifique des Neutres est une histoire tragique. La nouvelle technologie d'alors, je veux parler des fusils que les Français apportèrent lors de la traite des fourrures, bouleversa toutes les traditions anciennes et les institutions. L'invasion des Iroquois amena la destruction des anciennes relations pacifiques et la conquête des Neutres aussi bien que celle des Hurons.

Les parallèles historiques ont des limites. Les différences sont souvent plus importantes que les ressemblances. Mais, si je ne m'abuse, un égal désir de neutralité entre les deux cultures qui s'affrontent à Montréal, anime plusieurs de mes amis juifs. Le rapprochement culturel avec la communauté canadienne française, une entente qui sauvegarderait la position des Juifs dans cette periode de changement rapide et permettrait de poser des gestes concrets susceptibles de montrer que nous ne sommes pas entièrement liés à la culture anglo-saxonne malgré les tendances historiques manifestées, telle est, je pense, la voie qu'envisage la communauté juive de Montréal.

Ce n'est pas pour renforcer des peurs et des soupçons que j'ai attiré l'attention sur cet épisode lointain mais pour signaler que le rêve de neutralité des Juifs ne pourrait être perpétué que si les Juifs et les Canadiens français pouvaient rester fidèles à leur foi passée et si un processus rapide de changement social n'avait pas commencé à agir avec autant de célérité.

De fortes ressemblances rapprochaient autrefois l'histoire des Juifs et celle des Canadiens français. Pour ceux-ci, le but primordial était évidemment la survivance. Certes, c'était un rêve arcadien d'une simplicité toute pastorale. Ce thème est bien connu. Citons pour mémoire le roman *Jean Rivard, le défricheur*, écrit par Antoine Gérin-Lajoie en 1862. Le but avoué de cette oeuvre était franchement propagandiste: souligner la vocation rurale du Canada français. "Emparons-nous du sol, c'est le meilleur moyen de conserver notre nationalité." Ce qui devint le signe de ralliement des nationalistes qui domina la pensée sociale des Canadiens français au cours du XIXe siècle.

Ce mythe de l'Arcadie eut son pendant dans la littérature juive du début du vingtième siècle: celui du "shtetl"; cette petite ville ou ce village de l'Europe de l'Est, où une vie simple, faite de piété, d'humilité et de soumission à la nature, devait rapprocher l'individu des intentions divines. Dans les écrits de Mendele, de Peretz, et de Sholom-Aleichem, on retrouve ainsi le mythe arcadien de la survivance. C'est celui-là que les Juifs immigrants apportèrent avec eux à Montréal et enseignèrent à leurs enfants.

Ce rêve inaccessible dans un centre industriel et urbain comme Montréal disparut de notre histoire pour les mêmes raisons qui entraînèrent la chute de la vocation rurale du Canada français. L'industrie moderne, les communications, la société technologique, ont mis fin à ces deux mythes et en ont créé de nouveaux. Voilà pourquoi, si nous revenons à notre parallèle historique, le rêve de neutralité dont j'ai parlé passe également du côté des mythes anciens. Voilà pourquoi je ne crois plus possible, dans le contexte actuel, une situation de neutralité entre les Anglais et les Canadiens français.

Ce point-là n'est pas une thèse que l'on puisse soutenir avec une rigueur toute scientifique. C'est plutôt le résultat d'une intuition personnelle que je tire de la connaissance du passé. Permettez-moi d'insister sur cet aspect. Les jeunes Juifs de ma génération ont vécu des situations cocasses, surtout lorsque nous avons été jetés au sein de deux cultures que nous ne partagions pas. Nous ne pouvions pas fréquenter les écoles françaises dont nous étions exclus faute d'être catholiques. Nous sommes ainsi devenus néo-protestants.

Je me souviens de ma première année scolaire. Je fréquentais le Bancroft School, rue St-Urbain, avec une trentaine d'autres élèves agés de six ans. Notre institutrice s'appelait Miss Cohen. Près de la porte de notre classe, se trouvait un grand drapeau, l'Union-Jack, et chaque journée débutait par des exercices matinaux tels le salut au drapeau et le serment d'allégeance que nous avons prêté au souverain et qui se terminait par cette phrase: "one king, one empire, one flag." Ce salut au drapeau était suivi d'oraisons dominicales et d'un hymne. Souvent Miss Cohen lançait sa classe composée de vingt-huit élèves juifs et d'un Ukrainien, sur la piste d'un refrain entrainant, "Onward Christian Soldiers!" Mais le caractère ironique des exercices matinaux ne nous échappait point. Il appartenait à un monde plus mythique que réel. La vie elle-même se déroulait au sein d'une communauté juive repliée à toutes fins pratiques sur elle-même. On nous enseignait les mythes saxons mais les contacts avec la communauté anglaise étaient pratiquement inexistants. Tout autour de nous, vivaient les Canadiens français. Ceux-ci demeuraient nos plus proches voisins.

Je conserve un souvenir vivace de la classe ouvrière canadienne-française et de son milieu. Je suis né et j'ai grandi dans l'est de Montréal et j'évoque toujours cette vie d'autrefois avec une certaine nostalgie.

L'été en était la saison typique—les longues veilles sur le trottoir dans un fauteuil à bascule, l'ombre des escaliers extérieurs grimpant comme des vignes, les pipes émettant leur bouffée de fumée, la bonne humeur qui présidait au bavardage sur le pas des portes. Les aînés se retiraient, ne restaient que les baisers des jeunes dans la lumière jaune des rues et parfois la voix rauque d'un buveur attardé. C'était un monde calme, résigné à son destin, incapable de comprendre les ambitions étranges comme les miennes, celles de partir.

A vrai dire, jusqu'à mon départ pour les Etats-Unis où, à vingt ans, je suis allé poursuivre mes études, je n'ai point connu d'autre Canada français. A mon retour seulement, j'ai pu découvrir cet autre univers canadien-français, la classe moyenne, fortement unie, intelligente et cultivée, familière avec la littérature, les beaux-arts et la cuisine, mais presque coupée des ouvriers. Pour cette classe moyenne, les gens de l'est de la ville suscitaient le dédain. Ils portaient une peste sociale dont il fallait prémunir les enfants.

Au cours des années récentes, ces deux univers canadiens-français se sont retrouvés. Je crois discerner maintenant une nouvelle affection commune, un désir subtil d'affirmation collective qui embrasse dans une même solidarité les deux mondes que j'ai connus.

Au coeur de la révolution qui se déroule au Québec, la communauté juive est confrontée à des problèmes complexes. La révolution en cours est en train de se structurer de façon originale et il est évident—il était évident depuis longtemps—que cette révolution est aussi bien politique et économique que culturelle. Celle-ci a déjà changé la situation du Québec qui continuera à évoluer dans le même sens. Il s'agit donc d'une révolution sociale radicale. Il faut d'ailleurs se préparer à des changements plus radicaux encore au niveau des relations qui unissent les groupes et les provinces. Le moment est donc venu, je crois, de discuter ouvertement l'ensemble des problèmes de l'adaptation à ces forces sociales nouvelles. Je parlerai ici des efforts qui m'apparaissent essentiels de faire sur les plans culturel et économique.

La tâche présente consiste à réfléchir sur les principes de la coexistence de la communauté juive et de la communauté canadienne-française qui est en train de se définir en fonction de ses objectifs sociaux et politiques propres. Sur le plan culturel, il faut penser aux moyens d'orienter l'éducation des élèves juifs en tenant compte du fait que le français est la langue principale de la province. L'important est de dépasser les simples gestes de bonne volonté. Il est nécessaire de préparer les enfants juifs à jouer un rôle spécifique dans la vie économique, professionnelle et politique de la province.

Il faut reconsidérer les liens qui nous unissent avec les écoles protestantes de Montréal, qui ont surtout constitué un moyen artificiel d'angliciser notre communauté. Les dernières déclarations du feu premier ministre, M. Daniel

Johnson, nous fournissent l'occasion de nous engager de façon différente et davantage profitable en fonction d'un projet si vital.

La communauté juive de Montréal a très bien réussi à hausser son niveau de vie économique grâce à ses propres efforts. Mais ce succès a lui-même créé une inégalité économique qui, à mon avis, ne s'accorde pas tout à fait avec les objectifs à long terme de la révolution en cours. Bien qu'il existe des droits sur lesquels il soit juste d'insister—droits civiques, droits culturels, droits aux services sociaux déjà existants—je ne pense pas que nous puissions considérer la répartition actuelle des biens comme s'il s'agissait d'un privilège sacré, même si en système économique capitaliste, les biens acquis paraissent dépendre directement des efforts personnels des individus. Il faut donc prendre conscience qu'à long terme, la révolution actuelle amènera une meilleure répartition des biens et des services sociaux pour l'ensemble de la population du Québec.

On ignore les plans et les projets de la réorganisation économique de la province. Mais nous sommes certains qu'aucune société moderne ne néglige la poursuite d'une meilleure distribution des biens en vue de créer une égalité plus réelle entre ses membres. Il faut surtout se garder de considérer le droit de propriété comme sacré car il ne l'est plus dans les sociétés modernes et il ne le sera certainement pas davantage dans l'avenir, que ce soit que Québec ou ailleurs.

Sur le plan du bien-être social, la communauté juive actuelle possède un réseau d'institutions sociales: services médicaux, services aux indigents, aux vieillards, système d'écoles privées qui dessert presque vingt-cinq pour cent des enfants juifs, Y.M.H.A. clubs privés, etc. Toutes ces institutions sont principalement financées par la communauté juive elle-même, de sorte que l'on peut espérer maintenir le niveau atteint. Mais il faut également prévoir que l'aide gouvernementale se tournera de plus en plus vers d'autres institutions moins bien développées ou situées dans des régions moins fortunées de la province.

Si nous confondons nos droits politiques et culturels justes et essentiels avec les soi-disants droits économiques et le droit de propriété, il en résultera que la communauté juive deviendra une force réactionnaire au sein du Québec nouveau. C'est pour éviter pareille éventualité qu'il importe de repenser les buts à long terme que notre communauté doit s'assigner. Toute nouvelle réorientation n'est pas facile. Notre communauté juive est bien organisée et hiérarchisée. Remarquons toutefois qu'elle repose surtout entre les mains d'une élite composée d'hommes d'affaires. Le moment est donc peut-être venu de repenser aussi la question de la démocratisation au sein de la communauté juive elle-même. Les professionnels, les jeunes diplômés, les intellectuels, n'ont pas encore pris toutes leurs responsabilités dans la communauté. En fonction de notre survivance, nous sommes encore dans l'attente de notre propre révolution sociale.

April 1969

AFTER THE FALL

The War Measures Act

There are a few of us left in the country who remain appalled and sickened by our government's response to the recent crisis in Quebec. Mr. Trudeau has gained unprecedented political support from both the populace and the media for the dramatic gestures of force as wielded by Parliament, the army and the police. Gestures they were, for we have yet to see what was achieved. It was conventional if belated police work that discovered the hiding place of the kidnappers of James Cross and turned up the suspected murderers of Pierre Laporte. For the rest, we have yet to be told what several thousand raids and over 400 arrests accomplished. We have yet to be told why. Ghosts of conspiracies still haunt this venture in political theatre.

What we gained vicariously in symbolic gratification, and whatever political objectives Mr. Trudeau has thereby fostered, carry with them a large price-tag over the long term.

After one of the gravest periods in this country's history the task is *not*, as some would suggest, to put it behind us with earnestness and good will and go on to cure the unemployment problem in Quebec. Sentiment and rhetoric have their place, but also their limits. The crisis must be revisited, without the mind-contracting drug of national hysteria and free of the shadow of political and military overkill. The crisis throws the 'normal' into sharp relief and our first task is to see clearly who and what we really are—under what kind of political structure we actually live, under what strains or threats it buckles, and above all, what sorts of illusions we have been entertaining about Quebec.

Quebec and Canadian Nationalism

Looking back on the fragile plant called English-Canadian nationalism, I feel that our broad analysis of the situation of Canada as a whole can be re-affirmed, while our position on Quebec has proved weak and illusory. On a position that I have attempted to define as 'the nationalism of the left,' our emphasis has been on the retention and the regaining of the crucial powers of decision in this country—the many realms of economic, social and cultural life. At stake is the integrity of the apparatus of the nation-state as a means for implementing the growing number of tasks assigned to it by its citizens, from mass education through social welfare and full employment. The nation-state is particularly important as a social counterforce to the spreading technological society in easing its disruptive costs and distributing more equally its benefits. In an age of rapidly spreading global corporations, only the nation-state remains as a regulatory power and safeguard of sufficient strength against the vast reorganization of resources and global planning carried on by these corporations in their own interests.

The underlying premises of such a position rest on a recognition of the realities of power in the modern world and the shared values and common interests of collectivities in directing that power to common purposes. In that sense, such a position stands opposed to the atomized individualism of the liberal view of society with its faith in the benevolence of blind market forces.

Recognition, however, of a separate community in Quebec, as an indigenous collectivity seeking many of the same powers of decision for itself as we sought for Canada as a whole, lacked a clear definition in this scheme. Many of us sincerely held the view that once Quebec had arrived at a consensus on its own course of action, we would be prepared to support it. Implicitly at least, we felt that the lethargy and indifference in English Canada to the issue would never bring us to use troops if Quebec should decide to separate.

But the irony of history is supreme. Could we ever have imagined that the leading convert in this country to Lord Acton and to Manchester liberalism would be the architect of unprecedented repression? Could we have foreseen that the prophet of nineteenth-century individualism would flex the political contours of our nation-state in a way that has never happened before, creating a national unity through fear and an almost limitless craving among the people for authority, for troops and for police?

Mr. Trudeau has been given undue credit for 'flexibility,' and for his ability to adapt his philosophy to 'circum-stances'. In reality, the road from Manchester liberalism to the repressive state leads in a straight line. The illusions of Lord Acton that centre on the non-recognition of power must in the end rediscover this reality with a vengeance and devoid of moderation. One example will suffice. American extra-territorial jurisdiction in this country that has accompanied American foreign investment has increasingly eroded Canadian sovereignty over a long period. Yet the Prime Minister has never concerned himself seriously with this manifestation of American 'parallel power'. It is a problem that has moderate and viable solutions, as the Watkins Report has demonstrated. Instead, the issue of 'parallel power' emerges full-blown as if it had never existed before the F.L.Q., and is dealt with through a national hysteria of political and military overkill. Thus our own totalitarianism—the ultimate warning of liberals to nationalists—turns out to be founded in that tissue of shallow nineteenth-century fictions about man and society which liberals regard as their ideal. Unable to recognize the legitimate demands of community and the integrity of the institutions of power that nationalists advocate, liberals thereby become the chief architects of the repressive society in a crisis. As their ideals collapse, their refuge in the apparatus of the state is uncritical and untempered.

If Quebec nationalists have given little thought to the political strategy of recreating their political framework, English-Canadian nationalists have offered little more than an empty good will and benevolence. The events of the past few months can be read in many ways. I draw my own lesson from the fact that English and French Canada appear unexpectedly to be interlocked and mutually interwoven in a way that permits no such easy restructuring of the status quo without an immense and complex political effort on both sides.

Some may prefer to cling to an old scenario. If Lévesque and the Parti Québecois had won the last election, would we not have acceded to separation with ease and good grace? It is a tantalizing question and now totally irrelevant. The frustrations that produced the moral climate in which the F.L.Q. emerged are now magnified and doubly embittered. The War Measures Act and the deployment of troops have created a precedent that will be more easily invoked a second time. Our politics have moved beyond the constitutional debates and the self-indulgent literary anguish of the two-solitudes epoch. A neanderthal addiction to force has surfaced and only a supreme romantic will expect our politics to retreat into the channels prescribed by Westminster code books.

Nationalists in English Canada can only regard this escalation with the deepest pessimism. We have introduced into the realm of legitimacy, and indeed probability, the use of military force and emergency powers to achieve *political* ends. The costs of Quebec remaining within Confederation may be as high as those of separating.

Quebec nationalists, of whatever persuasion, must now recognize that they cannot achieve their objectives at any reasonable cost without active support from English Canadians. Nationalists in the rest of the country must realize that the continued repression of Quebec will only create a society which is not worth inhabiting.

Our mutual interests must be recognized. The old empathy

and passive moral support are no longer sufficient. We must now travel in tandem to create in English Canada active legal, political and institutional channels that support and foster Quebec's legitimate aspirations. It is our only hope of mitigating the impact of the collision which looms ahead.

Our dialogue must be reopened in a serious rather than a sentimental vein; our emphasis must be on techniques, on institutions, and strategies that deal evenhandedly with the interests of two emerging nations. But no one can be optimistic about the future.

Symbolic Formula for Quebec

What effective alliance are English-Canadian nationalists offering to their French-Canadian fellow-countrymen? How could this alliance be expressed in an immediate way on the chessboard of political forces?

Claude Ryan's editorial questions move as always, to the heart of the matter. Shortly after his words were written, an alliance that called forth national attention, sprang up within one portion of the Canadian political spectrum. We refer to James Laxer's formula on Quebec which has been adopted by the Quebec wing of the N.D.P. and has produced an alliance between that group and the Waffle. This has become the subject of a major debate by the five N.D.P. leadership candidates in their trek across the country.

The heart of the new formula is that Quebec has the absolute right to self-determination up to and including independence.

The full significance of the formula is elusive. It originally came to us, couched in the language of socialism and as part of the Waffle programme for the N.D.P. convention. But the formula has little to do with socialism as such, and the outer covering fell away quickly.

Within the N.D.P. it was received with bitterness and political apprehension. David Lewis claimed that the party had been driven to consider an irrelevant and false issue. Of course Quebec had the right to self-determination, we were told, when and if she chose to exercise it through the ballot box. But why should separatism be encouraged? "These are hypothetical situations," Lewis continued, "in a language not understood in French or English Canada." The formula was clearly no magic road to success at the polls. Mr. Trudeau and his politics of polarization hovered in the background, and the N.D.P. leadership had visions of a massive electoral defeat if the Liberals tagged them with the label of "soft on separatism."

The reception in Quebec of this new approach was a different matter. It received a much wider endorsement and seemed to strike some responsive hidden chord in the province. Some commentators reacted by suggesting that if the resolution were approved, then Quebec would likely not go all the way to separation from Canada. An acceptable relationship could be envisaged on a fundamentally new basis. This did not seem like a cunning political move; there was something entirely genuine surrounding this prognosis.

The notion of "give us the right to independence, and we will likely not use it," is peculiar and unprecedented. It would be difficult to find a single independence movement anywhere that phrased its position in quite this way. Not Ireland, not the new states of Africa, not the Flemish nor the Welsh.

Some hidden symbolism surely surrounded this issue and we were hard put to find it. The *symbolic* right to independence seemed absolutely crucial. English Canada was being tested for something. . . .If we failed the test, the major thrust in Quebec might revert to a clear demand for outright independence. Claude Ryan stated recently that the issue teetered at the half-way point—the possibility of Quebec separation, in his view, was given a fifty per cent chance.

Leaving aside the tactical political issue as it comes up internally within the N.D.P., is this new formulation simply a Machiavellian gesture, an inching along of separatism, or does it carry instead a hidden plea? If so, what is that plea?

Perhaps the issue runs deeper than it appears to on the surface. The moral burden of the past for Quebec, sits as a shadow cast on its history—the constriction of its inner sense of freedom, the spiritual albatross dragging down its growth and its vision of the future. It originates, in my view, with nothing less than the fatal formative moment when the die was cast in its future relation to English Canada. In one word, what the new formula pleads for is the symbolic liquidation of the Conquest of 1759—the spiritual release from the permanent burden of its history as a conquered people.

Raymond Laliberté, the new leader of the Quebec N.D.P. was right when he stated that this resolution at the N.D.P. convention was at a level of importance such that it might one day head off a civil war in Canada.

Nothing less, in our view, is at stake. A united Canada has a chance of surviving only if English and French Canadians begin again: begin from a point of symbolic separation and come together in the full freedom and genuine equality of the two nations. It is a superior moral basis for a new Confederation.

As partial evidence of our interpretation, we cite the fact that the adherents of this new formula in Quebec refuse to place themselves prematurely in some definite locus on the spectrum between federalism and separatism. They opt out for the moment from taking a concrete political stance until the symbolic issue is fully tested in English Canada. Their political response will then follow.

Our answer to Claude Ryan's challenge is to articulate explicitly the symbolic nexus of this question. The symbolic issue must first be recognized in English Canada and its implications fully accepted. We will then be in a better position to speak of new political alliances between English- and French-Canadian nationalists.

Whatever the outcome of the N.D.P. leadership convention, the Waffle group's stand on the Quebec issue becomes a contribution to this country of primarily educational rather than political significance. I have disagreed with their policies in other areas. On the issue of Quebec they embody in its highest form, the conscience of the country and the response to the burden of our history.

November 1970
January 1971
March 1971

Beyond the Pale: Canada's Foreign Policy

9

PEARSON

Question: What is so rare as an independent Canadian foreign policy?
Answer: A day in June when Mr. Pearson supported Gaullism before an American audience.

Or so it would have seemed from the press reports of his Springfield speech:

> France is not, has not been, and will not be, satisfied with an Atlantic Organization, or an Atlantic Alliance of independent states, dominated by America. France, and not only France, feels that Continental Europe is now strong enough. . .to be given its rightful share in the control of the policies of the alliance.

It was all the more surprising since for the few months preceding the Nato conference, Mr. Paul Martin's righteous rebukes of Gaullism had ventured beyond the call of 'duty'. Even the U.S. State Department had been pursuing a discreet silence about de Gaulle. Had Mr. Pearson launched a new foreign policy?

The actual text of the speech indicated how false the hope was. Not Gaullism, but that hardy perennial, Atlantic Union was the main theme—"a federal union of the peoples lying on both sides of the North Atlantic as a step to an even wider union of all men."

The speech was sentimental and evasive. Clarence Streit, the original Atlanticist of the early 1940's was invoked as a 'visionary', France was offered sympathy as the victim of "a kind of nationalism from which [she] has suffered as much in the last fifty years as any country in the world." The hard-core problems of Europe such as German unification were ignored entirely.

It remained for Mr. Rusk to point out the contradiction a few days later when he testified before the Senate sub-committee on national security affairs. He noted that Mr. Pearson had called for greater Atlantic unity, "and at the same time indicated some sympathy for President de Gaulle's view, which is moving in exactly the opposite direction."

Mr. Pearson's sympathy for de Gaulle is governed by his wish to keep France within his scheme for an Atlantic Community. But Mr. Pearson's Atlanticism would involve major concessions of sovereignty by its members, and neither the United States nor any other principal member of Nato has indicated any willingness to make the concessions which an Atlantic partnership involves. If an Atlantic Alliance cannot move beyond sentimental declarations and remains structured as it is at present, then the erosion of Nato will simply continue.

The basic reluctance in Ottawa has been to face up to the alternative to an Atlantic Community—a movement toward a European Community where Gaullism and resistance to American influence would play a key role. With the growing autonomy of Eastern Europe and the major détente between the U.S. and the Soviet Union, such a scheme becomes the more likely alternative. M. de Gaulle's successful visit to Moscow and the new plan for German unification advocated by an eminent German parliamentarian, Herr Barzel, brought a European settlement much closer.

The possibility of an independent Europe poses the real challenge to present Canadian foreign policy. For if an eroding Nato cannot be transformed into an Atlantic Community, there is seemingly no other fate for Canada but continentalism. Whatever view Canadians may have of their own independence from the United States, a European community drawn together in large measure by the attempt to curtail American influence, would be unsympathetic to any important relationship with Canada. Europe, especially Paris, regards us as already too closely tied to the United States to be much more than an American stand-in.

The alternative to both the illusive policy of Atlantic Community and continentalism is independence. The pursuit of this objective must necessarily begin with a fundamental shift in *domestic* policy, and in particular, a change in our passive attitude to the level of American investment in this country. This is a minimum requirement if we wish to create the image of an independent Canada abroad. As Melville Watkins argues cogently, we might find a greater potential for autonomous action in foreign policy by following Mr. Gordon on the problem of foreign investment. And as Stephen Clarkson has suggested, there are ways in which we can profit from de Gaulle's initiatives and experiments while avoiding his more flamboyant and dangerous gestures.

Mr. Pearson appears to have missed his opportunity both at home and abroad. The link between an independent domestic policy and an independent foreign policy today is central.

If Mr. Pearson could capitalize on the growing sentiment for more economic independence on the domestic scene and move toward independent initiatives in foreign policy—cutting loose from the United States in its Vietnam and China policies for example—he might at last produce a policy that would rally the country.

July 1966

TRUDEAU

Premier Kosygin's visit to this country put into clearer focus the federal government's strategy in response to the Nixon economic measures. It was to be mainly a response in the area of foreign policy. Kosygin reminded us, in his candid way, of the injustice of the American policies, though in more moderate language than that used in defence of those policies by the U.S. Secretary of the Treasury, John Connally. The rest of the world was now being called upon to pay the financial cost of America's blunders in Vietnam and her acquisition of the economies of other countries. Far from rebuking the Russian premier or disassociating himself from his statements, the Prime Minister replied that he hoped that Canada could develop ties with the Soviet Union which would be as close as those with the United States.

Meanwhile, our Minister of External Affairs repeated his appeal to American public opinion over the heads of the United States government. While the speech to the Inter-American Union in New York contained a mixture of pleading and rebuke, calling for the re-establishment of the cozy 'special relationship', his interview on N.B.C. threatened, albeit hesitantly, 'retaliation'. He was backed up by Jean-Luc Pepin's suggestion that we would begin to run hard for new markets in Eastern Europe.

At the moment, the main thrust of our response to the Nixon measures, therefore, is in the international arena and in the context of a system of signals and symbolic responses. If the Prime Minister now goes off to visit China and keeps the energy talks with the U.S. in their present state of suspended animation, he will have adopted an inexpensive strategy toward the United States with a potentially high political pay-off in electoral appeal.

A symbolic stance is not to be underrated. The U.S. State Department has received the message although it seems to be making less impact on the U.S. Treasury Department. The Russians, in turn, are taking the matter of a realigned Canada very seriously; the Russian delegation at the U.N., we are told, is making more consistent and serious approaches to the Canadian delegation for joint initiatives and serious co-operation.

If an independent line in foreign policy now strikes an appropriate note, the question arises whether Mr. Trudeau has indeed outflanked the nationalists at home and left the question of costly and risky domestic proposals conveniently dormant. But we might well ask how long such a symbolic posture can be sustained, given the great vulnerability of this country's economy to the new American proposals? How easy would it be for the Americans to call our bluff in a period of very high winter unemployment? Can Mr. Sharp, for example, live up to his position (on the N.B.C. programme) that we will not bargain on the removal of the surtax and can he continue to decline continental energy talks? What will the DISC (Domestic International Sales Corporations) proposals do to exacerbate further the present unemployment problem? When, in short, will our foreign policy symbolism need to be supplemented by the substance of domestic policies?

In the realm of the things that urgently need doing by the government, nationalist policies have become a first line of defence, not by virtue of ideological or symbolic considerations, but because of the practical requirements that are needed to sustain this country's economy. Lower interest rates and an expanded money supply underline the need for more stringent controls of wages, prices, and profits. The danger of inflation must be removed as a constraint during a period when diverse and unorthodox policies may be needed. To meet the DISC proposals (which offer substantial tax incentives to multinational corporations to withdraw production from Canada to the United States) a variety of techniques, from countervailing tariffs to export subsidies, may be attempted. But what is needed most is expertise on the internal structure and modes of operation of our multinational corporations. Otherwise, any policy pertaining to the control of their operations would be difficult to administer. The Special Agency advocated by both the Watkins Report and the Wahn Report is desperately required as a sophisticated arm of any government policy in this area.

Some will argue that it is already too late to expect substantial results from such an agency, relying as it would on expertise accumulated over a long period. The larger issue that has been demonstrated however, is that the United States will continue to use the subsidiaries of these corporations, directly and indirectly, as an instrument of its economic policy when its own problems require it. DISC is not the first such instance; it follows the same line of conduct, in principle, as the previous Balance of Payments Guidelines (from which we were supposedly exempted by decree and not, it seems, in practice, as revealed by the balance of payments statistics for 1968). DISC is not the first nor the last legitimate instrument of their foreign economic policy. The rules of the game in economic affairs still run to exporting your economic problems to another country whenever you can, and we should continue to expect new difficulties within the framework of a strained international monetary system. If a new agency to deal with multinational corporations is to be baptized under fire, we shall still be far better off in the long run than with the present policy of endless delay in producing a foreign investment code or in activating the Canada Development Corporation.

The Prime Minister has himself done the best job of linking the question of trade with the United States and the question of foreign investment policy. He pointed out in his interview with Charles Lynch that we could not expect to meet our annual obligations to multinational corporations of about $1.5 billion for dividends, interest payments and so on unless we had a trade surplus. If the Americans insist on cutting into this surplus through their trade restrictions, then we could only continue to meet our debts by selling off more of the country. The Prime Minister found this course unacceptable and let fly with terms such as 'imperialism'.

The real danger is that we shall continue to protect ourselves with symbolic phrases only and vary their militancy for purposes of domestic consumption. Given our no-policy policy toward multinational corporations thus far, we are still David in a bathing suit making gestures against the well-armoured Goliath to the south. Mr. Trudeau may find this a convenient pose to take for the purposes of the next federal election. But he would serve us all much better if he realized that the protection of employment in this country in the long run requires some effective controls on foreign investment and a new policy of more autonomous economic development in our manufacturing industries.

November 1971

STRATEGIES

Retaliation has not been a noticeable feature of Canadian-American relations. This hardly allows us to conclude, however, that it will necessarily be ruled out in the future. We have enough instances of the Americans using retaliatory devices in their relations with other countries to know that it is a common instrument of U.S. policy. Their external aid to Egypt moves up or down every six months depending on the political climate; trade concessions to the Communist bloc are alternatively granted and withdrawn. American economic relations with Poland and Yugoslavia over the years are clear examples of the use of policy to reward or punish other nations for their behaviour. These techniques are used effectively by the Americans to secure their own interests, and justifiably so.

In their relations with Canada, the point is simply that part of the chess board has not been brought into play. Together, we operate on a narrower and more benign area of the board. Canada does not do things which might provoke retaliation; the Americans in turn are very leery of engaging in any actions which would set the retaliatory process in motion. Those powerful chessmen on the board have not been involved and perhaps will not be used in the future if the old patterns persist. The levels of independent initiative and risk that have been taken by Canadian policy-makers in the past have not been high, and therefore a series of retaliatory steps has not been necessary. I suppose that the pattern is governed by what Professor Fred Watkins at McGill used to call "the law of anticipated reactions": a policy is decided in terms of expected responses from those it will affect.

But if Canadians become restless with the old pattern of docile (or voluntary) compliance with American foreign policy, we cannot assume that retaliation may not become an important factor in our future relations. The question which I personally find interesting is this: What are the prerequisites, given this relatively benign situation in which we find ourselves, for carrying on an independent Canadian foreign policy? In order not to beg the question, however, I would ask: What conditions are necessary to permit us to take foreign policy initiatives which may have economic repercussions in our relations with the United States? The issues I have in mind, for example, are China and Vietnam.

I would like to suggest that there are three important requirements to make an independent Canadian foreign policy possible. The first is the development of support for such a policy among Canadian public opinion. The present state of Canadian public opinion is, on the whole, uninformed, too fearful and reticent; this makes an independent policy difficult for domestic reasons. I regard as very promising, therefore, the emergence of such groups as the United Church in an active role in foreign policy pronouncements. I think there should be other groups: university professors, trade unionists, and women's groups. I think public opinion should be conceived (potentially) as a network of such groups rather than what we sometimes think of—a collection of well-read individuals.

On this issue it is important to pay more attention to the use of media in the formation of public opinion. I found, for example, that an unusual feature of present-day life in Ottawa, is the role played by Executive Assistants to Ministers who are not bound, as I understand it, by the oath of secrecy. They are the ones therefore, who can originate leaks to the press and thus create some public interest and support for a certain policy. Press leaks have also been used in Canadian-American relations such as the Mercantile Bank case. If there is a deliberate press leak, public opinion may become aroused, and if I were sitting at a desk in the U.S. State Department, I would take this to mean that here is an issue on which the Canadian government is going to take an independent line and is not going to back down. I would suggest that if we want an independent foreign policy, some of these ad hoc and informal techniques should be looked at closely. An articulate and informed Canadian public, aware of the issues, is the first important prerequisite to an independent foreign policy. Any Canadian government which set out on an independent course and got into continuous trouble with the United States, would not last long. The Canadian public in its present condition would not tolerate such a policy.

The second prerequisite is to survey in advance the possible counter-moves that may be made by the United States and to have prepared policy positions on which to fall back. The most serious criticism I have about our relations with the United States, is that these relations are at present viewed as an 'all or nothing' game. I mean, in effect, that the web of relationships is very wide and should the web be damaged by some retaliatory move from the United States we are utterly unprepared to deal with the consequences. We have no clear idea where we are most vulnerable nor what we would do in the event of any specific act of retaliation. Consequently, we always fear the worst—that everything would be lost and that the cost would be infinite. I find it incredible, for example, that when the U.S. adopted its balance of payments policy (which had nothing to do with retaliation), the Canadian government was utterly unprepared to cope with the situation. There were no prepared positions, and it came like a bolt from the blue creating general panic and confusion. A second requirement for independence, therefore, is a far more sophisticated approach to research, policy-planning and prepared positions on every important issue where the chessmen may be brought into action. We may then discover that this is not an 'all or nothing' game, but that there are limited risks, that we can assess potential costs, and that we know how we would act in particular contingencies. It should not be difficult to estimate the cost to us of retaliation on oil concessions, the lumber agreement, the automobile agreement, etc. We could then examine the alternative possibilities open to us.

The third requirement is for a more sophisticated view of American public opinion itself. If we realized, as so few of us do in Canada, the many different levels of foreign policy formation in the United States, we might deal with Congress or the Senate in our own interests, and also with other relevant groups in the policy-formation process in order to back up any moves we might make toward an independent foreign policy. I am advocating a skilful and enlarged use of diplomacy on many levels to back up genuine moves to independent positions.

I should mention one assumption in the above remarks. There is no merit in ruffling the feathers of the eagle for its own sake. Nothing that I have said here implies such gratuitous activity. I am simply talking about a greater degree of elbow-room in the world for Canada, about a much wider horizon toward which we would be able to move. My plea is for a solid appreciation of the fact that there would be costs, of precisely what these costs would amount to and how we could cope with the consequences. If politics is the art of the possible, it remains to extend our view of the possible.

June 1968

Trade and Politics

10

THE FUR TRADE

In the warlike environment of North America in the seventeenth and eighteenth centuries, politics took precedence over trade, for it dealt with the life and death issues of inter-tribal relations. Trade functioned within the context of political relations and institutions and was subordinated to the overriding requirements of security. Economic life had not yet been differentiated as a separate and relatively independent sphere of social existence as in modern society. The coming of the market system with its anonymous buyers and sellers and its impersonal transactions had still to await the development of peaceful conditions, adequate and reliable policing, and a common legal framework.

It is true that the European trade partners of the Indians came from a Europe that was no stranger to shifting wars and hostile relations between countries. In the whole of the seventeenth century, there were only seven years of general peace in Europe. Thus mercantilist Europe did not happen upon an environment in North America to which it was completely alien.

Yet there were important differences, concerning trade more than politics. European traders were oriented towards profits which depended on fluctuating prices for their staples in Europe and tended to regard economic transactions as arms-length and impersonal activities. None of this was true for the Indian tribes which they encountered. Trade was a highly personal activity, an encounter of two political groups or their representatives (not of individuals) and followed established political patterns. A council was held, gifts had to be exchanged and most important of all, a political bond, a 'peace' or 'alliance', had to be established or confirmed. The rates at which European goods were exchanged for furs tended to be fixed throughout the eighteenth century.

The different conditions of Indian trade have been noted by the eminent historian E.E. Rich who indicates that the "Indians' habits of trade. . .were quite alien to a European trade system." He adds that at Hudson Bay, "the English accepted the Indians' habits" and that "much that was formal and social rather than primarily economic found a proper place in such interchanges." (1960:42)

An analysis of these 'formal and social' features of the trade reveals how closely embedded they were in Indian political institutions. Most of these features revolved around the central concern prerequisite to any economic transaction, namely, security.

Early European travellers through North America frequently noted the warlike inclinations of the Indians and their training for battle. Carver wrote that "they are early possessed with a notion that war ought to be the chief business of their lives, that there is nothing more desirous than the reputation of being a great warrior." Carver referred to this as an Indian propensity, but whether the propensity was an inborn trait or culturally determined, Indian wars did have concrete objectives. Usually they centred on the goals of vengeance for injury or murder or the acquisition of territory, "usually," wrote Father Jouveney, "in order that they may avenge an injury inflicted upon themselves or their allies."

Sagard-Théodat explains this as follows:

If one amongst their own people has injured, killed or wounded another, he is absolved by a present, and there is hardly any corporal punishment (which they don't employ for their own people) if the parents of the deceased do not revenge themselves, which rarely occurs. For they seldom do harm to each other. But if the injured person is from another tribe, then war is invariably declared between the two nations if the nation to which the offender belongs does not redeem itself with large presents drawn from its people for the injured party. In this way, two nations very frequently make war due to the fault of a single person, and they are continually in fear of a surprise [attack] from each other. . . .(1865: 153-54)

The expiation of murder by presents was common not only to the Indians of North America but to tribal societies generally, such as the Germanic tribes with the institution of *wergild* and *lex talionis* in the Old Testament. "An eye for an eye and a tooth for a tooth," refers in fact to the compensation for injury, not literal revenge as is sometimes assumed.

The second source of wars concerned territory. It may come as a surprise that in the vast underpopulated lands of North America, boundary disputes played a significant role in intertribal relations. However, the evidence leaves no doubt. Jonathan Carver for example, remarks that:

Notwithstanding it is generally supposed that from their territories being so extensive, the boundaries of them cannot be ascertained, yet I am well assured that the limits of each nation in the interior parts are laid down in their rude plans with great precision. By their's, as I have before observed, was I enabled to regulate my own; and after the most exact observations and inquiries I found but very few instances in which they erred.

Lahontan quotes an Iroquois spokesman in the year 1684 as follows: "We fell upon the *Illinese* and the *Oumamis*, because they cut down the trees of Peace that served for limits or boundaries to our Frontiers."

Territories were thus demarcated among the Indian tribes, but wars did not arise from motives of straightforward territorial acquisition but from problems of hunting rights and rights of passage. Carver notes:

The extension of empire is seldom a motive with these people to invade, and to commit depredations on the territories of those who happen to dwell near them. To secure the rights of hunting within particular limits, to maintain the liberty of passing through their accustomed tracks, and to guard those lands which they consider from a long tenure as their own, against any infringement, are the general causes of those dissentions that so often break out between the Indian nations, and which are carried on with so much animosity. (171)

F.G. Speck has shown that the Algonkian tribes of New England allocated hunting territories to their various clans and these territories were inherited patrilineally by succeeding generations. Trespassers could be punished, in some cases even by death. Concerning the Algonkians of the Lake of Two Mountains Alexander Henry also notes in 1761 that they

claim all the lands on the Outaouais [the Ottawa River] as far as Lake Nipisingue; and that these lands are subdivided, between their several families, upon whom they have developed by inheritance. I was also informed, that they are exceedingly strict as to the rights of property, in this regard, accounting an invasion of them an offence, sufficiently great to warrant the death of the invader. (23)

Murder and territorial rights are problems which in their nature antedate the coming of the Europeans. Whatever wars the fur trade was later to generate, it is safe to assume that the patterns of war and peace, and the intertribal institutions for dealing with them had already been set.

In such a situation of precarious peace and frequent skirmishes and wars, intertribal political institutions were of primary importance. The chief of these institutions, besides the Council, was the alliance system.

Unlike the system of international relations of the modern world where peace is assumed to exist unless war is declared, an Indian tribe was in a state of latent or active hostility with other tribes unless peace had been formally declared. Such a declaration of peace had various names—a covenant chain (among the Iroquois), an alliance, a friendship, a league, or merely 'a peace'. Predatory actions of neighbouring tribes might be expected at any time unless a formal political understanding had been reached. As Hunt remarked, "an Indian nation might be technically at 'war' with all nations not in actual alliance." (20)

Such an alliance was designed to provide mutual security against surprise attack, but also involved military obligations. A tribe would invoke the armed help of its allies to fight its battles. Such alliances might in fact be contracted with a common enemy in mind, a point which the Europeans soon came to understand. "You and they may join together against the French" the English Governor at Albany advised the Iroquois with regard to the Ottawa Indians, "and make so firm a league that whoever is an Enemy to one, must be to both."

Alliances existed in clusters or chains, linking various regional groups of Indian tribes. A systematic table of these alliances in the West was compiled by Zebulon M. Pike in his expedition to the head-waters of the Mississippi in 1805-1807. Seven major tribes of Indians are listed in his chart, and among other information there is included a column "With whom at peace, or in alliance." A second column indicates "With whom at war." The Sauks, for example, are shown as being in alliance with seven other tribes and "all nations of the Missouri," and at war with the Chippeways. Sagard-Théodat remarked with great precision that the Petun Indians of the Bruce Peninsula had "seventeen nations that are their enemies." In 1751 Governor James Glen enumerated the Indian tribes in alliance groupings in both the northern and southern parts of the United States. Before 1650 the Huron system of alliances north of the Great Lakes confronted the Iroquois alliance system centred in northern New York State. One of the earliest Jesuit missionaries, Father Le Jeune, discovered that it was the Huron policy to encircle the Iroquois by alliance as well as to attempt to divide the league.

"The relations into which the Europeans entered with the aborigines," wrote George Ellis, "were decided almost wholly by the relations which they found to exist among the tribes on their arrival." The dominant feature of these relations was the alliance system. European nations quickly became linked to one of these alliance networks with crucial consequences for both the military history of the continent and for the fur trade. Fiske, for example, notes that "the pivotal fact in early American history was the alliance between the Five Nations and the White men on the Hudson River, first Dutch, afterwards English." Likewise, we may recall Rich's remarks that

> The tribal alliances and hostilities to which the French were committed during Champlain's regime were to last throughout their rule in Canada and were to affect all that the French did.

Of the Indians allied to the French, Tailhan speaks of "the invariable fidelity of these savages to our country." He adds, perhaps with some exaggeration, "this devotion to France never once deviated, from the end of the seventeenth century to the Treaty of Paris (1763)." The Indian attack on the British in Michilimackinac in 1763 and on other British posts around Niagara by Pontiac was the manifestation of this long-standing alliance.

In the ebb and flow of intertribal relations, security was the main problem. Old murders might serve as an excuse to begin new wars, migration of hunting tribes would produce territorial disputes about hunting rights and a shifting network of intrigue and diplomacy (accompanied by presents) marked the day-to-day relations of the various tribes.

The major political institution to settle disputes and to create peace was the Council. This was a highly formal meeting among two or more tribes with an elaborate ceremonial procedure which included the presentation of gifts consisting of wampum belts or beaver skins, and the smoking of the peace pipe or calumet. Finally, if negotiations were successful, a treaty was agreed upon to settle the issue in question and an alliance was formed to create peace among the tribes concerned.

The Council was held not only for settling intertribal disputes but also on regular occasions. "They meet every

Spring and Fall," said Oldmixon, "to settle the Disposition of their Quarters for Hunting, Fowling, and Fishing." Councils might be held among clans within the tribe and Carver notes that within the Council,

> with the hereditary chief at its head, the supreme authority appears to be lodged; as by its determination every transaction relative to their hunting, to their making war or peace, and to all their public concerns are regulated.

Sagard-Théodat gives an account of the proceedings of such a Council among the Hurons. When one of his fellow priests was threatened with injury by a Huron, a Council was called of everyone in the village, where Sagard-Théodat openly laid his complaint, followed by an elaborate speech of apology by the chief on behalf of the tribe and a present to the priests of several sacks of corn. In the course of his speech the chief mentioned that only recently one of the members of his tribe had seriously injured an Algoumequin Indian while at play and the issue had been resolved without war through a present.

On a larger scale, he notes, are the "assemblés générales" or general councils of the various districts of the Hurons which take place annually where there occur

> great festivities, dances, gifts given to each other, and among these caresses, rejoicings and compliments they renew their friendship and discuss how it is to be secured, and how they will be able to dispose of and to ruin their common enemies. . . .

A detailed account is available of a Council of Hurons and French which occurred in 1684 after the murder of a young Frenchman, Jacques Douart, by the Hurons. This Council followed entirely the Indian ceremonial procedures. The detailed account by the Jesuit father is prefaced by the remark that "it might be a reasonable curiosity to wish to know, in this matter, their particular customs," which were, in this case, scrupulously followed by the French. The Council proceeded as follows:

Our Christians had informed us of all their customs, and exhorted us to observe them exactly, unless we would arouse prejudice not only against ourselves, but also against the cause of God and the faith. The Captains divided the sticks among them, so that every nation should contribute toward the presents which we asked. For this purpose every one went to his own village. No individual is obliged to make this contribution, but they vie with one another, according as they are more or less rich, in sharing those public burdens, in order to show their devotion to the common weal. A day was therefore set for the return, in order to perform the ceremony with all the solemnity of the country. This was the 11th of May. . . .These gifts are mostly of those beads of marine shells which the French, as we have said, have called *porcelaine,*—and similar trifles, utterly valueless in Europe, but much esteemed in those countries. . . .

The following morning, in the presence of a great multitude assembled from every direction, they made a sort of stage in a public square, where they suspended 50 gifts, which form the principal satisfaction: the remainder, already referred to, being only a sort of accessory. For a Huron slain by another Huron, they usually content themselves with 30 presents. For a woman, they ask 40. This is partly because they cannot defend themselves like the men, partly, too, because they people the countries,—on which account, their lives should be more precious to the public, and their weakness should have greater support from justice. For an alien they ask more; because otherwise, they say, murders would be continuous, trade would be ruined, and war would easily occur with foreign nations. . . .In return, we also made gifts to each of the eight nations, to bind up again and to confirm the old friendship; to exhort them to be always united and at peace, both among themselves and with the French, in order the better to resist their enemies; to prevent slanders which were current against the faith and the Christians, whom they accused of every disastrous accident; to console them for the loss of some of theirs, killed by the enemies; and finally, to assure them that the most Illustrious Signor Governor, who was the Signor Chevalier de Montmagni, and all the French, would forever forget that murder, for which they had, according to their custom, made full satisfaction.

It is thus that they punish murders; and, when presents are not forthcoming at the second or the third time, wars are declared among the nations.

A second instance may be cited where the intertribal Council was used to settle a territorial dispute. Peter Pond at St. Peter's River in Wisconsin recounts in 1744 how a "Grand Counsel" was arranged at Michilimackinac to resolve the hostilities between the Nottaweses and Chippewayan Indians concerning their hunting grounds. The terms of the treaty included an agreed territorial boundary between the two tribes, namely, the Mississippi River. This Council was held under English auspices after the French defeat. The immediate objective was to achieve peace in order to allow trade to continue. But the Council might also be used to mobilize Indian forces for war. One such large Council was held in Michilimackinac by the French in 1753 and is described in detail by "J.C.B.," the anonymous author of *Travels in New France*. This Council involved sixteen different tribes and some twelve hundred men. When they were all assembled the French military commander addressed the Indians as follows:

I was sent to you by your Father Ononthio (i.e., the French Governor) to tell you he loves all his children, and wishes to give them a token of his love by the presents that I was charged to bring you in his name. But I am also instructed to let him know your views about pledging yourself to raise the hatchet, and to go with your French brothers to fight the English.

Each of the Indian chiefs replied in turn that he would support the French and would march with them against the English. The entire proceedings lasted a week. Tobacco and presents were distributed, Indian dancing and pantomimes took place. Two further sessions of the Council were held to confirm the decision that was reached and to reaffirm the loyalty of the Indians to the French.

Evidence of the political significance of the Council in war and peace is abundant. The English, for example, renewed their alliance with the Iroquois frequently. On July 10, 1742, the Lieutenant-Governor of Pennsylvania, George Thomas, met the Iroquois at a Council held at the Great Meeting-House in Philadelphia. He invoked the name of William Penn and the "League of Friendship" Penn had made which "has often since been renewed by friendly Treaties." Presents were then given to the Indians.

La Verendrye tells of a Council with the Assiniboine and Mandan Indians where "a friendship" was formed and the Mandan Indians asked the French for military help in fighting the Sioux Indians, to which request La Verendrye consented.

While the main Indian political institution was the Council, attention should also be drawn to certain subsidiary features, namely, the exchange of gifts, the use of the calumet and the wampum belt. All had a role in the formal procedures of the Council and also in the trade ceremony. We refer here to their symbolic functions.

Among the Indian tribes, the exchange of presents served as a confirmation of a political agreement, usually an alliance or the propositions of a treaty. Colden, for example, notes that

> After the Seneka Speaker had done, the Wagunha Presents were hung up in the House, in the Sight of the Whole Assembly; and afterwards distributed among the several Nations, and their Acceptance was a Ratification of the Treaty.

These presents among the Indians usually consisted of beaver skins or a wampum belt. It was a custom which both the French and English followed. Referring to English negotiations with the Iroquois, Colden alludes to "laying down either Beaver, or any Belt of Wampum, as we always do, when we make Propositions." In political negotiations, presents had a binding character. One Jesuit described the gift of beaver skins from the Iroquois in negotiations with the French as follows: "according to the custom of the country...the term 'present' is called 'the Word', in order to make it clear that it is the present which speaks more forcibly than the lips." More than a century later in 1767 Major Robert Rogers, the English commandant distributed presents in political negotiations with the Indians at Michilimackinac. Several officers signed the accounting statement of expenses for these European goods and added that these presents to the Indians "were absolutely Necessary and well Timed. Otherwise an Indian War must have taken place in this Country Instead of a peace. . . ."

Presents were also used in distant diplomatic negotiations among the Indians. A Huron chief explained to Champlain that he had sent furs to neighbouring tribes of the Iroquois, not in order to trade with rivals of the French but to secure his political position.

> It was sieur de Caen, who believed that I had sent Beavers to the foreigners; I sent to those quarters a few Moose skins, not in trade, but to cut off the arms of our enemies. Thou knowest that the Hiroquois have long arms; if I had not cut them, we should have been taken by them long ago. I send presents to tribes who are their neighbors, to the end that they should not unite with them; it is not to offend the French, but to preserve ourselves.

A detailed description of the calumet and its function is given by Lahontan as follows:

> The calumet of peace is made of certain stones, or of marble, whether red, black or white. The pipe or stalk is four or five foot long; the body of the calumet is eight inches long, and the mouth or head in which the tobacco is lodged, is three inches in length; its figure approaches to that of a hammer. The red calumets are most esteemed. The savages make use of them for negotiations and state affairs, and especially in voyages; for when they have a calumet in their hand, they go where they will in safety. The calumet is trimmed with yellow, white and green feathers, and has the same effect among the savages that the flag of friendship has amongst us; for to violate the rights of this venerable pipe, is among them a flaming crime,

that will draw mischief upon their nations.

Colden notes as well that the calumet is used "in all the Indian Treaties with strangers, and as a Flag of Truce between contending Parties, which all the Indians think a very high Crime to violate." Colden adds that the calumet was "in use before the Indians knew anything of the Christians."

A general description of the ceremony using the calumet or "pipe of peace" in establishing an alliance is given by Jonathan Carver:

> As soon as it is sufficiently lighted, he throws off the coal. He then turns the stem of it towards the heavens, after this towards the earth, and now holding it horizontally, moves himself round till he has completed a circle; by the first action he is supposed to present it to the Great Spirit, whose aid is thereby supplicated; by the second, to avert any malicious interposition of the civil spirits; and by the third to gain the protection of the spirits inhabiting the air, the earth, and the waters. Having thus secured the favor of those invisible agents, in whose power they suppose it is either to forward or obstruct the issue of their present deliberations, he presents it to the hereditary chief, who having taken two or three whiffs, blows the smoke from his mouth, first toward heaven, and then around him upon the ground.

Wampum played a role both as currency and as a means of ratifying the articles of a treaty. Colden gives the following description:

> Wampum is the Current Money among the Indians: It is of two Sorts, White and Purple; the White is worked out of the Inside of the great Conques (i.e. shells) into the Form of a Bead, and perforated, to string on Leather; the Purple is worked out of the Inside of the Muscle Shell; they are wove as broad as one's Hand, and about two Feet long; these they call Belts, and give and receive at their Treaties as the Seals of Friendship; for lesser Matters a single String is given. Every Bead is of a known Value, and a Belt of a less Number, is made to equal one of a greater,

by so many as is wanting fastened to the Belt by a String.

J.C.B. describes the use of the wampum belt as follows:

> In an assembly, an orator never makes assertions, without
> giving illustrations by each string or belt, and sometimes
> both, that he presents. If he discusses several matters he
> will present a string for each one, and will take great care
> to remember, on any similar occasion, all that he said,
> and when he spoke, in regard to each string and belt. Their
> speeches are always as laconic as they are symbolic. They
> are often propounded in the assembly of the village or
> tribe. Each councillor holds a string or belt to serve as a
> reminder, when necessary, to the orator who is the
> spokesman. When the question of answering arises, strings
> and belts are given them in the same way, according to
> the circumstances. But we always take the precaution of
> writing down the speeches and replies to make sure of
> recalling them at need.

In the protocol for establishing an alliance, the calumet
and wampum are used as follows:

> When the chiefs who are intrusted with the commission
> for making peace, approach the town or camp to which
> they are going, they begin to sing and dance the songs and
> dances appropriated to this occasion. By this time the
> adverse party are apprized of their arrival, and, at the sight
> of the Pipe of Peace divesting themselves of their wonted
> enemy, invite them to the habitation of the Great Chief,
> and furnish them with every conveniency during the
> negotiation.
>
> A council is then held; and when the speeches and debates
> are ended, if no obstructions arise to put a stop to the
> treaty, the painted hatchet is buried in the ground, as a
> memorial that all animosities between the contending
> nations have ceased, and a peace taken place. Among the
> ruder bands, such as have no communication with the
> Europeans, a war club, painted red is buried, instead of
> the hatchet.
>
> A belt of wampum, is also given on this occasion which

serves as a ratification of the peace, and records to the latest posterity, by the hieroglyphics into which the beads are formed, every stipulated article in the treaty.

These Indian political traditions were consistently observed both in periods of friendly relations as well as in periods of a hostile political climate. When a deputation of Iroquois Indians visited Quebec City in 1694 for an audience with Count Frontenac, the French Governor, it proposed a step towards reconciliation of the two parties, namely, that the Christianized Indians attached to the French (the "Praying Indians"), would be allowed to travel unmolested to the English in New York state and to the Iroquois territory. This proposal took the form of three propositions, accompanied by the usual three belts of wampum. Count Frontenac mistrusted the good faith of the Iroquois however and assumed that this was only a ruse to win over the converted Indians to the Iroquois side. He rejected the proposal (in M. de Cadillac's words) as follows:

> The Count kicked away these three propositions or Belts, and by this mark of contempt and haughtiness, indicated to the proudest nation throughout this New World, his indifference for peace. . . .

M. de Cadillac goes on to add that in the past the haughty manner of the Iroquois was expressed as follows: "The Iroquois presented formerly but two Belts; one of war; the other, of peace. Choose they used to say; it is equal to us which."

Treaties and alliances formulated in the various Indian Councils resulted in opposing networks of Indian tribes spread over a wide area across the North American continent and engaged in frequent wars. It was in this political setting that the fur trade took root and these political institutions governed the basic patterns of the trade.

Nathaniel Atcheson of the North West Company wrote in 1811:

> It is to be understood, though it may be difficult to convey the idea, that the relations of buyer and seller, of trader and consumer, hardly enter into the view of the Indian—of

the Indian, at least, who lives remote from European settlements;. . .he hunts, and, through friendship and in the spirit of generosity he brings his furs to the trader: the trader he regards as a representative of His Majesty, through whose friendship and goodwill manufactures are permitted to be brought, and to be presented to him in return. Here, therefore, are less of the cold relations of trade, than of the warm one of national and individual attachment:. . .such are the springs of this trade, and the sources of the political influence possessed by the North West Company.

Rather than anonymous buyers and sellers, two political groups or their representatives were involved in the fur trade. Trade was embedded in established political procedures and casual trade between individuals of different tribes did not exist.

A stranger from a distant or hostile tribe turning up un-announced to trade would be taken as a spy. Instances exist of spies or scouts who attempted to use "the pretext of trading some beaver-skins." The Huron Indians, in fact, confined even legitimate visitors to their country to "special cabins to which they must retire; if they found them else-where, they would do them grievous harm." McIlwain notes that

In the eighteenth century trade with an Indian nation meant an alliance with it, and an alliance meant trade. The nations that traded with New France would fight against the English colonies, and the ones who brought their furs to Albany instead of Montreal could be counted on to fight the French.

A concise summary of the integral connection of trade and alliances was that given by an Iroquois spokesman at Albany in 1735, when he stated "Trade and Peace we take to be one thing."

The first Europeans did not find it easy to understand the formal institutions and the protocol which the Indians had established to deal with the requirement of security. In 1616 Pierre Biard, in an uncomprehending way, took these formal institutions of the Indians to be a sign of impertinence since the Indians wished nothing less than to ally themselves with the mighty King of France:

> ...you may be sure they understand how to make themselves courted. They set themselves up for brothers of the King, and it is not expected that they will withdraw in the least from the whole farce. Gifts must be presented and speeches made to them, before they condescend to trade; this done, they must have the Tabagie, i.e., the banquet. Then they will dance make speeches and sing *Adesquidex*, *Adesquidex*. That is, that they are good friends, allies, associates, confederates, and comrades of the King and of the French.

The all-embracing character of the Indians' notion of the alliance is reflected in the welter of synonyms in the above passage: "good friends, allies, associates, confederates, and comrades." It is reminiscent of Father Le Jeune's statement a few years later about the Indians, that "If any stranger, whoever he may be, unites with their party, they will treat him as one of their own nation."

The alliances had many effects on trade and largely they were used as devices to obtain furs by excluding rival European parties. In the early days of the Hudson's Bay Company, Oldmixon (404-405, italics mine), writes that

> The Company, by their Governours and Agents, made such Compacts with the Captains or Kings of the Rivers and Territories where they had Settlements, for the Freedom of Trade there, *exclusive of all others*. . . .These Compacts were render'd as firm as the Indians could make them, by such Ceremonies as were most sacred and obligatory among them.

But if the Europeans were concerned with the exclusive trade privileges of the alliance, the Indians were, in turn, interested in the military assistance to which they presumed an alliance entitled them. At the Rapids of St. Louis on the St. Lawrence, near Montreal, a meeting place for trade, Champlain was told in 1615 by the Hurons of "their hopes that we would give them some of our number to help them in their wars against their enemies," to which he readily assented. Champlain's participation in the wars against the Iroquois was not an incidental decision, nor was it independent of the French trading interest. It was an obligation that grew out of the alliance formed with the Hurons, without which no trade could have taken place.

Colden speaks frequently of the link between "Commerce and Alliances," of Indians coming "to Albany to trade, and settle Peace and Friendship," of the Indians who "not only desired a free Commerce, but likewise to enter into a strict League of Friendship." Peter Wraxall (144) remarks that "Trading is the Only Cement to bind the Indians to our Interest." The strategic import was clear:

> If all these Nations. . .be brought to have a Dependance upon the English. . .the French of Canada, in case of War, must be at the Mercy of the English.

As the Iroquois attempted to draw the Western tribes into the English trade network it was clear, as McIlwain points out, that "to induce these other Indian tribes to take English goods often meant to induce them to take up the hatchet against the French." (Wraxall, xliii)

The ceremony for the establishment or renewal of an alliance in trade had a highly formal character closely related to the procedures of the Indian Council. First, alliances were formed or renewed to satisfy the requirement of security for both groups. The peace pipe or calumet was smoked; gifts were exchanged such as beaver skins, wampum, food and liquor. A banquet or feast was often held and the whole occasion was one of high diplomatic protocol. The close resemblance of the way trade was carried on to the conduct of a political Council lends substantial weight to the contention that the fur trade was embedded in the political institutions of Indian tribal society.

The most complete description of the trade ceremony is given by Edward Umfreville (following closely the account of James Isham for the Hudson's Bay Company in the early eighteenth century). The common features of the trade included the renewal of "the league of friendship," the giving of gifts and the plea of the Indian chief, not for low prices, but for accurate measures.

When they arrive within a few hundred yards of the Fort, they discharge their fowling-pieces, to compliment the English; who, in return, salute them by firing two or three small cannon. The leaders seldom concern themselves with taking out the bundles, but the other men will assist the women. The Factor being informed that the Indians are arrived, sends the trader to introduce the leaders with their lieutenants, who are usually their eldest sons or nearest relations. Chairs are placed for them to sit down on, and pipes, etc. are introduced. During the time the leader is smoking, he says very little, but as soon as this is over, he begins to be more talkative; and fixing his eyes immoveably on the ground, he tells the Factors how many canoes he has brought, what Indians he has seen, asks how the Englishmen do, and says he is glad to see them. After this the Governor bids him welcome, tells him he has good goods and plenty, and that he loves the Indians, and will be kind to them. The pipe is by this time removed, and the conversation becomes free.

During this visit, the Chief is drest out at the expence of the Factory in the following manner: a coarse cloth coat, either red or blue, lined with baize, and having regimental cuffs; and a waistcoat and breeches of baize. The suit is ornamented with orris lace. He is also presented with a white or check shirt, his stockings are of yarn, one of them red, the other blue, and tied below the knee with worsted garters; his Indian shoes are sometimes put on, but he frequently walks in his stocking-feet; his hat is coarse and bedecked with three ostrich feathers of various colours and a worsted sash tied round the crown; a small silk handkerchief is tied round his neck, and this completes his dress. The Lieutenant is also presented with a coat, but it has no lining; he is likewise provided with a shirt and a cap, not unlike those worn by mariners.

The guests being now equipped, bread and prunes are brought and set before the Captain, of which he takes care to fill his pockets, before they are carried out to be shared in his tent; a two gallon keg of brandy, with pipes and tobacco for himself and followers, are likewise set before him. He is now conducted from the fort to his tent in the following manner: In the front a halberd and ensign are carried; next a drummer beating a march; then several of the Factory servants bearing the bread, prunes, pipes, tobacco, brandy, etc. Then comes the Captain, walking quite erect and stately, smoking his pipe, and conversing with the Factor. After this follows the Lieutenant, or any other friend, who had been admitted into the fort with the leader. They find the tent ready for their reception, and with clean pine brush and beaver coats placed for them to sit on. Here the brandy, etc. is deposited, and the Chief gives orders to some respectable person to make the usual distribution to his comrades. After this the Factor takes his leave, and it is not long before they are all intoxicated; when they give loose to every species of disorderly tumult such as singing, crying, fighting, dancing, etc. and fifty to one but some one is killed before the morning. Such are the sad effects of the vile composition they are furnished with upon these occasions.

After continuing in a state of intoxication, bordering on madness, for two or three days, their mental faculties return by degrees, and they prepare themselves for renewing the league of friendship, by smoking the calimut. The ceremony of which is as follows: A pipe made of stone is filled with Brazil tobacco, mixed with a herb something like European box. The stem of the pipe is three or four feet long, and decorated with various pieces of lace, bears claws, and eagles talons, and likewise with variegated feathers, the spoils of the most beauteous of the feathered tribe. The pipes being fixed to the stem and lighted, the Factor takes it in both hands, and with much gravity rises from his chair, and points the end of the stem to the East, or sunrise, then to the Zenith, afterwards to the West, and then perpendicularly down to the Nadir. After this he takes three or four hearty whiffs, and having done so, presents it to the Indian leader, from whom it is carried round to the whole party, the women excepted, who are not permitted to smoak out of the sacred pipe. When it is entirely smoaked out, the Factor takes it again, and having twirled it three or four times over his head, lays it deliberately on the table; which being done, all the Indians return him thanks by a kind of sighing out the word Ho.

Though the above ceremony made use of by the Indians, in smoking the calimut, may appear extremely ridiculous and incomprehensible, yet when we are made acquainted with their ideas in this respect, the apparent absurdity of the custom will vanish. By this ceremony they mean to signify to all persons concerned, that whilst the sun shall visit the different parts of the world, and make day and night; peace, firm friendship, and brotherly love, shall be established between the English and their country, and the same on their part. By twirling the pipe over the head, they further intend to imply, that all persons of the two nations, wheresoever they may be, shall be included in the friendship and brotherhood now concluded or renewed.

After this ceremony is over, and a further gratification of bread, prunes, etc. is presented, the leader makes a speech generally to the following purport:

You told me last year to bring many Indians to trade, which I promised to do; you see I have not lied; here are a great many young men comes with me; use them kindly, I say; let them trade good goods; let them trade good goods, I say! We lived hard last winter and hungry, the powder being short measure and bad; being short measure and bad, I say! Tell your servants to fill the measure, and not to put their thumbs within the brim; take pity on us, take pity on us, I say! We paddle a long way to see you; we love the English. Let us trade good black tobacco, moist and hard twisted; let us see it before it is opened. Take pity on us; take pity on us, I say! The guns are bad, let us trade light guns, small in the hand, and well shaped, with locks that will not freeze in the winter, and red gun cases. Let the young men have more than measure of tobacco; cheap kettles, thick and high. Give us good measure of cloth; let us see the old measure; do you mind me? The young men loves you, by coming so far to see you; take pity, take pity, I say; and give them good goods; they like to dress and be fine. Do you understand me?

As soon as the Captain has finished his speech, he with his followers, proceed to look at the guns and tobacco; the former they examine with the most minute attention. When this is over they trade their furs promiscuously; the leader being so far indulged, as to be admitted into the trading-room all the time, if he desires it.

The principal things necessary for their support of an Indian and his family, and which they usually trade for, are the following: a gun, a hatchet, an ice chizel, Brazil tobacco; knives, files, flints, powder and shot, a powder horn, a bayonet, a kettle, cloth, beads, and the like.

These institutional features of the trade economy were not restricted to trade at established European forts or settlements. Since they derive from Indian culture traits it is not surprising to find the same patterns in Indian inter-tribal trade. As part of the establishment of peace between the Cheyenne and the Kowa, Comanche, and Prairie Apache, the latter tribes reciprocated the civilities the Cheyenne had shown them the previous day. This was described as follows:

After all had eaten, High-Backed Wolf called out to his people that now their guests were through eating and they should bring their presents. "Those of you who are bringing guns must fire them in front of the lodges: not here close to these people." He spoke to the chief guests, saying: "Do not be frightened if you hear shots; it is our custom when we are going to give a gun to anyone to fire it in the air." Then for a little while it sounded like a battle in the Cheyenne camp—a great firing of guns. The Cheyennes brought guns, blankets, calico, beads, brass kettles— many presents.

After all these had been presented, High-Backed Wolf said to the guests: "Now, we have made peace, and we have finished making presents to one another; tomorrow we will begin to trade with each other. Your people can come

here and try to trade for the things that you like, and my
people will go to your camp to trade." It was so done, and
this was the beginning of a great trade.

The peace then made has never been broken. (Jablow 74-5)

Numerous observers in different periods of the fur trade
attest to the persistence of reciprocal gift-giving as an essential
feature of the trade. This was the French practice from earliest
times, for as Denys states:

> There is given the Indian every time they come to the
> establishments a drink of brandy, a bit of bread and of
> tobacco as they enter, however many there may be, both
> men and women.

Alexander Henry notes in 1776 that "We made presents of
tobacco to the chiefs. . .who brought us beaver-skins, in
return for which we gave a second present," prior to the
beginning of trade. These presents seem to have been a regular
institution, for Henry (196) notes earlier that "I gave them
their spring presents; to some clothing, to others large kegs
of mixed liquor." Richard White testified before the Parliamentary Committee of 1749 that

> he has known 11 Canoes leave the Factory at Albany
> Fort at One Time for want of a Present of a Bottle
> of Brandy.

The significance of these gifts was more than a formal
courtesy. As we have noted previously, gifts in a political
context served as a pledge or a way of ratifying a treaty.
Du Chesneau suggested in 1681 that these presents in the
trade were made in order to "confirm their words," pre-
sumably the alliance or friendship:

> As these tribes never transact any business without making
> presents to illustrate and confirm their words, should their
> voluntary offering not be kindly received. . .they en-
> deavour to enter into arrangements among themselves.
> (O'Callaghan, 161-62)

Elements of this relationship between trader and Indian
persisted through the nineteenth century. As late as 1892,
Indians coming to a Hudson's Bay post "had to be given a

little tobacco, flour, tea and sugar before furs were mentioned. Then the whole story would be repeated how the Company had always looked after its red children and fed them. . . ."

April 1972

BIBLIOGRAPHY

Atcheson, Nathaniel. *On the Origin and Progress of the North West Company of Canada with a History of the Fur Trade as Connected with that Concern.* London: Cox, Son and Bayles, 1811.

Blair, E.H. (ed.) *The Indian Tribes of the Upper Mississippi Valley. . . as described by Nicolas Perrot.* Vol. 1. Cleveland: Arthur H. Clark, 1911.

Carver, Jonathan. *Travels Through the Interior Parts of North America in the Years 1766, 1767, and 1768.* London: C. Dilly, 1781.

Champlain, Samuel de. *Voyages and Explorations.* Vol. II. E.G. Bourne (ed.) Toronto: The Courier Press, 1911.

Colden, Cadwallader. *The History of the Five Indian Nations of Canada.* London: T. Osborne, 1747.

Denys, Nicolas. *The Description and Natural History of the Coasts of North America (Acadia).* W.F. Ganong (ed.) Toronto: Champlain Society, 1908.

Great Britain, Parliament, House of Commons. *Report from the Committee Appointed to Inquire into. . .Hudson's Bay.* London, 1749.

Henry, Alexander. *Travels and Adventures in Canada and the Indian Territories.* James Bain (ed.) Toronto: G.N. Morang, 1901.

Hunt, G.T. *The Wars of the Iroquois, A Study in Intertribal Trade Relations.* Madison: The University of Wisconsin Press, 1940.

J.C.B. *Travels in New France.* S.K. Stevens (ed.) Harrisburg: Pennsylvania Historical Commission, 1941.

Jablow, Joseph. *The Cheyenne in Plains Indian Trade Relations 1795-1840.* Monographs of the American Ethnological Society 19. Seattle: University of Washington Press, 1966.

Lahontan, L.A. *New Voyages to North America.* Vol. I. R.G. Thwaites (ed.) Chicago: A.C. McClurg, 1905.

La Potherie. "Savage Allies of New France," *The Indian Tribes of the Upper Mississippi Valley. . .as described by Nicolas Perrot.* Vol. II. E.H. Blair (ed.) Cleveland: Arthur H. Clark, 1911.

La Verendrye, P.G. *Journals and Letters*. L.J. Burpee (ed.) Toronto: Champlain Society, 1927.

O'Callaghan, E.B. (ed.) *Documents Relative to the Colonial History of the State of New York*. Vols. VI and IX. Albany: Weed, Parsons and Company, Printers, 1855.

Oldmixon, John. *The British Empire in North America*. Vol. I. London: J. Nicholson, B. Tooke, 1708.

Pike, Z. *The Expeditions of Zebulon Montgomery Pike*. Vol. I. Elliot Coues (ed.) New York: F.P. Harper, 1895.

Rich, E.E. "Trade Habits and Economic Motivation Among the Indians of North America," *The Canadian Journal of Economics and Political Science*, Vol. XXVI, 1960.

———*Montreal and the Fur Trade*. Montreal: McGill University Press, 1966.

Rogers, R. "Rogers's Michilimackinac Journal," *Proceedings of the American Antiquarian Society*, Vol. XXVIII, 1918.

Rotstein, A. "Fur Trade and Empire: An Institutional Analysis." Unpublished Ph.D. thesis. University of Toronto, 1967.

———"Karl Polanyi's Concept of Non-Market Trade," *The Journal of Economic History*, XXX:1, 1970.

Sagard-Théodat, G. *Le Grand Voyage du Pays des Hurons*. Paris: Librairie Tross, 1865.

——— *Histoire du Canada et Voyages*. Paris: Librairie Tross, 1866.

Speck, F.G. *Family Hunting Territories and Social Life of Various Algonkian Bands of the Ottawa Valley*. Memoir 70. Ottawa: Department of Mines Geological Survey, 1915.

——— "The Social Structure of the Northern Algonkian," *Proceedings of the American Sociological Society*, XII, 1917.

Thwaites, R.G. (ed.) *Jesuit Relations and Allied Documents*. Cleveland: Burrows Brothers. Vol. I, 1896. Vols. III, V, VI, X, 1897. Vol. XXI, 1898. Vol. XXXVIII, 1899.

——— *The British Regime in Wisconsin*. Wisconsin Historical Collections, XVIII, 1908.

Umfreville, Edward. *The Present State of Hudson's Bay*. W. Stewart Wallace (ed.) Toronto: The Ryerson Press, 1954.

Wraxall, Peter. *An Abridgement of Indian Affairs. . .in the Colony of New York*. C.H. McIlwain (ed.) Cambridge: Harvard University Press, 1915.

ECONOMIC COEXISTENCE: CANADA'S TRADE RELATIONS WITH THE SOVIET BLOC

"Peace through trade" is the watchword proposed for Canada's trade relations with the Soviet-bloc countries.[1] It forms the theme of an editorial by a leading national newspaper:

> The United States is entitled to preach, and for its own part to practice, the economic isolation of countries with Communist forms of government. But most Canadians believe that peace is better served by trading back and forth with these countries in commodities of a peaceful nature.[2]

There is much to be said for such a sentiment. The economic advantages of trade are universally recognized, and beyond these are the political advantages. Trade creates situations of interdependence and personal contacts that increase confidence and reduce fear and suspicion.

The editorial continues:

> The exchange of goods brings nations closer together, makes them more dependent upon each other and so reduces the danger of conflict between them. This has become an essential point, and indeed now stands as a prime point, of Canadian foreign policy.

Again, most of us would agree. But this article is neither about the material advantages of trade nor the increased confidence which flows from personal contact. It is about the middle stage between the two, when individuals and organizations try to come to agreements about exchanging goods; it is about the rules of the game that prevail and the translation of sentiment into reality. When Soviet-bloc state trading organizations deal with Western private firms and businessmen, different rules, different motivations and different practices may be involved. A basic reciprocity of interest cannot always be taken for granted. Some even maintain that such a reciprocity of interest cannot permanently be achieved—that the two systems are at bottom irreconcilable.

It may be too early to offer a definitive answer on this

matter. The search for a minimum framework for economic coexistence is best served by the separation of domestic ideology from international business practices. In this regard, the Soviet-bloc foreign trade system, surprisingly enough, may be at less of a disadvantage than we are. Whatever factors may inhibit its accommodation to a changing international economy, socialist principle is not one of them. The same cannot be said of Western countries where the linking of international trade practices to domestic ideology inhibits not only necessary innovations but a recognition of the potentialities of institutions already developed.

We shall explore the general features of this problem and then turn to the specific Canadian context. The substantial wheat sales to Russia and to China were a happy event for this country but only a windfall. We cannot assume that Soviet-bloc harvests will always be poor nor that their basic agricultural problems are incapable of solution. Our trade relations at present depend on our buying if we are to continue to sell. Thus far, at least, we have been relatively unsuccessful in matching their purchases with our own, and no one can be optimistic about the permanence of what is essentially one-way trade. It is in the interests of this country to explore new approaches and new initiatives for the sake of both peace and trade.

Yet there are pitfalls and a chequered history with which to contend. The Cold War is thawing and a short memory may be a useful contribution in order to make it thaw further. But we might pause to recall that while the notion of 'peace through trade' is an old theme, it is relatively new in relation to trade with Russia. After all, it was only as recently as 1958, that a former Prime Minister was asserting the opposite, when he told an audience in the Albert Hall in London that

> Trade has become a major weapon in the communist world offensive. First it was the U.S.S.R. and now red China has joined in an Asian onslaught, intended to capture markets and with and through them, the minds of men. The communist drive is designed to undermine the economic strength of the free world.[3]

Even stronger expressions of dismay came from other

Western countries at the prospect of increased Soviet-bloc trade. In the late 1950's, Soviet-bloc trade did significantly increase political tensions in the West and was then regarded as a prime threat. Such tensions, actual and latent, were more typical of trade relations with Russia in the forty years that followed the revolution than the 'peace through trade' which we hope for today.

The solution to this paradox lies in distinguishing between the two basic political situations within which the trade relations of the two systems may take place, namely the competition inherent in the Cold War and the co-operation inherent in coexistence. We shall discuss each situation in turn. Let us begin, however, with a review of the formative influences and objectives of the Soviet foreign trade monopoly.

The distinctive features of the Soviet system of foreign trade have traditionally been: a monopoly of all foreign trade by a special state agency, an emphasis on self-sufficiency through the acquisition of imports that cannot be produced within the country (autarchy), and the conduct of trade through bilateral agreements.

It is these features of Soviet foreign trade, particularly the unusual powers of the foreign trade monopoly, that have given rise to difficulties and fears in market economies and are generally thought to be typically socialist devices. Yet it was not doctrinaire socialism that was in Lenin's mind when he created the Russian foreign trade monopoly in 1918, since socialist doctrine had little to say on how foreign trade should be organized and nowhere specified these particular features.

On the other hand, foreign trade monopolies were not unprecedented in history. They had, for example, been the hallmark of the mercantilist organization of foreign trade some several hundred years earlier, although never as unified as in the Soviet instance. In 1664 Colbert established the giant *Compagnie des Indes Occidentales* for French trade with America and Africa. Although private participation was welcomed, the bulk of the funds came from the royal treasury, making the company, in effect, an agency of the Crown. One economic historian, K.G. Davies, concludes that "the company must be regarded as little different from a department of state." Colbert had actually modelled his company on the Dutch West India Company founded in 1621, whose "chief purpose. . .was to wage hemispherical war."[4] (In Canada, the often-challenged but persistent monopoly of the Hudson's Bay Company in the fur trade is well known.) It was the frequent warfare and shifting diplomatic situation of the mercantilist period that called forth such state agencies to carry on trade. Economic historians have noted that trade in this period was also accompanied by strong tendencies toward autarchy and bilateral trading.[5]

Roughly similar problems of an unstable international environment (over and above an unstable domestic situation) confronted the Soviet Union in 1918, and it is not surprising that there was a similar response. The Russian government had to contend with problems of political turmoil, enormous economic change, instability of the international economy and foreign animosity due partly to its repudiation of the foreign loans contracted by the Czarist and Kerensky regimes. The Russian foreign trade system was an ad hoc response to these actual conditions rather than the fulfilment of socialist principles (even though it may seem, on the face of it, to be consistent with these principles). While the nationalization of industry *was* a matter of socialism, the nationalizing of the imports and exports of these industries through a separate central monopoly was to nationalize them twice over. This was not the only possible way to administer foreign trade and was challenged within the Communist Party. But Lenin feared above all that capitalist countries would use foreign trade as a weapon to undermine the new Soviet state industries. He declared:

> Strengthen and regulate those state monopolies which have already been put into effect and then prepare the monopolization of foreign trade by the state; without this monopolization we shall not be able to separate ourselves from foreign capital and from paying tribute.[6]

The novelty of this measure can be seen in the debate that followed. Other Russian leaders such as Bukharin advocated a more conventional solution to what was thought of simply as an infant industry problem, even though these were infant state industries. Bukharin put forward a proposal for high tariffs against foreign goods. He thought that state industries could then conduct their own foreign trade as separate corporations under tariff protection. Lenin, however, vigorously disagreed:

> Bukharin does not see that no policy of tariffs can be effective in the imperialist epoch when there is a monstrous difference between the poor countries and those of unbelievable wealth. Bukharin refers to protection by tariffs, failing to see that under conditions referred to, any one of the wealthiest countries can break down this protection.[7]

Lenin feared that capitalist countries might offer export subsidies on goods exported to Russia and these subsidies could overcome any tariff protection. The fears of foreign trade against which no tariff wall, however high, would provide adequate protection, prompted the formation of the Russian foreign trade monopoly. Lenin's decree of April 22, 1918, stated:

> All foreign trade is nationalized. Contracts for the purchase or sale of all kinds of products (the products of mines, of industry, of agriculture and others) with foreign governments or individual enterprises abroad will be carried out in the name of the Russian Republic by specially empowered organs. Apart from these organs every contract for trade, for purchase or sale abroad is forbidden.[8]

Lenin's fears turned out to have been justified. The early years following the revolution saw an economic blockade of the Soviet Union by Western countries. Many hostile and discriminatory provisions were put into practice. Soviet ports and borders were blockaded, Soviet exports and ships abroad were frequently seized and a 'gold blockade' was instituted which refused to accept gold payment from the Russians or else would accept payment only at a twenty-five per cent discount. More peaceful trade relations began with the signing of a trade agreement with Great Britain in March 1921, although embargoes and discriminatory restrictions on Soviet exports continued.[9]

Only later did the foreign trade monopoly acquire ideological status when it became for Stalin one of the "irremovable foundations of the 'platform' of the Soviet Government." This was not by virtue of socialism but for the same reasons that Lenin had given, namely, the fear of the consequences of trade with capitalist countries. In an interview with a visiting delegation of American trade unionists in 1927, Stalin declared:

> The abolition of monopoly for foreign trade. . .would mean abandonment of the industrialization of the country. . .it would mean that the U.S.S.R. would be flooded with goods from capitalist countries, the destruction of our industry because of its relative weakness; increase in unemployment, deterioration of the material conditions of the working class, and the weakening of their economic and political conditions.[10]

The main function of the foreign trade monopoly was to *import* the goods needed for the current economic plan. As the matter was put by one Soviet foreign trade official active in this early period:

> . . .the U.S.S.R. participates in foreign trade, but acting on different motives and with different aims [from capitalist countries]; it has to import many things; it requires machines that are not produced in the country, it requires raw material and manufactured goods, which either are not produced in the country at all or are produced in an insignificant quantity. As it is necessary to pay for the imported goods, the U.S.S.R. exports a corresponding part of its products, thus covering the payments for the imported articles.[11]

This was the approach of self-sufficiency or autarchy in Soviet economic development. Again, substantial economic interdependence with capitalist countries could not be relied upon because of the disruptive consequences to the Soviet economy that would follow if this trade were suddenly to be cut off. There is, indeed, nothing intrinsically capitalist about an international division of labour, nor intrinsically socialist about autarchy.

It is only in the postwar period when other countries became part of the socialist camp that the principle of autarchy began to be challenged and an appreciation of the benefits of the international division of labour became apparent, not only for trade between socialist countries, but between socialist and capitalist countries. An important state-ment of this position was that of two Hungarian economists in 1954:

> According to the classical formulation of the theory of autarchy, as given in all publications on foreign trade, the main task of foreign trade is, through exports, to procure imports of those commodities which cannot be produced within the country. This, in fact, was the way the problem arose in the emergency that once faced the Soviet Union, alone and under blockade in a capitalist world. . . .

They went on to add that:

> In foreign trade, then, it is not imports which are the end and exports the means; exports and imports alike are means, and means of equal importance in developing the socialist economy. . . . The economic returns from foreign trade can be determined only by a comparison of national and international values.[12]

The same general reasons lay behind the traditional bilateral organization of trade. The attempt was made (with some exceptions) to balance exports and imports with each indivi-dual country on the basis of a trade agreement. The alterna-tive, namely, to engage in a wide network of multilateral trade, with credits earned in one country being used to pay for goods in another, requires a greater degree of confidence and trust than was present. If such a network were disrupted at some point through the hostile actions of one of the parties, dangerous economic consequences might ensue. Bilateral trade agreements, then, were a means of partitioning the political risks and controlling the degree of inter-dependence.

While the Soviet foreign trade system was shaped as a defensive response to a hostile international environment, it nevertheless had unsettling effects on market economies when, unexpectedly, its latent powers became apparent in the direct confrontation of the two systems.

The Soviet foreign trade monopoly functions in practice through twenty-nine trading corporations many of which engage in both import and export activities. Each corporation specializes in certain classes of commodities and equipment.

For example, *Exportkhleb* deals in grain, pulses and oilseeds, and *Machinoimport* imports power, mining and transport equipment. This form of trade organization is roughly similar in all Soviet-bloc countries and China.[13]

The main function of these state trading corporations, as we have noted, is to procure the materials and equipment from abroad to help fulfill the current economic plan, and imports are planned accordingly. But "the best laid plans of mice and men gang aft agley." When deficiencies, bottlenecks and crises occur, the relevant trading corporation is called upon to import the necessary goods to solve the problem. With the growth of the socialist camp in the postwar period the goal of self-sufficiency has been broadened to include a division of labour within the bloc through the Council of Mutual Economic Assistance (Comecon).

Foreign exchange to pay for imports from abroad is obtained through the sale of domestic surpluses, or of commodities that may, for the moment, be less urgently required than the ones being sought. Alternatively, foreign exchange may be obtained through the sale of gold.

While the state trading corporation would prefer to obtain the highest possible prices for its exports by selling at established world market prices, it may be forced to undercut world prices when foreign exchange is needed urgently or in large amounts. So-called 'losses', in so far as these can be established at all, are spread over the entire domestic economy. More important, the state trading corporation does not know, nor does anyone else, what the domestic cost of production actually amounts to.

Accounting costs of each item are known but these omit factors such as interest charges and ground rent at some stages of production, while the pricing of labour and other factors such as machinery and natural resources often does not reflect their productivity. In addition, the mark-up for profit varies substantially on each product. Thus accounting costs bear no clear relation to economic costs and the extent to which they differ is unknown.[14] The state trading corporation knows whether the price at which it exports is above or below its accounting cost but not whether it is above or below the real cost of production. In addition, the corporation may and does set its export price at any level it chooses whether it turns out to be above or below its accounting cost. The fact that the ruble rate of exchange is an arbitrary rate set by Soviet authorities while trade agreements are concluded in foreign currencies adds an additional complication in cost calculation.

The extent to which Soviet-bloc trade differs from Western economic practice thus becomes clear. Further, it cannot be established in the Western importing country whether or not Soviet-bloc goods are being 'dumped' since Russian domestic costs cannot be compared with the price at which the goods are being offered.

Even if adjustments could be made in the cost data between accounting and economic costs, would the principle of comparative advantage or relative costs be followed in planning which items to produce domestically and which to import? This is currently a subject for debate within the Soviet bloc, but in some countries it is clear that a different principle is being followed, namely the concentration on heavy industry whether that happens to be the most efficient allocation of resources or not. For example, the chief of planning in Rumania, M. Constantinescu, writes:

> The all-round development of the machine-building industry is a major necessity for all the countries. Without this, it is impossible to achieve technical progress and greater mechanization of all branches of the economy or to ensure proper care of existing equipment and its constant improvements. . . .Lenin developed the Marxist tenet that accumulation in Department I (production of the means of production) is a factor making for the proportionate development of these two departments and consequently Department I must play the leading role in extended reproduction.
>
> . . .Only if this condition is observed can Socialist reproduction on an extended scale be assured. From this springs the need for accelerated rates of development of heavy industry, a need that is common to all countries building Socialism.[15]

Two different sets of objectives in trade thus stand in sharp contrast in the international economy. Soviet-bloc trade as carried on by state agencies is geared to certain objectives such as obtaining the imports necessary for industrial growth. Western foreign trade reflects the comparative advantage or relative efficiency of certain domestic production as determined largely by the price system and is carried on, in general, through firms and individuals which must sell above cost.

The existence of different objectives in trade may create latent or actual situations of instability with harmful consequences. For example, the state trading corporations may undercut world market prices with ease if they either choose to do so for political reasons, or are forced to do so in order to obtain foreign exchange. The first major manifestation of this difficulty came in the drive to reorganize agricultural production and to build an agricultural machinery industry after 1929. Exports of Soviet wheat and lumber were sold at less than existing world market prices in order to obtain urgently needed foreign exchange even though these raw materials were in desperate shortage at home. These exports aggravated the already existing crisis in world trade considerably. This led in turn to a world-wide press campaign against "Soviet dumping" and "the use of forced labour" and to an increase in political tensions.[16] It was the first major instance of the political difficulties associated with Soviet trade which were to come up even more sharply some thirty years later.

Two events coincided in the late 1950's to create dismay in the West around the issue of Russian trade. The first was a foreign currency shortage in Soviet-bloc countries, and the second, a heightened development of the Cold War.

To obtain urgently needed foreign currency, Rumania undercut world market prices for oil, Poland did likewise for farm produce, and Russia undercut the price of tin and of Canadian aluminum (by about twelve per cent) in the London market. In the latter case, Alec Nove has suggested that these Russian exports were linked to the acute balance-of-payments problem which had developed with the sterling area in 1957 when the Russians imported rubber from Malaya, cocoa from Ghana, wool from South Africa and New Zealand, and copper from the London market. Aluminum and tin proved to be the commodities most easily spared at home and so they were sold at less than world market prices in order to earn sterling quickly. Nove writes that "the decisions to sell these products do not seem to require either a more subtle or a more sinister explanation."[17]

The intention to disrupt deliberately the international economy need not be read into these instances. Yet the climate of the Cold War had also become more severe. Former Premier Khruschev stated in 1957 that "We declare war upon you [the United States] in the peaceful field of trade." Soviet trade agreements were being negotiated with Burma, Egypt and other developing countries, offering long-term barter arrangements which Western private firms could not match and which gained political advantages for the Soviet bloc. In competitive situations, the weakness of the West, trading as it generally does through private firms, became dramatically apparent. Mr. Nathanael V. Davis, President of Aluminium Ltd., issued the following statement at the time of the undercutting of the aluminum market:

> Although we are ardent supporters of free trade and competition among friendly nations, we are convinced that a private industry alone cannot compete against the resources of a state.[18]

A similar conclusion was expressed by Mr. Desmond Donnelly in a recent study of Soviet-bloc trade:

> The specific danger here is that the resources of the bloc are always sufficient to place any individual Western industrialist at a hopeless disadvantage. . . .[19]

In Washington in 1958 there was fear and dismay surrounding the question of Russian trade. James Reston reported:

> A high official of the United States Government discussing the problem of meeting the Communist offensive, commented this afternoon:
>
> "It is politically impossible for us to discuss in public

the radical changes we shall have to make to deal effectively with the Soviet economic offensive.

"They control all of their trade. They can use it as a political instrument regardless of cost. They can take losses to drive competition out of a given market precisely as large producers once were able to do to eliminate small competitors in this country.

"We have been discussing quietly inside our own Government for six months the need to establish an overseas trade monopoly to compete with the Soviet monopoly on equal terms, but this is so foreign to our normal way of doing business that we dare not mention it in public."[20]

Unexpectedly, Lenin's fears of foreign trade had found their exact counterpart forty years later during a period of political tension and, uncritically, the same response was being considered as the one to which Lenin had turned.

This trade monopoly was not implemented. A year later the U.S. State Department declared:

Creation by the United States of a trading corporation would be an imitation of Soviet state trading methods and contrary to traditional U.S. encouragement to and reliance on free markets.[21]

This was a curious confusion of domestic ideology and international practice in view of the fact that a U.S. government agency, the Commodity Credit Corporation, has been exporting abroad over $1 billion a year of U.S. agricultural produce, in effect making the United States the leading state trader in agricultural commodities.

The events we have outlined led the former general counsel of the International Monetary Fund, J.E.S. Fawcett to conclude:

No reciprocity between the systems is possible. Both aim to achieve a universal division of labor by methods which are mutually exclusive, and hardly adaptable to international rationalization.[22]

This conclusion may be an exaggeration. Western governments already possess the means to deal with possible economic disruptions caused either directly or unwittingly by the Soviet-bloc foreign trade monopoly without resorting to the radical measure suggested in the United States. Government agencies exist in every Western country for commodity agreements, foreign aid and military procurement. If necessary, they could be used to counter the actions of the foreign trade monopoly either by an individual government or on some intergovernmental basis. Not all such disruptions require government action, but extensive price-cutting, for example, might be met by equivalent price reductions of Western goods financed by such an agency, if this was felt to be in the national interest (for the sake of domestic employment) to safeguard markets. One of the benefits of such a standby policy might be its deterrent effect on the foreign trade monopoly. Other measures by government agencies are also possible, and a far simpler solution would be to ease the foreign exchange position of a Soviet-bloc country through some currency or credit arrangement if this was politically feasible.

But none of this has proved to be necessary. The crisis passed and the Russians have since eased the situation by attempting to work within world commodity agreements, by paying for imports in gold and by purchasing large agricultural surpluses from Western economies.

The heightened tensions and the foreign exchange difficulties in the 1950's have been superseded by two developments. A general thaw has occurred in the Cold War due in part to the nuclear test ban treaty, and in the economic sphere, long-term credits have been granted to the Soviet Union for the purchase of machinery and equipment to meet the crisis in the chemical and fertilizer industries. The granting of such credits by Great Britain and Japan, disregarding U.S. policy in this matter, and the reports of imminent action by other Western governments to follow suit, will relieve pressure on Russia's foreign exchange reserves.

The Russians are not unaware of the serious political consequences that their foreign trade monopoly may create and have no economic reason to cause disruptions if long-term credits are available.

Predictions about the course of international politics are hazardous, but the present turn of events may open a period of political co-operation where 'peace through trade' may have the chance to become a substantial reality if remaining difficulties can be resolved. We will offer suggestions on how this may be achieved in the Canadian situation.

Rigidities and difficulties exist on both sides which inhibit long-term co-operation of the two different trading systems in the international economy. The hoped-for changes on the side of the Soviet bloc over the long run would centre on abandoning autarchy in favour of a more permanent division of labour with capitalist countries, and on abandoning bilateralism in favour of multilateralism, where credits earned in one country would be regularly available to purchase goods in another. (There are indications of the beginnings of such a process in Russian trade today.) The foreign trade monopoly might also be made more flexible to allow greater direct contact and negotiation of Western businessmen with Soviet-bloc domestic industries. Since these traditional features of the Soviet-bloc trading system are not fundamental matters of socialist principle but the response to a hostile political climate, we may have reason to think that the easing of international tension and the growth of mutual confidence will create such greater flexibility in the Soviet-bloc foreign trade system in their own economic interest.[23] The necessary administrative tasks of co-ordination of imports and exports and currency control are not precluded by such changes. The rationalization of economic administration and accounting methods now taking place in the Soviet Union and other Soviet-bloc countries will also assist in the rationalization of foreign trade.

But we have only the power to change our own policies to meet the present situation. We must deal with the system as it is today while remaining aware of future possibilities.

Exports to Soviet-bloc countries have been about ten times the volume of imports in recent years. Under a system of complete multilateralism, such an imbalance might be of little consequence. The task today, however, is that of increasing Canadian imports in order to provide a basis for the preservation of long-term trade.

Limitations on trade are set by the similarity of geography and natural resources of Canada and the Soviet Union. On the other hand there may be a significant basis for trade due to relative transport costs. Soviet officials have suggested that Canada might ship up to 18,000,000 bushels of wheat (or 500,000 tons) annually to the Soviet Far East since that would prove more economical than rail shipments from their central regions.[24] These exports would be contingent on Canadian imports, however.[25] Canadian industrial equipment may also have a market in the Soviet Union, as evidenced by the recent sale of an asbestos manufacturing plant valued at $7,000,000 on the basis of a five-year credit agreement. Soviet officials have also expressed interest in purchasing Canadian farm machinery and equipment for the pulp and paper and food industries. These officials have also suggested that the following goods might be of specific interest to Canadian buyers: mine-drilling equipment, coal-cutting combines and excavators, diverse metal-cutting and wood-working machines and bearings, welding equipment, cranes, hoisting mechanisms and printing machines. In addition, pig iron, chromium ore and ferro-alloys would be of interest to the Canadian steel industry. Other goods might include watches, and optical equipment.[26]

What, therefore, inhibits trade between the two countries? It is not differences on the Soviet side in international business procedures. The state trading agencies follow the traditional international practices regarding letters of credit, financial arrangements and bills of lading, insurance, c.i.f., f.o.b. and f.a.s.

Some of the difficulties reside in the relationship of the Canadian private firm to the Russian state trading agency, and not enough attention has been given to how they are to deal with each other.

Soviet state trading corporations are not adept at merchandising and selling techniques particularly in competition with private firms from other countries such as England, France and the United States.

Private firms in turn are apprehensive about the risks involved in dealing with such foreign state agencies. Concern centres on the reliability of deliveries, spare parts and servicing of equipment, the difficulty of interim negotiations on technical matters,[27] and the possibilities of renewed orders when markets have been established in Canada.

Some of the risks may be reduced and difficulties of negotiation lessened if, on the Canadian side, a government agency were available for the task of mediating and for liaison functions between the private firm and the Soviet-bloc agency on a voluntary basis. Information and advice would be available to both parties on drawing up contracts, with provision perhaps for standard penalties in cases of failure to meet deliveries of goods or spare parts, and to fulfill other functions of mediation.

Some of these functions of providing information are presently performed on a limited and informal basis by the Department of Trade and Commerce. They might be extended and formalized, although no new government agency would be required.

I am suggesting nothing more, in fact, than the application of our present policy of a mediating agency which we already follow in relation to other foreign Western governments engaged in direct economic transactions in this country. Following the end of the Second World War, the Canadian Commercial Corporation took over in 1946 the functions of the Canadian Export Board which had until then carried out various procurement functions in Canada on behalf of foreign governments and the United Nations Relief and Rehabilitation Administration. Its functions as set out in the Canadian Commercial Corporation Act and its amendments include:

1. To assist in the development of trade between Canada and other nations:
2. To assist persons in Canada
   (a) to obtain goods and commodities from outside Canada; and
   (b) to dispose of goods and commodities that are available for export from Canada.[28]

The principal functions of the Corporation are to enable

the procurement by foreign governments of defence supplies. Other functions include the purchase in Canada of supplies and equipment for foreign aid projects such as the Colombo plan. The total value of contracts which the Corporation has entered into from its inception in 1946 to March 31, 1962, was $3 billion, of which the value of U.S. military contracts amounted to $1 billion. The Corporation has also purchased defence and other supplies on behalf of some eighteen other countries as well as for agencies of the United Nations. In some cases the Corporation acts as agent for the foreign government and in other cases buys and sells on its own account.

This first proposal, therefore, is that advisory and mediating functions be formally provided on a voluntary basis by the Canadian Commercial Corporation. In cases of difficulty, Canadian importers will have the backing, up to a point, of their own agency rather than standing in an isolated and vulnerable position vis-a-vis a foreign state agency.

The second proposal concerns the easing of the bilateral character of Soviet-bloc trade which poses awkward rigidities for both sides. As a first step we might turn our attention to three-cornered or tripartite solutions on the eventual road to multilateralism. This step is not unprecedented. In 1954 for example, a tripartite agreement was reached involving trade between Poland, Italy and Indonesia, and other such cases exist. More recently the Chinese have come up with a tripartite proposal vis-a-vis France and the former French colonies in Africa. According to press reports,[29] the notion involves the shipment of raw materials from the African countries to France, the shipment of French oil to China, and the shipment of Chinese equipment and consumer goods to the African states.

The Canadian situation offers perhaps roughly similar possibilities vis-a-vis Britain and the Soviet Union. The latitude offered by the administration of existing tariff policy in Canada and in Britain may permit either a formal or informal agreement with Britain and the Soviet Union on specific commodities. Under such a scheme, Canada would adjust the application of her tariff procedures on specific

British goods, in accordance with various domestic considerations; Britain would do likewise on certain Soviet goods, and the Russians would thus sell more to Britain to partially increase foreign exchange earnings for Canadian wheat purchases. Numerous practical considerations are involved here, and while Britain has a balance-of-payments deficit with both Canada and Russia, such a scheme may still be to her economic advantage. This scheme does not depend on exact calculation of the increased sales which would result. We may start with very rough estimates and make later ad hoc adjustments. A different type of three-sided solution with another country, perhaps France, may be appropriate for trade with China (and with Russia), and tripartite agreements may be possible with, for example, Czechoslovakia or Poland and Russia. Such proposals need more detailed investigation, of course. Although such a scheme may raise questions with regard to the General Agreement on Tariffs and Trade (G.A.T.T.), administrative leeway may exist for its implementation. (The larger question of the relation of Soviet-bloc trade to G.A.T.T. still remains to be settled, and a Canadian initiative in this regard may be advisable.)

However, all proposals on increasing imports of Soviet-bloc goods into Canada are contingent on the way our tariff policy is applied. The way in which domestic industries are protected from 'dumping' is through the application of the 'third country' criterion. Soviet-bloc goods are assigned a value by our customs authorities which reflects the selling price of such articles when exported by another Western country with an economy similar to Canada's. Dumping duties are levied equal to the difference between the Communist country's selling price and the price as quoted by the third country. Normal tariffs are then paid in addition, on this newly computed value.

Admittedly, as we have discussed above, no effective way exists to determine whether Soviet-bloc countries are selling their goods in Canada below domestic cost price (i.e. 'dumping'), so this 'third country' criterion may be a useful administrative substitute in principle. However, much depends on the way in which it is applied. One of the areas for administrative discretion is the choice of the relevant third country and the related product produced there. The Department of National Revenue, under whose jurisdiction this valuation falls, should exercise this discretion to permit goods to enter, rather than setting higher valuations so as to exclude them. An important element of uncertainty would be eliminated if tariff rulings from this department could be obtained in advance on the basis of sample goods; otherwise importers remain uncertain about a significant portion of their costs until goods have actually reached this country.

Closer co-operation of the Canadian government and business is required if progress is to occur. Our trade agreement with the Soviet Union has in recent years specified that the Soviet government would purchase twice as much from Canada as Canadians did from the Soviet Union up to a total of $25 million. The proportion has in fact been very much higher, as we have seen, due to the Soviet purchases of wheat. The commitment to purchase Soviet goods by the Canadian government is only nominal, since it depends on private firms to do the purchasing. The former Minister of Trade and Commerce, Mr. Churchill, has declared that:

> We are not a state trading nation, and the Canadian government cannot ensure that the proportion desired comes into the country from Russia.[30]

Perhaps the existence of the Canadian Wheat Board slipped Mr. Churchill's mind, as a result of ideological wishful thinking. The general result has been that no progress has been made since by the government on this question. We have thus far got no further on the matter than Mr. Churchill's notion that:

> . . .the Soviet export organizations, if they wish to expand their sales in Canada, will have to make the necessary effort to ascertain what Soviet products may be saleable in the Canadian market and how these sales can be developed on an orderly basis.[31]

The result of our passivity has been that Canadian trade with the Soviet bloc is planned, not by Canadians, but by the Soviet-bloc governments.

The spirit of these proposals suggests an approach to the tasks of long-term economic coexistence as they may arise in the future. It is difficult to specify what these tasks will be, but they may include world-wide commodity agreements, currency agreements, partitioning of supplies of scarce raw materials in order to avoid a scramble, and joint investment projects in underdeveloped areas. Canadian government agencies already exist whose functions can be adapted to these tasks in cooperation with private business. These include the Export Credits Insurance Corporation, the Exchange Stabilization Fund, the Canadian Wheat Board, and the Canadian Commercial Corporation which we have mentioned. The Soviet state trading corporation would have a partner of equal power and stature and Canadian private business would have a shield.

It is clear that we shall have to continue to live in an international economy which is not of our own design. It will not be a question either of mercantilism or of free trade and if our analysis is correct, the degree of change in the Soviet-bloc foreign trade system is likely to be even greater than in our own. In the light of other changes as well, such as the evolution of the European Common Market, and the accommodations necessary for underdeveloped areas, no one can predict the nature of the institutional framework that will ultimately emerge. But the rapid growth of the U.S.S.R. to fifth place in world trade in recent years indicates that we are on the threshold of a major realignment of the international economy similar in scope perhaps to the change from mercantilism to free trade. Many maintained during that transition that new trading arrangements could not be implemented. Free traders were at first regarded as a nuisance, subject to designations such as 'interlopers'—with connotations of piracy and poaching. These complaints about threats to established trading institutions were in vain.

In this regard, one lesson in Canadian economic history should be recalled. Just over a hundred years ago in Canada, the merchants of 'The Commercial Empire of the St. Lawrence' fought a rearguard action against history. They tried desperately to preserve their mercantilist tariff privileges in England against the tide of the free trade movement. Their strategy went down to defeat in bitterness and frustration, but their trade prospered even more under the new system than it had previously.

Trade is not a universal solvent for peace, or history would have run a different course. Yet Canada is offered today opportunities that make for both peace and trade. The words of Hegel come to mind:

Besseres nicht als die Zeit,
Aber auf's Beste sie sein.

We are bound to what the times allow us,
But let us live up to the best that is offered.

January 1965

NOTES

1.   I am indebted to the late Professor Karl Polanyi who first drew the subject of economic coexistence to my attention. I have benefited greatly from discussions with him of his general ideas on this matter. Preliminary views on this question were presented in two talks on the C.B.C., Feb. 23 and 24, 1959, and in an article in *The Canadian Forum*, Feb. 1964.

2.   *The Globe and Mail,* Nov. 20, 1963, 6.

3.   Cited in *House of Commons Debates*, Third Session, 1960, Ottawa; Queen's Printer, 239.

4.   K.G. Davies, *The Royal African Company*, London, Longmans Green and Co., 1957, 19 and 22.

5.   Klaus E. Knorr, *British Colonial Theories 1570-1850*, Toronto, University of Toronto Press, 1944, esp. 23, 103, 127-28.

6.   V.I. Lenin, *Sochineniia* [Collected Works], Moscow, third edition (1928-37), Vol. 22, 449. Cited in J.N. Hazard, "State Trading in History and Theory," *Law and Contemporary Problems*, 24:2 (Spring 1959), 245.

7.   *Sochineniia,* Vol. 27, 381. Cited in "State Trading in History and Theory."

8.   [1918] *Collection of Codes of the R.S.F.S.R.*, No. 23, item 432. Cited in "State Trading in History and Theory," 246.

9.   Cf. A. Baykov, *Soviet Foreign Trade*, Princeton, Princeton

University Press, 1946, 7, 18.

10.   J. Stalin, *Questions and Answers to American Trade Unionists*, New York, Worker's Library Publishers, 1927, 28. Cf. also *Voprosy Leninizma*, [Questions of Leninism], tenth edition, 1933, 179.

11.   J.D. Yanson, *Foreign Trade in the U.S.S.R.*, London, Victor Gollancz Ltd., 1934, p. 18.

12.   Tibor Liska and Antal Marias, "A gazdaságosság és a nemzetközi munkamegosztás á (Optimum Returns and International Division of Labour), *Közgazdaşàgi Szemle*, No. 1 (1954), 78. Excerpts in English are given in United Nations, Economic and Social Council, Economic Commission for Europe, *Economic Survey of Europe in 1954*, 131-35. The above passage is on p. 132.

13.   Cf. Alec Nove and Desmond Donnelly, *Trade With Communist Countries*, London, Hutchinson, 1960, 165 ff.

14.   "Our present price system...does not reflect values because it considerably undervalues producers' goods.... A further complication arises from the fact that the proportion by which producers' goods are undervalued is not constant. The price of many producers' goods contains an element of turnover tax, whereas many other producers' goods are priced at less than cost." *Economic Survey of Europe in 1954*, 133.

15.   M. Constantinescu, "On the Road of Building Socialism, Some Problems of Economic Development in Rumania in the Light of the Economic Tasks of the People's Democracies," *For a Lasting Peace, for a People's Democracy*, Bucharest, Sept. 9, 1955. Quoted in Nicholas Spulber and Franz Gehrels, "The Operation of Trade Within the Soviet Bloc," F. Holzmann (ed.) *Readings on the Soviet Economy*, Rand McNally, 1962, 147, n.15. Rumania's position on this matter has been consistent and has recently been the source of a disagreement with Comecon, which assigned to Rumania the role of an agricultural and petroleum producer in the Soviet bloc's division of labour. Cf. *The New York Times*, June 3, 1964, 5.

16.   *Soviet Foreign Trade*, 18.

17.   Alec Nove, "Soviet Trade and Soviet Aid," M. Bornstein and D.R. Fusfield (eds.), *The Soviet Economy*, Homewood, Ill., Richard D. Irwin, Inc., 1962, 286. Cf. also the comments of the London *Economist*, July 5, 1958, 12: "The Poles who lately charged clumsily into the London butter market, helping to push down the price to the chagrin of New Zealand, did so not to undermine the Commonwealth but because, with the bottom fallen out of the coal market, they are desperate for foreign exchange."

18.   *The New York Times*, Sept. 27, 1958, 27.

19.   *Trade With Communist Countries*, 161.

20.   *The New York Times*, Dec. 2, 1958, 17. A further indication of the temper of the time in Washington is given in the following excerpt of a speech delivered by the then U.S. Secretary of Commerce, Lewis L. Strauss, to a Canadian audience at the Chateau Laurier Hotel in Ottawa on February 18, 1959:

> ...there is now a new kind of Soviet threat facing both our countries—the Soviet declaration of economic warfare. For the first time in history, so far as I know, we see commerce perverted. You and we who engage in business for the incentive of legitimate profit now have competition from a monolithic exporter—a government which employs the labour of slaves and cares not a whit for profit. It dumps even the goods it needs at home if thereby it can damage or destroy our market or penetrate underdeveloped countries with its products and its technicians. We shall have to meet this new weapon with an effective countermeasure. It is an insidious kind of warfare because it is less dramatic than a shooting war but it can be just as lethal.

(Lewis L. Strauss, "Strengthening the Foundations of the Canada-United States Partnership," address to the Canadian-United States Business Conference, sponsored by the Canadian Chamber of Commerce, the Ottawa Board of Trade with the cooperation of the Chamber of Commerce of the United States, Feb. 18, 1959, mimeographed.)

21.   Senate Committee on Foreign Relations, 86th Congress, First Session, *U.S.-U.S.S.R. Trade Relations*, 1, Washington, 25, n.1.

22.   J.E.S. Fawcett, "State Trading and International Organization," *Law and Contemporary Problems*, 24:2 (Spring 1959), 349.

23.   Partial and indirect confirmation of our view of the Soviet-bloc foreign trade system comes from a Canadian source. When the League for Social Reconstruction issued its volume, *Social Planning for Canada*, in 1935 (Toronto, Thomas Nelson and Sons), it proposed that foreign trade should be planned "because of the impossibility of leaving socialized industries at the mercy of foreign capitalist sabotage" (247). In the absence of such a threat to a planned Canadian economy by either foreign or domestic capitalists, the League envisioned that:

> ...any special foreign trade policy would be superfluous. Within the limits laid down by the national plan and commercial treaties, and under the control of the national bank, the various socialized industries and services might be left to manage their own importing and exporting. (361)

24.   *The New York Times*, May 14, 1964, 32.

25.   See the report of remarks by Soviet Agriculture Minister J.P.

Volovchenko on his recent Canadian tour. *The Globe and Mail*, Aug. 21, 1964, B-2.

26. *The Globe and Mail*, Oct. 14, 1964, B-6.

27. The following description of these difficulties is given in the London *Economist*, July 12, 1958 (143-44):

> In the formal pattern of trade with Russia, the supplier deals with a central purchasing agency that is helpless to make any technical decision without referring it back, which can blur or delay negotiation to an infuriating degree.
> [In Moscow] underlings abound and typists; but there is usually nobody who admits to knowing where a person is, when he will be back, or whether it is worthwhile ringing again. . .if he has gone down the corridor, to Sochi, Siberia, or indeed Valhalla, he leaves no forwarding address.

Perhaps continual contact through a Canadian government liaison agency will provide a better path through the maze.

28. Canadian Commercial Corporation, *Annual Report, 1960-61*, 3.

29. *The New York Times*, Dec. 27, 1963, 1, and *The Globe and Mail*, Jan. 15, 1964, B-1. Other examples of tripartite agreements include Finnish agreements with Russian and eastern European countries and joint construction projects by Hungary and Austria in Lebanon, India and Italy. Cf. "Hungary's Rising Trade with the West," *East Europe*, Oct. 1964, 13: 10, 18.

30. *House of Commons Debates*, Third Session, 1960, Ottawa, Queen's Printer, 3136. He also declared in reference to this trade agreement that:

> . . .the terms of the arrangement are better than those offered by the U.S.S.R. to any other country (6105).

31. *Ibid.*, 6106.

Binding Prometheus

11

Of all peoples on earth, Canadians are least able to understand the process of Americanization. America is total environment: it envelops us as a mist, penetrating every sphere of our cultural, political, economic, and social environment. For that very reason we seem to feel powerless, unwilling and unable to achieve the perspective necessary for an appraisal of our situation. It sometimes seems as superfluous to ask what should be done about the Americanization of this country as it is to ask what should be done about the weather.

It may well be that an assessment of the ground that we have already lost and of the process which continues to overwhelm us would lead any objective observer to declare 'game over' in the battle for Canadian independence. But there is a moment at which the purging of illusion and even the deepest pessimism can beget the firmest resolution to survive.

The global significance of this country's fate should not be over-looked. Americanization is today a worldwide process and Canada is both the sharpest example and the clearest early warning system to many countries who are still on the fringe of a universal process that is proceeding with enormous impetus. A global perspective may also offer a better focus on our own dilemma. A preoccupation with Canadian-American relations as a bilateral process tends to create a mood which is introverted and myopic. We are thus inclined to miss the salient features and forces that transcend this bilateral relationship while still having a substantial effect on it. I refer particularly to the political and social consequences of industrialization as carried forward by the present thrust of the American multinational corporation which has become the single most dynamic economic force of our time. It is the latest episode of the interplay of society and the machine.

The value of the production of all multinational corporations in countries outside their home base in 1967 exceeded $214 billion. This makes the aggregate production of these corporations abroad the third largest economy in the world, second only to the domestic economies of the United States and the Soviet Union. To throw further light on the magnitudes involved, this production exceeded the total volume of world trade in 1967 (according to figures from G.A.T.T.) and exceeded as well the combined gross national products of the United Kingdom and Japan. One forecast by the International Chamber of Commerce suggests that multinational corporations abroad will grow at a rate of no less than twenty-seven per cent per year.

Obviously this is the major challenge to the independence and national integrity of countries such as Canada.

This essay attempts to seek out what is in the industrial experience of western societies that may offer some basis for action and for hope without illusion in our present circumstances. Our itinerary roams far afield, our argument is condensed and elliptic, not to say arbitrary, and the possibilities that are sketched out for Canadian independence against the tide of Americanization are at best intuitive. An uncompromising assessment of the Canadian political psyche must go hand in hand with an appraisal of the chequered course of the industrial experience of the West. There are grounds for believing that no determinism whether economic, ideological, or technological can properly encompass or predict the social, political, and moral eruptions which we have already witnessed in the unexpected century and a half of the machine age. Hope rooted in the tides of both historical experience and historical uncertainty may be brought to bear on the present impasse of an eroding Canadian independence.

The First Industrial Revolution

Americanization and industrialization today are closely intertwined and require a historical perspective to appreciate the range of forces at work. Discussions of the consequences of industrialization tend to centre on the confining effects of the machine on social existence, the tendency for a proliferating bureaucracy to force daily life into a straitjacket. In backward perspective, however, other forces can be discerned; some social effects veered in exactly the opposite direction. Three main phases can be noted: the immediate social consequences of the industrial revolution in Europe, the effects on the colonies, and the larger tidal wave of moral forces that were released later in the nineteenth century.

In the first stage of the industrial revolution, the institutional requirements at the time centred on the regular provision of the voluminous quantities of raw materials and labour to feed the new industrial factories and machines. It appeared then that only a free labour market, accompanied by a free market for raw materials and land, could organize an automatic flow of a self-adjusting kind, for the new industrial order. The social transformation which this implied was novel, indeed revolutionary. The removal of a centuries-old system of social welfare at the parish level was required in order to establish a free labour market, for example. The unrestricted faith in labour as a commodity implied the most pernicious consequences for social organization. Child labour, employment of women in the mines for long hours, the disorganization and demoralization of the early factory towns, all of these social phenomena are too well known to be recapitulated here. (The full story of the social history of the nineteenth century is best told in Karl Polanyi's *The Great Transformation*.) What was striking about the social history of that century, however, was what we may call the 'double movement'. The extension of the free market system for genuine commodities was accompanied by a simultaneous attempt to restrict the market for such 'fictitious' commodities as labour and land, neither of which was originally 'produced' for the market. This spontaneous counter-movement was the natural response of society to safeguard the two basic ingredients of social existence, man and his environment. What seemed to some in that century a conspiratorial attempt to restrict the nascent 'free economy', was in reality the self-mobilization of society to protect the essential features of its existence. It is this social dialectic which is the most impressive feature of our adjustment to the first round of the industrial revolution. A network of social institutions arose, whose primary aim was to restrict and to thwart the unrestricted effects of an automatic social order (the market economy) running along its own rules, grinding out production in response to maximum profit possibilities and the needs of the market. In the end, the market economy of the nineteenth century was indeed humanized: child labour laws, housing and zoning regulations, safety regulations in the factories, the whole trade union movement, as well as the rise of tariffs and monetary restrictions in the international economy. It was also the era of the birth of socialism. All of these institutional devices were designed to insulate and protect the social order from an attempt to crowd society into the confines and rules represented by the market economy. What characterized that century, we repeat, is the unexpected renaissance of social institutions that were meant to free society from the juggernaut organized to feed and extend the new industrial order.

The impact of the industrial revolution on the colonial areas of Asia and Africa had a different history. During the first centuries of contact with outlying countries, the European presence was limited and strictly confined to trading enclaves in coastal areas. Numerous examples exist in West Africa and on the Malabar Coast of India. Local rulers maintained full sovereignty and jurisdiction even though Europeans were from time to time engaged in political and diplomatic intrigue in the areas in which they landed and traded. On the whole, this assertion of sovereignty—the creation by local rulers of a body of restrictive regulations concerning foreign European merchants—safeguarded their societies from the disruptive effects which were to come later.

The collapse of indigenous regimes came in a great rush after the middle of the nineteenth century. European powers seized political control of the Asian and African continents, each eager to carve out a sizable empire. Complex political forces were at work, but certainly one of the features of this drive for colonial empire was the attempt to secure total control over land areas which were producing the growing volume of raw materials needed to feed the European industrial machines. Another consideration was the large markets these areas represented for European manufactured goods which were forthcoming in a torrent of new production, following the widespread industrial organization of European economies. But it required the force of arms to end local independence.

In the present period, in a second and much more powerful round of what we may call the New Mercantilism, the moral of this story should be apparent. The new multinational corporations threaten the survival of the indigenous cultures and political integrity of the countries which they penetrate. Again, a well-conceived programme of regulation and careful accommodation should go far in restricting these effects of the second round of global penetration, the result of which is the rapidly increasing Americanization of the world. The areas of economic regulation and control may range widely: the policies of these multinational corporations toward local management, the extent of domestic production facilities and export policies, the participation of local capital and entrepreneurs, policies on expansion and new investment, and finally the protection of the local country from the extension of American law through extraterritorial legislation.

This type of broad approach may benefit from the lessons of the first round of mercantilism at the margin of Europe. There was in these areas a stand-off relationship rigorously maintained whereby chartered companies and trading agencies were confined and restricted in their operations. They had specific rights and they were met by an existing legal and political containment, which was amazingly strong even in the very small African potentates and in the small principalities of India. Countries such as Canada and other Western European countries should be able to muster at least as much initiative and imagination in the protection of their own independence and cultural survival as was demonstrated over a century ago by much weaker and often semi-literate small countries.

The third important lesson to be drawn from this first round of industrialization concerns the unexpected release of new moral forces within Europe itself which resulted in the transformation of traditional societies to the beginnings of what we now call modernization. In backward perspective it would appear that tidal forces of a moral and ideological character arose, which altered the most basic assumptions on which society was organized and had dramatic effects on institutions and life-styles at the grass-roots level. It seemed that a strange dialectic with the machine released these new forces to create the modern West. The institutional change was enormous: the rapid development of mass literacy, mass education, universal suffrage, the development of new forms of public opinion and communication such as the daily newspaper, and a much more democratic and responsive society moving forward from the control of the traditional aristocratic élites which had been at the helm of European countries for many centuries. It is at this level that the lasting effects of the first machine age can be perceived. New premises of democracy and freedom and new axioms of political theory became an unexpected heritage of industrialization.

Summing up, the social history of the first century and a half of the machine offers a curious perspective. It began in such areas as Manchester in the 1840's, with the gin mills, the shocking conditions in the factories, the disruption of local networks of welfare and protection in society. In turn, a series of counterforces emerged to the point where a new conception of life and society eventually burst the bonds of the confining elements of the market economy. This should offer some evidence of the strength of the inner resources which the human social response may bring to bear at the present juncture, as globe-girdling networks of computers and complex technological processes penetrate once more in a second global invasion under the aegis of the American multinational corporation.

The Second Round: Messianism v. Despair

Two divergent faiths confront the new technology today: a fervent messianism and an absolute despair.

For the adherents of the first faith, the new global thrust of technology has become identified as the very essence of progress. This tradition rests on a curious marriage between a messianic strand long characteristic of western thought, and the feeling that technology itself is the main vehicle for the establishment of the good life which is embodied in our vision of 'the end of days'. The feeling is widespread today that any new discovery in science or technology and any mechanical or electronic advance that promises a greater degree of efficiency can only bring us closer to that future. The notion abounds that as we ride the crest of an ever-proliferating technology, we ride the light and the progress which is the promise of our civilization. In a world of growing urban chaos, ecological devastation and pollution, and the nuclear threat, such a view needs no lengthy rebuttal.

The second group regards the stringencies of the new technology with the deepest pessimism. At stake is not only the independence of individual countries but the survival of the major values of western society. Modern bureaucracy, necessary for co-ordination and control of technology, has become a network of anonymous tyranny, the chief threat to the continuity of a tradition of freedom. The institutions which are the spearhead of this technology, such as the multinational corporation, easily displace and shatter indigenous cultures in the course of the technical onslaught.

Simplistic answers fail to meet the situation. The trite observation that "man has created technology, and so he can control it" does justice neither to the complexity of the accompanying social organization nor to the stringency with which we have committed ourselves to ongoing technological change. Technology is not born naked in the world but in

a social context. There are questions of who controls technology, how technological change is co-ordinated, how
technology expands and renews itself, and how its costs and
benefits are distributed. These questions require an institutional solution, for they deal with the social cocoon in which
technology is nurtured. Technology, in short, comes in a
social and political package which necessarily will determine
its consequences. The demands for proper co-ordination of
the various inputs, raw materials, information, and the proper
ordering of society in order to accommodate complex
mechanical and electronic systems produce a stringency of
their own. The feeling arises of man encompassed in a
bureaucratic network running away on its own tracks.

Realism is needed in appraising the depth and complexity
of the problem, but total despair may be premature. In so
far as we find that the new technology is clothed in the laws
and values of the Stars and Stripes, we are still able to
counter and to contain, even if only in the near-term, the
special effects and political thrust of the multinational
corporation. The creation, at least through close regulation,
of the equivalent of the old enclave for the multinational
corporation is still possible. But it is sentimentality of the
first order to pursue a policy, as has recently been followed
in Canada, of enlisting the corporation in a set of 'guidelines'
for good corporate behaviour on a voluntary basis. This is
only the latest example of the consistent history of uncertainty and vacillation in regard to the question of the
multinational corporation. We have been preoccupied with
only one set of consequences, namely the economic boon
which these corporations offered to the development of the
Canadian economy.

It must appear to be the greatest of paradoxes to a foreign
observer to note the passive and quiescent way in which
Canada has dealt with the penetration of its economy up to
the present day. To take one example, the popular book, *The
American Challenge*, by the French author J.J. Servan-
Schreiber, rang the alarm bells in France when the level of
foreign ownership of industry had hardly reached one tenth
the level in Canada. The fact that this country vacillates in a

lethargic discussion of the issue is a mark mainly of the impotence of the Canadian political culture—the weakness of the 'will to survive' in this country.

The 'Will to Survive'

The greatest weakness in the set of requirements for preserving Canadian independence is the peculiar intellectual and political tradition that forms the present basis of the Canadian political culture. In brief, we are the legatees of a transplanted political tradition stemming from classical English liberalism. While we have gained the legal trappings of sovereignty and independence, we are unable to muster the symbols and the political vocabulary necessary to understand the vital interests of this country and to act for its preservation. The essential weakness of the Canadian political culture lies in its derivative liberalism. This is the heritage of an intellectual colonialism, concepts and symbols of which are inadequate to our dilemma and bypass the major problems surrounding Canadian independence.

Stepping back for a moment to view the question of the political culture which liberalism in general has produced, let us examine several contemporary problems and the liberal pronouncements about them. Centred as it is on a philosophy of nurturing and granting freedoms to the individual, liberalism has glossed over or failed to recognize some fundamental issues which relate to society as a whole and to the structure of its institutions. In the first instance we may examine, for example, the question of 'the nation' as seen in liberal philosophy. The 'nation' *per se* has no specific or recognized place in this outlook. It becomes in practice the source of obstruction to the free flow of goods and capital through instituting tariffs and restrictions. It is further regarded as a source of chauvinism and of parochial and irrational ideas which obstruct the free flow of natural good will and disembodied 'ideas' from man to man across the globe. The nation in its own right has no recognized existence as an aggregate or collective entity. There is consequently almost no way to mobilize liberal opinion in defence of the nation except in cases where either civil liberties or direct military threat is involved. The threat today, however, is from a different direction, and consequently is unrecognized in a liberal perspective. The modern phenomenon of nationalism is totally incomprehensible and can only be seen by liberals as a demonic force.

A second major issue is the question of poverty. In this case, classical liberalism simply proclaims that in a free society (organized as a market economy) each individual has an equal opportunity to seek his just reward on the market. Thus poverty, at least in this formulation of the philosophy, remains a problem for which the individual himself must accept responsibility. As he has been given equal opportunity to make his way among his fellows, in principle there is no responsibility accruing to society for his lack of success.

A third illustration is provided by the problem of race. Liberal philosophy indicates only that "we look at the individual and not his 'background.'" The problem of race, in short, is negated by a focus which necessarily begins with a view of society and its components as an aggregate of the individuals of which it is composed and their rights. There is a basic non-recognition of a vital problem which in its essence cannot be understood within the confines of an individualistic philosophy, but can only be seen as that of a collective entity.

These three issues, nation, poverty and race, curiously enough have arisen with a vengeance in the twentieth century, while at the same time they are the central blind spots of the liberal philosophy. One of the reasons that we have failed so badly to cope with them is that fundamentally we are unable to understand them because of ideological myopia.

The paradox is all the more striking since the questions at least of poverty and race are as old as mankind itself and have been problems ever since the existence of recorded history; the nation as we conceive of it today is certainly several hundred years old. It is therefore worth reflecting on why they have remained so deliberately obscured in the political theory fostered by liberal tradition. Today, moreover, these problems carry with them an urgency and a demand for virtually overnight solutions. The very fierceness of the claims made upon us may derive in part from the obscurity with which these problems were viewed previously. Add to this the fact that Canada has never had a historical moment of the actual creation of its national existence, and we may begin to understand why the combination of a colonial mentality (in the intellectual sense) and a quiescent history have created no firm basis for an independent political culture in this country.

The only two issues which succeed generally in creating popular and vigorous reactions are, on the one hand, territorialism (viz. the public uproar in regard to sovereignty in the Canadian North) and on the other, extraterritoriality. Both of these issues which are alive in the popular imagination are, however, nineteenth-century in their essential importance. For the principal issue which confronts us today, in the sense of being of vital national interest, is necessarily rooted in the major features of twentieth-century life, namely, technology, computers, electronics, all of which find their home in the economy. And it is the economy, of course, over which Canadians have lost virtually all control and with which they demonstrate only a sporadic and partial concern.

In the absence of a vision of our nationhood, and of a political culture possessed of symbols to evoke and protect our independence, it is no cause for wonder that the ideological pull of the United States has been strong and attractive throughout our history. We have found no alternative vision to sustain us in terms of our own political culture.

As a result, our social policy has also been largely derivative. It is a fact that most Canadian innovations and public policies, virtually since 1840, have been imitative of the United States: the building of the canals, the railroads, the land-grant system that was necessary in the settling of the Canadian West, anti-combines legislation (imitating the anti-trust philosophy of the United States) and finally the 'war on poverty'—all have been derivative of American legislation. The seal of approval in Canada originated from the earlier attempts at such legislation by the United States. This has both minimized the risk and created a source of legitimacy sufficient to endorse equivalent policies in this country. Admittedly, this legislation has often responded to similar problems, but it is true nevertheless that our sense of social innovation has been timid and substantially restricted because the premises of our national existence have been derivative and inadequate.

What we understand least is the nature of power, particularly as it applies to the economy. Power has generally been treated with deep suspicion and arm's-length reservation in English political philosophy, culminating in Lord Acton's famous *obiter dicta*. We have relied instead on a faith in the built-in harmony of the market society, in accord with Adam Smith's maxims about the individual pursuit of self-interest. The effect has been to gloss over or to negate the importance of the locus of economic power.

Thus when the power to make decisions shifts outside the country by virtue of foreign ownership of the economy, we are barely conscious that anything of importance has happened. We are unable to meet the challenge of the new technological thrust centring on huge economic and bureaucratic systems and external control. The world of atomistic individualism has faded away everywhere but in our minds.

Strain and Transformation

The global strains of the technological society are becoming apparent everywhere. There is not only the contradiction between affluence and poverty (both domestically and internationally) but also the contradiction between nominal independence and real independence of nation states. The heritage of colonialism is being restored by technology, but the urge to attain genuine freedom continues unabated in many countries.

There are other strains as well that centre on the social constrictions of the great bureaucratic networks. We have never been more passionate or more militant in the attempt to awaken the counter-forces for local control.

We can see already the signs of what appear to be volcanic forces arising as a counter-movement to this global extension of the technological network. We are witnessing the most important feature perhaps of this new round of technological penetration, namely the second eruption in the great dialectic between the machine and the moral forces which are induced and released by its extension. If we can contain and channel the effects of these immense moral passions which are rapidly expressing themselves in continuing and seemingly mysterious waves of unrest, we may witness a new institutional transformation.

In France, the student rebellion of May 1968, in the United States, the eruptions against racism and militarism, and unrest and dissent in many other countries—such political upheaval seems present everywhere. Even in Canadian politics, the weak whisper of the slogan 'participatory democracy' has become a theme of our political life. These internal moral tides have begun to disestablish all our major institutions, religious as well as secular, churches as much as universities. Global forces, often blind and unfocused at first, have penetrated the political processes of most countries. It may be too early to discern whether creative and lasting institutional change will result from this political eruption. Nevertheless, it should give pause to those in despair about the effects of technological change, who prophesy only an increasing erosion of democracy and freedom.

I have attempted in this essay to place the problem of Americanization and Canadian independence within a global perspective. I have also attempted to show that there are good reasons for avoiding premature pessimism or indeed capitulating to the spread of the technological society spearheaded by the multinational corporation. The essential features of the history of the machine from the beginning have been the remarkable counter-movements on both the institutional and the moral levels, which have transformed human society. I do not doubt that in Canada these forces will operate—as they will elsewhere—as the technological society continues its advance. The political forces which have been let loose are of enormous power; no established institution (and this includes the multinational corporation) will remain exempt from their effects.

It is apparent, however, that I have made no particular

case for the survival of the nation-state within the context of these changes. In fact, the question may well be asked, "why do I see major institutional change everywhere except here?" The nation-state has become synonymous in our own day with the protection of the indigenous culture, institutions, and traditions of a particular society. It possesses the major political power and the means to resist, to modify, and to humanize the technological process. I fail to see how the nation-state can become obsolete and merged in a larger international setting as is sometimes predicted, when the additional functions and responsibilities which we attach to it increase almost daily. One need only list the tasks of economic growth, full employment, education, housing, control of pollution, and the number of other tasks continually thrust upon the nation-state, to see that it can hardly become obsolete at this time. If it remains a suitable agency for the performance and realization of these tasks, it must survive and assume a more democratic (and less class-ridden) role in carrying out these objectives.

The nation-state remains, in the end, the central locus of power and authority in our society and, until such time as transcending institutions have been created, we may envisage that it will remain to protect its members by moderating the intrusion of such technological forces as the spreading American corporation. For this reason, I remain a conservative in regard to Canadian survival and a radical in regard to the emergent institutions necessary to achieve this task.

Prometheus, the god who brought fire and the technical arts to mankind, was chained to a rock by Zeus where he remained during the greater part of human history. Now that he has freed himself in the century and a half of the machine age and tried to render the earth his own, it will be necessary for man to chain him once more.

November 1969

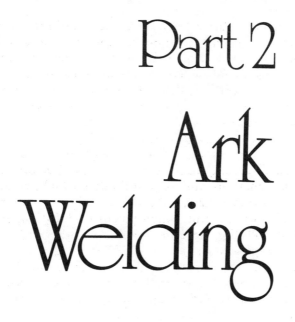

Part 2
Ark Welding

Secondary Relays

12

THE OUTER MAN: TECHNOLOGY & ALIENATION

No civilization has been as rich as ours. Yet few have been as apprehensive.

Modern concern centres on our irreversible commitment to technology. Has a Faustian bargain been struck with the machine?

The most general theory of technology which we have is that of Marshall McLuhan. Technology is the extension of man. The wheel is an extension of the foot, the axe is an extension of the arm, print is an extension of the eye, radio an extension of the ear, and the computer an extension of the nervous system.

Technology is regarded as an extension of the *individual*— his limbs, senses and psyche. In McLuhan's world, man stands naked in the jungle of his technology. No institutions intercede to mediate or amplify the severity of the consequences. Social change is a stringent function of a changing technological environment. The progressive extension of man's being through his evolving technology rigidly sets the course he must travel.

Individualism, for example, is the product of a particular technology which generates a characteristic set of institutions. Print created literacy and increased specialization. This division of labour extended the process of exchange and the market system. Starting with the printed Bible and the Protestant Reformation, there developed the cult of achievement, accumulation and capitalism. With print, came the literate voter, the 'informed public' and liberal democracy. History is trapped in the ramifications of technology.

For Karl Marx, institutions intercede to mediate the effects of man's technology. Under the rubric of Marx's concept of externalization (*Entäusserung*) man projects his person naturally through his productive and creative activity; through his technology as well as through art, law and politics. But when a specific institutional framework, i.e., capitalism, despoils his human tie to these productive efforts through the impersonal and exploitative nature of his institutions, man becomes alienated. Alienation, or estrangement (*Entfremdung*) is not inherent in a given technology but only a consequence of the way that technology is instituted. "The estrangement of man," Marx states, is "realised and expressed in the relationship in which a man stands to other men." Thus, at least in the case of capitalism, institutions intrude between man and his technology so as to increase the social burden of his existence.

Marx is an optimist on the inherent consequences of technology itself. The fault under capitalism is purely institutional. He remains largely innocent in the area of technological constraints that transcend specific institutional forms whether capitalist or socialist.

A more general theory of technology and alienation proceeding beyond both Marx and McLuhan might begin by positing as the central proposition a mutual extension between man and his technology: while technology is an extension of man, man in turn may become an extension of his technology—the driver becomes an extension of the automobile, the factory worker an extension of the assembly line. The group of individuals linked to a given technology becomes a collectivity operating under the actual constraints and ties of that technology. In a technological society, institutions cease to be the voluntary contractual associations of individual atoms, but rather express in various ways the concrete concerns and constraints of persons tied by the hard realities of specific technologies.

The new technology erodes individualism and sets the central apprehension of the modern age—the loss of individuality. Symbol of the new technology is electricity, operating as pure information in the form of the computer. It also creates the power grid on which the very sustenance of life depends. Food, heating, transport, light and production rely on the grid. This overriding constraint of daily life effectively wires us all into the common circuit. Information moves with the speed of light and compresses time and space. Vital interdependence creates the collectivity as instant common fate.

Yet everywhere today we see not centralization and uniformity but protest—Quebec, Berkeley, Albania. The effective unit of action is the group, not the individual. The emerging pattern is the self-definition as well as the interdependence of collectivities. The result of the erosion of individualism is the creation of many tribes in the global village. Tribal involvements have become the prerequisite of personal identity.

All technology is man's externalization. To 'outer' oneself is to create new power and to risk losing control of it. Alienation is latent in the process of 'outering' but only comes to the fore with the machine. Karel Capek, in the play *R.U.R.*, anticipated the final limits of 'outering' in the robot. The alienation of man from himself is complete. But it is the trauma of the individualist—the total externalization of the individual man.

Externalization today proceeds in the creation of the immensely complex and pervasive technologies and institutions of collective power. The robot, in fact, has a hundred thousand heads. With this insight Huxley and Orwell laid the basis for the modern vision of negative utopia. But the vision is necessarily a nightmare so long as one equates loss of individuality with totalitarianism and refuses to admit of meaningful collective existence.

Technology is not simply our environment. It is parts of our individual and collective being rendered in material form. It has been created by ourselves. We are not prepared to disown it, and cannot reasonably be expected to do so.

Alienation is mass guilt. The technology that we have initiated, and assented to, may constrain not only ourselves but others. But we can neither relinquish it, nor contract out of our responsibility in an attempt to safeguard the sanctity of our individual consciences. The new institutions with their inherent potential for compulsion flow from the modern technology to which we have given our assent.

The moral issues of today are matters of the collective conscience; we are all involved in Hiroshima. The effective response to collective guilt is collective action.

The commitment to technology must be distinguished from the relinquishment of control over technology. It lies within our power to direct the process of invention and to mediate the social consequences of technological change. The absolute commitment to efficiency prevalent in North America amounts to saying 'let technology run free.' This is a cross that we need not bear.

With the new technology have come new philosophies. Existentialist philosophy focuses on the guilt and despair of the individual and misses the point. The philosophers of the absurd push our social diseases into high definition, thereby heightening social awareness and collective solutions. The philosophers of the new technology, notably McLuhan, make us aware of the environment, and thus increase our freedom to deal with it.

Technological determinism is fostered, albeit unintentionally, by those who merely cultivate apprehension in the name of the old moral absolutes of the individual conscience or who remain utopian with regard to the machine.

On one level, social reform focuses on existing patterns of income distribution, the paramountcy of property rights, and the premature lethargy of an affluent society. This affluence is itself the result of a more integrated and more interdependent industrial order, and thus provides a moral basis for institutional change. The new moral order bypasses the individualism of a competitive market society, but also challenges the individualism of our ethical commitments.

But the reform of the cash nexus can become a myopic

endeavour if it ignores the hard and irrevocable reality of the machine nexus. On this level, the potential, if not the actual, endeavours toward reform of both capitalism and socialism draw more closely together. Neither can be utopian about the inherent consequences of the machine.

The human condition today is given by the certain commitment to technology and the uncertain limits of the loss of freedom. For those who are neither utopian nor in premature despair, these limits can only be known in the abiding commitment to social reform.

With Mel Watkins
August 1965

NATIONALISM IN A TECHNOLOGICAL SOCIETY

The hallmark of the future is the technological society. This essay is mainly concerned with the political features of the technological society in so far as we can discern them. The role of nationalism will be examined as an aspect of the tasks of creative politics in such a society.

Nationalism is usually applied to the sharper, more assertive expressions of national sentiment and national interest in the modern period. But the nation itself has been invoked, more or less directly, during many diverse periods of social change which have swept over society: the restoration of monarchies and their overthrow, the 'new Jerusalem in England's green and pleasant land', as well as *Blut und Boden*; the pastoral idyll of nineteenth-century Catholicism in Quebec, as well as Russia's 'socialism in one country'. In this broad context, social movements that have invoked the nation in some way, have been responsible for both virtues and crimes as extensive as those, for example, that have been committed in the name of religion. Sweeping judgments in either case may be pointless.

But today, nationalism, as a self-conscious and direct political force, is with us much more. Indeed, in recent times, it would not be an exaggeration to say that the heightened self-consciousness and intense introspective awareness which accompany nationalism often amount to a virtual *discovery* of the nation.

We do not propose to present a rationalization of the traditional concept of the nation. The nation itself is undergoing rapid social change and the nationalism of the future will be an assertion of the character, the values and the institutions of the national society of that time, a very different national society from that of the bourgeois nation in the first phase of industrialization.

The maturity to which a technological society impels us, if we are to survive in it, will demand basic revisions of our view of social existence. This is not to suggest that a reassertion of nationalist values in itself contains the entire basis for such maturity. But the integral character which a human community acquires through the new technology and the new communications—through ribs of steel and nerves of electronic impulses—transforms the old slogan of interdependence from a benign manifestation of individual good will into the hard reality of the new social framework. Nationalists of the left should find themselves at home in this new society.

Through a Grid Darkly

Jonathan Swift was hardly the prophet of the new technology, yet he left, unwittingly, a graphic image of the electric society. Lemuel Gulliver, while asleep in Lilliput, has been tied to the ground with thousands of threads by the fearful and industrious Lilliputians. When he awakens, he discovers that he has been rendered immobile and the struggle to free himself is in vain.

A society dependent on the pervasive wires for virtually all vital tasks of daily life—light, heat, food, transport, production, communication and education—may also be tied down by its electric grid in a way not unlike that of Lemuel Gulliver. With this vital dependence on electricity, we ourselves become, in an important sense, plugged into the grid.

The point was brought home in a dramatic fashion on November 9th, 1965, when at the height of the rush hour in the late afternoon, the lights flickered and went out in the eastern half of North America. It was the beginning of the most massive and puzzling blackout that had yet occurred. In the industrial heartland of the United States and Canada, extending over some 80,000 square miles, the daily lives of thirty million people were temporarily disrupted—in some regions for as long as fourteen hours.

The blackout was only a brief moment in the twentieth century, yet it lit up the characteristic shape which existence had taken. We could suddenly 'see' the all-encompassing electric grid. Some imagined that since the grid had become the central nervous system of our society, people might turn to panic and hysteria if it should cease to function. Others wondered whether the blackout was the result of sabotage, and still others wondered whether there would be violence and looting.

None of these fears was warranted. There were no indications of sabotage nor of violence and looting. Instead of panic, quiet camaraderie filled the air. Life suddenly ceased to be harried and frantic. Languid conversations took place in darkened offices. A light-hearted grace flowed everywhere, particularly in the normally rude and belligerent New York City. Those who managed to reach home had dinner by candlelight; many who did not whiled away the hours at a local lounge, not overly concerned with their fate. Businessmen stepped in with relish to direct traffic. Those who were stranded in subways, elevators and railway stations found the blackout less pleasant, but courtesy, calmness and an easy tolerance prevailed everywhere.

A political philosopher might even have been tempted to draw some conclusions about this facsimile 'state of nature' of an industrial society. Notwithstanding Thomas Hobbes, people had turned out to be lambs rather than wolves.

We had a brief glimpse of a more benign world, but it was an artificial world and irretrievable. When the towering pylons and the ubiquitous wires sprang to life once more, and we had again donned the technological harness, peculiar questions still remained, not the least of which was the unsolved mystery of what had caused the blackout. There were also other questions: had we any assurances that it would not recur, and what, in any case, was this extensive Canadian-

U.S. grid that bound the two countries together like a prolific vine? Thus, together with the questions about the interruption of the grid, there emerged questions about its normal operation. Perhaps in the blackout there lay a paradigm for the evolving technological society, some of whose features flickered briefly in high definition.

For five days following the blackout, hundreds of experts in Canada and the United States were engaged in searching for the cause of the disruption. Once the possibility of sabotage had been ruled out, the assumption became prevalent that some technical or mechanical failure was at the root of the trouble. As matters turned out, the difficulty was not in the malfunctioning of the technology (it worked exactly as was intended) but in the human element. There was, in short, an organizational rather than a technological flaw. The separation of technological and organizational aspects is revealing. Technical constraints and the discovery of flaws bring about a certain kind of organization and reorganization for the more efficient functioning of the system.

One of the conclusions of the investigations that were carried on both in Canada and the United States made it clear that, however unexpected such a massive blackout had been, no reassurance could be given that this event would not recur. The report of the Federal Power Commission in the United States concluded:

> There can be no absolute assurance that outages of the November 9 magnitude will not recur. On the other hand, there is no apparent reason why operating equipment and techniques cannot be improved to the point where the likelihood of recurrence would be so remote that it would not constitute a major worry to either the industry or the public.[1]

In Canada, a statement on the power failure issued by the Minister of Trade and Commerce on December 9, 1965 noted the following:

> There is, however, no such thing as perfect security in power supply, any more than in any other activity directed by humans. The question is how to achieve the highest practicable degree of security.[2]

In the attempt to achieve the 'highest practicable degree of security', as well as economy, two kinds of adjustment had been under way. First, local electrical systems were being integrated in order to provide emergency power to counteract temporary failure of any part of the system. This also allowed power to be shunted from one area to another during peak periods which fell at different times, so as to put the generating capacity to greater use and thus provide cheaper power. These factors were creating larger and larger grids, with a continent-wide grid now being advocated as the next step forward. In the face of these compelling technical and economic advantages, increasing Canadian participation in the American grid had seemed 'obvious', and had gone quietly forward with little public awareness or debate in recent years. At the same time there was a shift from private power companies to large governmentally-organized power grids operated by administrative boards. This was a shift from market organization to administrative organization, to promote the efficient extension of the system.

But this trend toward greater efficiency and security of the system in the past made the cause of this spectacular failure even more mysterious. As it turned out, the matter was a vestigial element of human oversight. The factors in this situation are worth recounting in some detail, for they may be indicative of the way in which complex technological systems remain vulnerable.

One of the technical problems which confronts electrical transmission systems is the protection of existing equipment from damage in case the system becomes overloaded with electrical power. To meet this particular problem, the device that is used is a circuit breaker, which operates in much the same fashion as a household fuse, namely, it shuts off the system when the power load becomes too great. In 1955, when a circuit breaker failed to operate in the case of a faulty transmission circuit at the Sir Adam Beck Power Station at Niagara Falls, substantial damage was sustained by the equipment. In order to prevent a recurrence, Ontario Hydro installed additional protective devices called secondary relays to make sure that the circuit breakers were triggered in time.

It was one of these relays, known as Q 29—a complex of coils and calibration devices no larger than a loaf of bread— which initiated the blackout. Since the installation of this secondary relay in 1955, it had worked perfectly. In 1963 the relay was set at 375 million watts, the maximum level beyond which the relay was to operate the circuit breaker. This figure included a safety margin over the average power load, but the average had been slowly increasing until the line was carrying a normal level of 356 million watts. When a simple upward fluctuation in the load occurred, the relay operated precisely as was intended, and shut off the circuit. This simple event set the blackout in motion in a grand domino sequence. The power on this particular line was shunted onto five other power lines of Ontario Hydro over-loading these in turn, and shutting them down as well. With no other place to go, the electric current normally used by Ontario was sent surging in an electrical torrent through the power system of upper New York state, triggering in turn automatic shut-downs all along the line right through to New York City.[3]

New York City might have been saved from a power failure if it had cut its own electrical system loose from the grid in time. When Edwin J. Nellis, the engineer on duty at Con Edison noticed the dimming of the lights at 5:16 p.m., he thought at first to check the condition of the electrical system of upstate New York. After two short telephone calls, he decided to separate the New York City system from the electric grid of New York State. The decision which he had faced was whether to try to protect the power supply for New York State as a whole, or alternatively, to take no risks and separate New York City from the system. At the end of the second phone call upstate, he had made his decision and stated "I am going to cut you loose." At 5:28 p.m. he began to push a series of eight buttons to separate New York City from the larger electrical system but he was seconds too late. Just 2.5 seconds after that, New York was completely blacked out. Thus when Nellis had been confronted with a significant moral decision and had actually exercised his discretion, it turned out that there had been insufficient time for such a decision to be made.

Other areas such as New Jersey had saved themselves because they had an automatic cut-off device. In the investigation that followed, one of the major considerations was whether the electric grid in the future, as it expanded its connections across the continent, could in fact tolerate these kinds of human decisions at crucial moments.

This example of the relatively insignificant flaw or unforeseen accident which disrupts a complex technological system is repeated frequently in military technology. Instances abound in the U.S. military and space programme—a small plastic disc comes loose to interrupt the fuel supply of a moon rocket; an electrical short circuit sends a space ship far out of orbit; a Strategic Air Command plane with a hydrogen bomb aboard makes a forced landing on American soil and it is discovered that six of the seven protective devices on the bomb have ceased to function; the crash of an American bomber carrying hydrogen bombs in Spain, contaminates Spanish soil, and one of these hydrogen bombs is lost for two months in coastal waters. But military technology is only the herald of the complex technology which will be increasingly widespread in society.

This new characteristic of the complex technological environment has been described as the 'fail-safe syndrome'. The fail-safe syndrome has wide implications and may become a crucial ingredient of twentieth-century politics. 'Fail-safe' is a popular term which has thus far been used only with regard to the danger of unintended nuclear war. The main concern has been the possibility that the world would be catapulted into nuclear destruction, not by virtue of a conscious decision of either one of the parties, but by virtue of some technological or human mishap.

For the evolving technological society, the 'fail-safe' problem may be a portent. For example, in the case of hydro-electricity, the statements of the two governments cited above make it clear that such a system cannot be made foolproof. A vast network of enormous importance to the survival of the entire continent must be regarded as having inherent features of uncertainty, however small this uncertainty may become. Secondly, in attempting to make this system more secure, we are increasingly required to hand over important decisions to automatic devices. Less and less human decision is tolerable because, for example, it cannot be made sufficiently quickly. Important decisions are shaped by technological rather than political considerations. For example, whether the Canadian and U.S. electric grids should be even more closely meshed will increasingly become a technological question.

As integration of technological systems proceeds, the lives of an ever growing number of people will be bound together by the vulnerability of a system that is immensely more disruptive, even though the frequency of breakdowns may be less. In short, the technological grid, including computers, electric circuitry and automatic devices eventually begins to form something resembling an enormous elaborate mobile suspended on thin threads.

In the process, a new political atmosphere or environment is created. The stake we have as a society in such technological systems becomes ever greater. The fears and apprehensions at the back of our mind centre primarily, not on the survival of our individual persons, but on social existence itself—the continuity and security of the urban-industrial-machine web. As we become wealthier and the machines and interconnections become more complex, our technological system increasingly becomes an all-or-nothing game with the stakes rising at some enormous rate. The backdrop of our social existence becomes transformed, and becomes, in a sense, the latent emergency. We have been made aware initially of this sense of the latent emergency by the mobilization of the new technology for military purposes. But the main feature of the technological society is the extension of this phenomenon into economic life, as the economy becomes more dependent on integrated, complex technological devices.

The Precarious Society

The social necessities of the nineteenth century centred on the institutional constraints of the market and brough forward countervailing political institutions.[4] The focus of concern in our own day has shifted much more to the inherent necessities of technology and technique. Admittedly, the forces and constraints of the new technology to which we are increasingly committed, may pose even more stringent difficulties of social adjustment than those posed by the institutional nature of the market system. Much has been said of the eroding effects of the new technology on our culture, our values and our institutions. Nevertheless, the very experience of the last century should be sufficient to indicate that creative political responses, in part spontaneous and in part deliberate, may form the human and social structure within which we will attempt to contain that technology, to control its rate of change and to distribute its human and social benefits. But cybernetics and self-regulating technical systems, organized and co-ordinated by computers, may present a different and more complex dilemma than the market society, and the solutions may require greater social ingenuity and imagination.

The political climate of the advanced technological society is still barely visible. In particular, we have pointed to the sense of latent emergency or precariousness. An ever more complex and fragile technological web is highly vulnerable to disruption and produces latent political responses to protect the continuity of life in such a situation. For example, the intuitive attempt to protect the institutional balance or technological continuity of the precarious society may give rise to conformist pressures against unpopular political positions. In that sense, every technological society has within it the seeds of totalitarianism, in so far as it is prepared to mobilize the resources of the state against even minor threats to the continuity of existence. The stakes become too high and the tolerances too small to permit genuine divergences that threaten the fragile technical-social equilibrium.

Another effect of the new technology is to upgrade economic life to the level of a vital national interest, similar in kind to such potential life and death questions as defence or foreign policy. The importance of the economy in a technological society contrasts sharply with an earlier period where the continuity of small, discrete individual enterprises never posed the same threat to collective existence which the new economic interdependence has created.

In a complex society, the necessity to co-ordinate as well as to humanize the technological maze has given rise to large-scale institutions with immense power to make decisions affecting the entire society. Corporations, trade unions, various levels of government, the military and even the multiversity are examples of the new topography of the political landscape in modern society. Interposed between man and the machine web, we have created new institutions capable of affecting decisively the character of our collective existence.

A discussion of the evolving technological society is necessarily speculative and only some suggestive notions can be offered. But it may be that these fears and apprehensions at the fringe of our mind, generated by the technological society, have found their sharpest expression in our literary imagination. Starting with simple legends such as *The Sorcerer's Apprentice*, to more ominous tales of Frankenstein, Karel Capek's play *R.U.R.*, Huxley's *Brave New World*, up to the embodiment of our worst fears in the novel *1984*, the advent of the machine—particularly the automated machine—has haunted our imagination. The end result of industrial technology is the progressive extension of man's being and power—a progressive 'outering' of himself to the point where there is loss of control by humans over automatic devices and the fear of the end of human existence as we know it.

This new political landscape is still evolving but its main features, as far as we can discern them, have been suggested: the fail-safe syndrome or the precariousness of such a society, the escalation of enormous power in the new political institutions, the escalation of anxiety, and the consciousness of interdependence or instant common fate.[5] These are the tendons and nerves of social existence.

Our immediate conclusion is that the old view of society, as an atomistic collection of self-seeking individuals concerned with their individual freedom and contracting together to form the institutions of the state, is an obsolete notion in the technological era. The pervasive elements of a precarious politics, the growing number of tasks assigned to the nation-state, the embodiment of society's values and goals within these tasks—point to a new view of existence centring on the indissoluble character of the social framework. This is not a matter of theory, sentiment, or blood, but a matter of collective common interest with regard to the use of the technology on the one hand, and the protection of society through its political institutions on the other. In this new environment, nationalists will feel particularly at home. This is not to say that the twentieth-century political landscape is the final vindication of an age-long nationalist myth. Nationalists, however, have always been concerned with the preservation of collective values, have asserted these in times of stress, and within the new political landscape are able to sense the importance of the locus of power and decision-making in the home in which it is located at present, the nation-state.

The Reality of Society[6]

Premature despair in the face of the new technology has been widespread recently. The erosion of institutions and human values in the face of the stringent artificial requirements of technique cannot be denied. But the proponents of despair too often are unaware of the varied and creative ways in which new institutional forms are interposed between man and his environment to ease the pressure and to safeguard social existence. In these prophecies of despair man usually stands alone, whereas the social history of the market society and the countermovement against the eroding effects of the free market is one instance of the tendency to collective self-protection through new institutional forms.

The essential ingredients of a mature approach to our new environment involve both a fundamental shift in our political values in recognition of the inexorable nature of technological interdependence, and a more conscious and deliberate attempt to protect the human character of our institutional and cultural endowment. No doubt the cost will have to be paid in terms of some technological efficiency.

We cannot be sure of meeting such a challenge, especially

when we have hardly staked out the full dimensions of the problem. At issue is the question of freedom in the technological society.

The moral shape of the individual in our society has, as its touchstone, the deep imperatives of individual conscience and their fulfilment. At this level, the commitment to freedom becomes the vindication of the very purpose and meaning of the Western tradition. While the technological era promises, in various ways, new possibilities for the fulfilment of the individual and a more beneficial material existence, it is at the moral level that the question of the possibility of freedom arises. It is here that the incursions of technology are bound to create substantial limitations.

At bottom, moral and political maturity will require a fundamental recognition of the nature of power in our society. Power, as David Hume once pointed out, rests ultimately on opinion. As long as we have consented to a technological society, we share in the responsibility for the institutions of compulsion and constriction to which it must necessarily give rise. The full promise of freedom rests implicitly on the assumption that the individual may contract out of situations where he participates in creating compulsion and constriction of others, in order that his conscience may not be violated. But it is this very possibility of contracting out which, in a technological society, is in question. The dilemma may not be new in principle, but it is focused more sharply and comes up substantially as a matter of degree in the maze of the complex society. In essence, no one who consents to live in such a society and surely no one who shares in the benefits of this technology can contract out of the pervasive institutional and bureaucratic web.

On one level, we may, through imaginative use of our institutions, create new concrete freedoms: ways of protecting the individual from bureaucratic mismanagement, new ways of providing alternative choices in labour and leisure, new facilities for enhancing the individual's self-development on both an educational and a material plane. But basically, the technological society will involve the individual morally as a direct consequence of his own aspirations. A ramified bureaucracy is an inevitable consequence of this society and the compulsion which it creates must weigh on the conscience of the individual to constrict the integrity of his absolute freedom. Directly and indirectly, the individual is compelled to compel. In a technological society, the individual has no way of contracting out and may be forced to betray the integrity of his conscience. In this moral sense, his freedom may be suspended.

The road to maturity that follows such awareness must recognize *the reality of society*. Just as we cannot contract out of the institutions of power that have been created, neither can we preserve the goal of the reform of society without recognizing the limits set by the implacable constraints of technique. While the possibility of an absolute moral freedom may thus be suspended, nevertheless the demands of conscience would require us to search for the limits to which such a society can be made more free and more just. These limits are unknown; but without the abiding engagement in such a search, no one can resign himself prematurely to the view that all is lost, that technology triumphant is the foreboding destiny about which nothing can be done.

A moral position which begins with this basic recognition of the reality of society must be accompanied by a commitment to search for its limits. These limits can only be found in action—action in the concrete efforts of social reform.

The Nationalism of the Left

The passionate moral fervour of 'the New Left' aims at total reform, disregarding the limitations and irreversible character of technological constraints. Wholesale references to our social difficulties are personified ubiquitously by the term 'the Establishment'. An absolute freedom is invoked which pretends to bypass the stringencies of the technological environment and its institutional complex, even though these remain a permanent feature of our social existence. This political philosophy of the New Left shares to a large extent the neglect and suspicion of power characteristic of liberal political thought in the nineteenth century and exhibited, for example, by the views of Lord Acton. Yet if we accept our commitment to the new technology as irreversible, we must also accept, at least in principle, the limitation on freedom in ways which we have yet to explore.

The 'Nationalism of the Left' presumes a different moral position on the possibilities of freedom. The chosen level of action is in the institutional sphere, and the centre of concern is the protection of the cultural integrity and political values of the nation. This is a commitment to conservatism only if we fail to recognize the changing character of the nation itself.

The feudal nation was committed to privilege at a time when aristocracy and status considerations were dominant. *The bourgeois nation* was committed to the preservation of private property, freedom of contract, and to the political values which sustained a market economy. In our own day the nation itself is transformed under the new commitment to greater equality, to measures of social justice already embodied in the evolving welfare state and to a more genuine democracy. *The democratic nation* increasingly embodies the values and purposes of our present society.

The recognition of the increased responsibilities and changing social character of the modern nation does not limit the possibilities of participating in the growing interdependence of nations. A troubled nation that is the victim of its own conflicts, uncertainties and vacillations is neither in control of its own destiny nor able to fulfill the international tasks which are increasingly placed upon it.

While new technological requirements and new demands for natural resources, including water, may increasingly tie Canada and her economy to a North American framework, the political consequences of these technological developments can by no means be presumed or allowed to follow a mechanistic pattern that simply treads in the footsteps of those technological interconnections. The function of a creative politics has always been to protect society, to ensure order, growth and the flourishing of national life itself. On other continents and in other countries the spread of technology has been accompanied by a fierce revival of indigenous cultures, a reassertion of national values and a countermovement to retain national control of decision-making power.

The creative response which man has often manifested to processes of rapid social change in the past offers some hope that technological determinism will not set the abiding pattern for future social existence. Of the various political and social responses that have thus far been offered to the challenge of the technological society, the Nationalism of the Left brings with it some rudimentary insights and values which will permit us to safeguard and to extend those features of social existence which we cherish and hope to preserve from the erosive forces of automation and technology.

March 1966

NOTES

1. *New York Times*, Dec. 7, 1965, 40.

2. Press Release, Department of Trade and Commerce, Ottawa, 90-65.

3. Details are given in the *New York Times*, December 7, 1965, p. 1 and the *Globe and Mail*, Toronto, November 17, 1965, p. 29.

4. This theme is discussed in the essay, "Binding Prometheus," pp. 185-87. The original version of this essay also develops this and other themes at greater length. See "The 20th Century Prospect: Nationalism in a Technological Society," in *Nationalism in Canada*, Peter Russell (ed.), McGraw-Hill, Toronto, 1966, 341-63.

5. Some of these thoughts draw on Douglas Lepan's essay "The Outlook for the Relationship: A Canadian View," *The United States and Canada*, John Sloane Dickey (ed.), Englewood Cliffs, 1964, 152-69.

6. I rely heavily in this section on Karl Polanyi's philosophical perspective.

Voices of Wisdom

13

ROBERT OWEN

In the maelstrom of the first days of the Industrial Revolution, portents of a new era studded the social firmament: mysterious and inexplicable increases in the number of the 'unemployed poor', a plethora of imaginative and ingenious schemes of social engineering to make profits or build new social communities with the poor, increases in wages accompanied by a multiplication of misery, deterioration of social and moral standards, crippling of children in the new factories and unheard-of notions of the animal character of man and his victimization by natural laws of geometric growth.

With vision and compassion, Robert Owen, alone among his contemporaries, sensed the meaning of the new era and the unyielding character with which it would vest society. His was a prophetic personality and within the first quarter of the nineteenth century, he ran the gauntlet of the next hundred and fifty years. It is the mark of his genius that he perceived the portent of the era from its first glimmerings. "Some change of high import," said Owen, "scarcely yet perhaps to be scanned by the present ill-taught race of men is evidently in progress."

The year 1771 ushered Robert Owen inconspicuously into the world in a small Welsh village, scarcely two years after Arkwright's waterframe and James Watt's patent on the steam engine made their equally inconspicuous entries.

The Manchester of the time, the site of Owen's first close acquaintance with machinery, was at the beginning of an expansion which was to increase the population six-fold in the next sixty years. Its growth paralleled the similar six-fold expansion in the value of England's cotton exports. Soon after the turn of the century, for example, the cotton trade was already estimated to be employing some 800,000 persons including children.

At school in his Welsh village, Owen was somewhat precocious, but his formal education ceased at the age of nine when he began to work in a neighbour's shop. He read a great deal, and was an introspective and weak child. He may have been frightened of working in a mill all his life.

About the age of fifteen Owen came to Manchester, and in a few years, with a hundred pounds of borrowed capital, he was launched on his first venture—manufacturing cotton spinning machinery. A year later he was directing one of the largest spinning mills in Manchester, employing some 500 people. He was an eminently able and successful manager, and before long, Owen writes of himself, he was regarded as "the first fine cotton spinner in the world".

The new economic torrent of the Industrial Revolution was cascading over England through the framework of the market. Owen's grasp of the laws of the new economy was poor (most of his major writings were formulated before 1820). He did not perceive clearly the intricacies and mechanics of a nascent market system, neither the dominant role of capital nor the hegemony which a self-regulating market was shortly destined to assume over society.

Only Aristotle, some 2000 years before him, had given expression to the inimical character of the market for the pillars of human community. In his time, however, Owen went further, and recognizing the market economy for what it was—a social artifact—he focused unerringly on the central features of the new age: machine and society.

A superficial assessment of Owen has left the general impression of a wistful dreamer concerned with some doubtful utopian colonies in England and America. Although many of his ventures were unsuccessful, they had a superb relevance for society. He was the first to see that the entry of the machine had brought "lamentable and permanent evils" and if the machine was to benefit the human race many things would have to change greatly.

His eminent success in business and practical administration did not prevent him from seeing the beginnings of the wider social drama around him centred on the machine. He pointed to its boundless role and indeterminate effects, while he struggled against the new reality and challenge which a technological society began to pose.

His story follows the progressive unfolding of the portent of the machine. From the beginning he was pushed by events from one stage to the next until he had faced up to the main issues of the following century. One by one he was forced against all of the major problems of a modern industrial society.

It was an unwilling progress towards the discovery of society, made at the behest of an overweening selfless passion. He was harassed by the fear that his insights might momentarily topple the social structure. He hoped, perhaps, that reticence, secrecy and a careful gradualism would save the day from the menace of chaos and revolution. But ultimately, he felt that he must state his case in its starkest and most uncompromising form. No one penetrated further into the problems of industrial life under a market system.

Robert Owen, the man, was at the least, unusual. He enjoyed an immense popularity, even though he was shunned by some as a dangerous radical, and later, as a religious heretic. He was the intimate of prime ministers and archbishops, Presidents and royalty. On many occasions they endorsed and even distributed his writings. Both the charm of his personality and his brilliant success as a manufacturer opened all doors to him. On his first visit to France, he was acclaimed as the 'lion of Paris'. It may have been his Welsh origin that allowed him, by exception, unrestricted entry across the aristocratic thresholds, even though he was a man of the people. Other commoners, such as Cobden and Bright, leading the powerful and influential free trade movement, could hardly get the public's ear. But Wales had no nobility of its own and Owen's humble origin was no hindrance to him.

Harriet Martineau tells us that much to the chagrin of his more conventional opponents, "when they were expecting, as they declared, to hear of his being in Bedlam, they heard of his being at Court, introduced to the young Queen by her Prime Minister, Lord Melbourne."

As one obsessed, Owen never knew a single doubt nor deviation in his own outlook on the world but nevertheless took absolute tolerance as his standard. He remained a persuasive democratic leader of Lanark village, yet was detached and autocratic with those who could claim to be his equals. He treated them as children to be patiently led to the fullness of the truth he had seen. His quiet and continuous insistence led to quarrels with many fellow workers in the movement and in his colony in America.

He maintained that the force of reason and the demonstration of his new truths were sufficient to recreate society immediately on new foundations. The age of co-operation which would follow could "ameliorate the condition of the producing class throughout Great Britain and Ireland in less than five years."

His personal qualities were unmatched: complete selflessness and lack of vanity, and abundant generosity. He had unlimited patience, and was utterly impervious to unjust accusations. He had an impersonal, detached faith in his cause and was unswayed and unimpressed by king or emperor. He was tactful and reserved but absolutely deaf to logical argument.

His work was often rendered in biblical imagery and his own commitment came to him as a revelation. "The whole, as though they had been delineated on a map, were laid open to me. Shall I now, at this eventful crisis, make the world known to itself?" People would be blinded by the truth "and their sight would be destroyed by the intensity of the day that is beginning to dawn upon them." The recognition was irreversible for "the principles on which the New View of Society is founded are true. . .never more but with life will they be removed from your minds, and your children's from the end of time." Man must be reborn: "the minds of all must be born again, and their knowledge and practice commence on a new foundation." He regarded his world-famous achievement at New Lanark as "the harbinger of that period when our swords shall be turned into ploughshares and our spears into pruninghooks; when universal love and benevolence shall prevail; when there shall be but one language and one nation; and when fear of want or of any evil among men shall be known no more." Throughout his writings were sprinkled such evocative passages as "from this hour," "from this day forward," henceforth," "the period is approaching" and the sentence: "I came not among you to establish a name, but to relieve you from the errors and evils of all names."

And yet with Owen, radical insight encompassed a total tolerance: "to blame and to be angry with our fellow-men for the evils which exist, is the very essence of folly and irrationality, and that notions which can give rise to such feelings never could enter into the composition of any human being that had been once made rational."

Being 'rational' meant having a knowledge of society: that it was society which formed the individual's character and this realization, through some unaccountable logic, removed the reasons for all anger and punishment.

He was opposed to violence and class war and was convinced that the rational demonstration of superior methods would win the day. If it failed to do so—and this, too, was part of his creed—there was no help, either on earth or in heaven.

His compassion for humanity was a dedication unto death: "whatever may be the consequence, I shall now perform my duty to you, and to the world; and should it be the last act of my life, I shall be well content, and know that I have lived for an important purpose." He made superlative sacrifices of fortune and family, and not a few concluded he was insane (which view, at one time, Owen considered favourable to his purposes and didn't wish to contradict).

His whole progress took place under an everlasting concern that chaos would accompany too rapid change. This was his abiding fear. He felt possessed of an insight which had the power instantly to change the world if he were to reveal it, yet at the same time he knew that he must take every conceivable precaution to prepare the way, and only bring about reform through "temporary intermediate arrangements." Always in his mind was the reminder of the French Revolution, or of an interregnum even more terrifying. "A reform of any of our great national institutions, without preparing and putting into practice means to well train, instruct, and advantageously employ, the great mass of the people, would inevitably create immediate revolution. . .and all Europe and the Americas would be plunged in one general scene of anarchy and dreadful confusion, of which the late French Revolution will give but a faint anticipation." It was a fearful dilemma.

Owen combined the vision of the prophet with the attention to detail of the administrator. He was an eminently successful business leader, entirely aware of practical necessities and careful steps. Harriet Martineau remarks about New Lanark that "the management of the mill and the farm, the school and the ball-room, everything requiring the exercise of the economic and administrative faculties, was of a rare quality of excellence under his hand." Change was to be allowed only after a convincing demonstration of its actual superiority: "it is absolutely necessary to support the old system and institutions under which we now live, until another system and another arrangement of society shall be proved by practice to be essentially superior."

This singular approach demanded, as we shall see, the maintenance of the existing class structure of society, in spite of his disdain of the empty life and parasitism of the rich. His was a message for the whole of society and he insisted that reform could occur within the existing institutional framework and might even be made to pay dividends: "as the New Lanark establishment belonged to parties whose views were various, it became also necessary to devise means to create pecuniary gains from each improvement, sufficient to satisfy the spirit of commerce."

Not until the end of the century would George Bernard

Shaw, in his reconstitution of human character in an industrial society, portray in his plays the figure of the 'saint' in a similar simplicity, modesty and selflessness of character.

Owen travelled everywhere with the positive assurance that he had seen the central question which the machine had raised. As his father-in-law often said to him, "Thou needest be very right for thou art very positive."

Owen's most memorable achievement was the transformation of the backwoods factory village of New Lanark into what his biographer called "the model factory, model school and model village of Europe."

Owen arrived at the turn of the century to take charge of the cotton mills of New Lanark which had been built some fifteen years earlier in the rough, uncultivated Scottish lowlands near the falls of the Clyde. It was a primitive community with bad roads and a few poor inhabitants. Owen recounts that on the trip from Glasgow to New Lanark, a distance of some thirty miles, three toll-keepers refused to take his goldpiece in payment of the toll, because they had never seen a gold coin before. "I concluded," said Owen, "that I had come into a very primitive district."

The mills were built near the falls to make use of water power for the spinning machinery. The population of 1300 consisted to a large extent of thieves, criminals, drunks and prostitutes. The self-respecting Scottish crofter of the lowlands would not work the long day of fourteen to sixteen hours in the unhealthy conditions of the new factories, nor would he send his children. Only the starving peasants from Ireland and the West Scottish highlands, made destitute by the enclosures, could be induced to work in the factories. They had acquired the characteristics of a rootless, displaced population—crude, destructive and brutalized.

The labour force consisted mainly of some 500 children, known euphemistically as 'the parish apprentices'. These were children, most of them seven to twelve years of age, who had come from the poorhouse and were in the care of the public authorities. The parish was pleased to shift the burden of their maintenance to the factory owner and few questions were asked about what happened to them after that.

The previous owner, David Dale, Owen's father-in-law, had made some provision for the children's education, lodging and medical care. He was a benevolent employer by the standards of the time, and when one of the mills burned down soon after opening, Dale continued to pay the wages of the workers until the mill was restored.

The general conviction of the day, however, was that England's prosperity rested on child labour, long hours and low wages. The work day rose to fourteen and sixteen hours, and both working and living conditions became more wretched than they had ever been before the introduction of manufactures. Workers were taxed far beyond their strength, and their only solace was found in the abundant gin mills. But the saddest offspring of the new era were the children—"feeble, pale and wretched," spindle-legged, often crippled, wracked by disease and with poor chances of survival during their relentless days in the factory. Employers forced wages down, so the entire family was required to work for a bare existence. As Owen put it, "we are unacquainted with any nation, ancient or modern, that has suffered its hundreds of thousands of children of seven to twelve years of age to work incessantly for fifteen hours per day in an overheated, unhealthy atmosphere, allowing them only forty minutes of that time for dinner and change of air, which they breathe often in damp cellars or in garrets, in confined narrow streets or dirty lanes." Owen called it 'white slavery' and thought conditions much worse than any he saw later among American and West Indian slaves. "I can make manufacturing pay," said Owen, "without reducing those whom I employ to misery and moral degradation."

Owen also discerned, soon after his arrival at New Lanark that "theft was very general, and was carried on to an enormous and ruinous extent, and Mr. Dale's property had been plundered in all directions, and had been almost considered public property."

At first, every change that he made was regarded with suspicion. Owen tried to seek out those workers in a position of influence to explain his point of view and objectives but he was still hindered at every turn. In 1806, however, the

Americans placed an embargo on the export of cotton, and most cotton factories had to suspend operations. But Owen continued to pay full wages to all for four months, amounting to some 7000 pounds, and this marked the turning point in his relations with the workers.

Owen's programme of reform at New Lanark encompassed the whole range of life in the community. He reduced the hours of work to twelve, including an hour and a half for meals, raised wages, provided free medical care, organized stores where first-quality food and clothing were sold at cost, and started a savings bank. In the factory, he devised a 'silent monitor' for each worker, a four-sided piece of wood, each side of which was a different colour to denote the behaviour of the worker, from 'bad' through 'indifferent', 'good', and 'excellent'. The previous day's conduct was openly indicated by the silent monitor placed beside the worker and was registered permanently in a book of character, "never to be blotted out." Before long, a great improvement was noted with the 'goods' and 'excellents' being in the great majority. Owen also carried through a rearrangement of production methods and replacement of machinery reminiscent of modern industrial engineering and scientific management.

He devised comfortable clothes for the workers who, till then, wore cumbersome frockcoats, tails and other elaborate clothing. For women particularly, he wanted to dispense with existing customs that sought to protect female modesty in elaborate layers of burdensome apparel.

The 'parish apprentice' system of child labour was abolished and Owen refused to hire children under ten years of age, while those between ten and twelve were to work only six hours a day.

Houses at New Lanark had been built by David Dale at the time that the mills were constructed, and they consisted of only one room to house an entire family. There were few sanitary facilities and refuse was piled high before the front door of each house. One of Owen's first projects was to add a second story to each house, thus providing another room. He also laid streets in the village and arranged to have refuse carted away regularly, forbidding it to be piled up again. He induced the workers to organize their own committee to raise the standard of health, cleanliness and general house-keeping. Without punishment, but in face of great opposition and indifference at first, living conditions and standards soon rose to what G.D.H. Cole termed "the cleanest and most sanitary manufacturing village in the country."

Owen recognized the workers' need for recreation and amusement as an essential relief from their work, and he encouraged such activities, throwing open the surrounding woods for public enjoyment. Temptations such as gin mills were removed from the vicinity, although good whiskey could be obtained in Owen's stores.

The heart of Owen's position, his entire hope for lasting reform, lay in education. It is the educational system of New Lanark which became its most important feature. It brought him his greatest renown and was the forerunner of the school reform movement of the twentieth century. For Owen, education was the means of character formation, which in turn was the basis of a well-functioning society, the achievement of happiness, the prerequisite for reconciling differences of creed and country, and instrumental in the promotion of the millennium. Education would allow the release of the vast powers of the machine, bringing abundance for all.

Education was not to be for a favoured few, serving to reinforce caste and class, but was to be the free universal right of all. No one was turned away from his school at New Lanark.

Owen anticipated virtually all the principles of modern education. His emphasis was on the training of individual ability and achievement, and independent thought rather than the rote memorization current at the time. He understood that the whole personality was involved in the educational process. He questioned the value of existing books, especially at the early stages of the child's training, and introduced charts, maps and models, instead. The curriculum included dancing, singing, gymnastic exercises, open-air activities, studies of surrounding natural objects and walks in the country. He made use of many types of games and devices reminiscent of the later Frobel techniques of coloured squares and blocks for learning. Visitors to New Lanark were greatly impressed and Owen remarks that "the dancing, music, military discipline, and geographical exercises were especially attractive to all except 'very pious' Christians." No rigid schedules were kept for each activity, but indoor work would be followed by outdoor physical exercise and games according to the teacher's judgement of the mood of the class.

Most homes, Owen felt, were unfit places for the young child, and he developed the idea of 'infant schools'. The very early years were the important ones for the formation of character, and Owen looked forward to the time when every child who was a year old would be placed in a 'rational infant boarding school.' When he visited Europe some years later, Owen saw the schools of Father Oberlin, Pestalozzi and Fellenburg, but his own schools were then well underway and seemed to him more advanced.

Later, when he was coping with the problem of the unemployed, Owen urged the combination of schemes for national employment with apprenticeship training of children.

His concern with education derived from the realization that simply changing the environment was not in itself sufficient to ensure permanent changes in character unless training was begun from infancy.

Owen was also a pioneer in adult education and his evening lectures and programmes were the first major achievement in popular education among the workers.

These projects received a great stimulus when, to house them, he completed a special building known as the 'New Institution', dedicated to a system "which shall give happiness to every human being through all succeeding generations."

Owen acquired an international reputation for his achievements at New Lanark, and some twenty thousand visitors came to see the results of his work in the years 1815 to 1825, including European royalty and American senators. They made the remote journey on the bad roads to see a factory community that was both humane and successful. His great experiment offered a demonstrable, overwhelming testimony on behalf of his beliefs. New Lanark exhibited the general appearance of industry, temperance, comfort, health and humanity. And moreover, as a financial venture it was a resounding success.

It demonstrated to Owen that the communities around the new factories, of which there were now many and many still to come, could be run in surroundings with infinite possibilities for good.

Owen's whole being revolved around the new import of the machine. He saw that its development would be boundless—that "its extension will go on ad infinitum." He felt almost personally responsible for having introduced the machine age.

Like John the Baptist, he emerged from his years in the wilderness with a mission: "I have been silently preparing the way for upwards of five-and-twenty years."

The first step in Owen's discovery of society was the recognition of the dominant influence of environment on character. Owen felt that the persistence of society's evils was due to a false belief that the individual was responsible for his actions and for his own character. But "the character of man is, without a single exception always formed for him." It was the environment which was instrumental in forming the individual's character, and therefore the solution to all evils lay in creating a healthy and favourable environment which in turn would mould individual character in the same pattern. "Any character, from the best to the worst, from the most ignorant to the most enlightened, may be given to any community, even to the world at large, by applying certain means; which are to a great extent at the command and under the control, or easily made so, of those who possess the government of nations."

This implied a crucial shift of responsibility from the individual to society. Owen's instinct had hit upon the vital point. He regarded society as more than a political aggregate of individuals; it had an independent and prior reality of its own.

The years of New Lanark saw Owen's best writing, and a

full statement of his outlook came forth in the years 1813 to 1821, years of continuous revelation. His essays were well received in the highest circles and widely distributed. His first work "A New View of Society: Essays on the Formation of Character," written in 1813, was distributed by Lord Sidmouth, Secretary of the Home Office to the leading governments and universities of Europe, and to each English archbishop and bishop. John Quincey Adams, the American ambassador, sent a copy to the governor of each state in the United States. At the conference of the great powers at Aix-La-Chapelle, Lord Castlereagh presented Owen's "Two Memorials on Behalf of the Working Classes." Owen also had reason to believe that the Prime Minister, Lord Liverpool, and many of his Cabinet, were converts to his views.

Man's basic motivation, thought Owen, was his "self-interest" or "desire to obtain happiness," and this could "only be attained by conduct that must promote the happiness of the community." In other words, man's self-interest could not be realized outside of society, and there, only by fostering the welfare of the community. This was the basis of Owen's doctrine of co-operation. "When these truths are made evident, every individual will necessarily endeavour to promote the happiness of every other individual within his sphere of action; because he must clearly, and without any doubt, comprehend such conduct to be the essence of self-interest or the true cause of self-happiness."

It was the limited focus on the individual and his responsibility which was at the root of Owen's violent stand against organized religion. Religion preached individual reward and punishment and held that not society, but the individual was to be reformed. This was directly contrary to everything that Owen stood for.

His feelings against religion were as vigorous in his autobiography written at the end of his eighty-seven years, as they had ever been.

"Religions are today the great repulsive powers of society; dividing husbands and wives, parents and children, brothers and sisters; and are everburning firebrands wherever they exist. For proof of demonstration of this—witness the present state of mind, feelings, and conduct, of all the religions in Europe, Asia, Africa and America. The being who shall devise the means to terminate these spiritual insanities will be the greatest friend to the human race that has yet lived. . . .There is no sacrifice at any period, which I could make, that would not have been willingly and joyously made to terminate the existence of religion on earth."

His major public denunciation of religion occurred at a public meeting in the City of London Tavern on August 21, 1817, which Owen called "that day the most important of my life for the public." He was conscious that it was one of the crucial declarations of his life. It also marked the beginning of his decline among the prominent and influential of the day.

Owen was himself, however, in essence a deeply religious person, and for him, the core of all religion consisted of "the desire 'to do good to all men'." He professed a broad tolerance and freedom and believed that "each man in existence has a full right to the enjoyment of the most unlimited liberty of conscience." Later in his life, he advocated a "rational religion."

Owen discovered capitalism and its laws through the problems of unemployment. Although the socialist norm was implied in his premises, he was only gradually forced to envisage socialism as a total solution.

The boom of the Napoleonic wars ended with the victory of 1815, and England was soon enmeshed in the grave perplexities of the depression years. Up to that time, no distinction had been made between the unemployed and the ordinary members of the labouring class known as 'the poor' who had presented a long-standing problem. Various imaginative schemes had been put forward to deal with pauperism and make it pay. From Bellers' 'Colleges of Industry' in 1696, a self-supporting community to number three hundred labourers, to Bentham's 'Industry-Houses', the notion persisted that social communities of the poor could produce profits as well as solve the problem of unemployment. Bentham himself had been a partner in New Lanark and had earned a dividend; Ricardo was on the committee to raise funds for it.

New Lanark had been superlatively successful: welfare improvements, increased productivity, a spectacular advance in the social and moral level of the community, and moreover, high profits.

But this had happened in the boom period of the Napoleonic wars. Owen had known a labour shortage only in New Lanark and was suddenly amazed to see the large number of unemployed whose membership continually varied. Sometimes there were more and sometimes fewer.

The term 'unemployment' itself was unknown and at first, Owen referred to the situation as "unusual general distress" for which he thought the machine was responsible. "The immediate cause of the present distress is the depreciation of human labour. This has been occasioned by the general introduction of mechanism into the manufactures of Europe and America, but principally into those of Britain, where the change was greatly accelerated by the inventions of Arkwright and Watt."

The situation did not call forth a single petition about the condition of 'the poor' and Owen was deeply troubled. Moreover, the Malthusian explanation which was frequently invoked to explain the proliferation of 'the poor' seemed to make nature responsible for the whole problem: population tended to increase in a geometric progression. It seemed that one could not solve the problem without controverting the laws of mathematics and biology.

Owen's reply was simple, namely, that man is born singly, and has the capacity of producing much more food than he requires. Malthus's theory, therefore must be a fallacy.

The annual increase of population is really one by one; we know its utmost limit—it is only, it can be only, an arithmetical increase; whereas, each individual brings into the world with him the means, aided by the existing knowledge of science, and under proper direction, sufficient to enable him to produce food equal to more than ten times his consumption. The fear, then, of any evil to arise from an excess of population, until such time as the whole earth shall become a highly-cultivated garden, will, on due and accurate investigation, prove a mere phantom of the imagination."

Falling prices added to the hardships, increasing the burden of both the war debt and the poor relief rates. A public meeting was called in the City of London Tavern to discuss the new array of economic problems. However, no one seemed able to offer any answer. As Owen put it, "All at the meeting appeared to be at a loss to account for such severe distress at the termination of a war so successful and the commencement of a peace so advantageous, as it was thought, to this country."

A committee was formed by the meeting and Owen testified to disbelieving ears on the extent to which the new machinery had now become widespread over England. That the committee was unaware of the extent of the growth of machinery is narrated by Owen as follows: "Here I was asked by Mr. Colquhoun—the celebrated city magistrate and political economist, who had lately published his 'Resources of the British Empire'—how much I thought this new mechanical and chemical power now superseded manual labour. 'It now must exceed the whole amount of manual producing power.' 'What! Mr. Owen!' exclaimed Mr. Colquhoun and many others—'exceed the labour of more than five millions! Five millions! It is utterly impossible.'"

Owen held on a different occasion, that the productive capacity of existing machinery was equivalent to a mature labour force of one hundred million persons. He saw that business was being stifled by the new Ricardian policy of regulating the issue of currency and credit in accordance with the domestic gold standard. He took a position against gold and considered currency reform a most urgent need.

Owen was forced against these problems of emerging capitalism, unemployment and currency and sought for a solution. It came in the form of his proposal to construct the Villages of Union.

The continuing unemployment after 1815 was a grave shock, and all the more so because no distinction was yet envisaged between the unemployed and 'the poor'. Although the urgent concern was the solution of 'mass unemployment', yet drawing on his New Lanark experience and his general views of the influence of environment on character, Owen put forward a proposal.

He thought that by organizing communities on the land within the scope of the Poor Law, 'the poor' would produce for each other's needs. In this way he approached the market as an 'artificial' institutional framework which could simply be bypassed, dispensing with the rich and their motive of gain. "There can be no doubt that it is the artificial law of supply and demand, arising from the principles of individual gain in opposition to the general well being of society, which has hitherto compelled population to press upon subsistence."

These Villages of Union were to contain some 1200 persons on 1000-1500 acres. The buildings would be arranged in parallelograms and the public buildings would include dormitories for the children over three years of age. Communal kitchens, joint lodgings and common land would be more economical than separate cottages and individual plots. There would be "the principle of united labour expenditure, and property, and equal privileges." Funds required to establish such a village were estimated by Owen at about 96,000 pounds or 80 pounds per inhabitant. The annual interest on such a sum of 4 pounds per head, would be cheaper than the per capita expenditure on the unemployed from the poor rates. These communities would then become the only form of public assistance to the poor.

Owen soon saw that the scheme had several weaknesses; it would institutionalize and stabilize the unemployed and even attract additional paupers rather than getting rid of them as the parish intended. Since the time of John Bellers' plan, 120 years before, the poor rates had multiplied some twentyfold although the population had only trebled. It appeared to Owen that if the depression were to grow, mass unemployment might prove too great a burden for the parish whose resources would run out, sweeping away the whole scheme.

No one showed interest in his idea so Owen then put

forward a second plan some six months later in September of 1817. His new scheme was more radical and extended the Village of Union to those classes already employed. He called for workers to indenture themselves for a seven-year period and receive a capital sum at the end of that time. He hoped thereby to stabilize employment by immobilizing the labour class. Employers would be attracted to the scheme by the absence of a basic wage commitment since subsistence from the land would enable low wages to be paid. The plan would however provide long-term job security, halt the spread of unemployment, and thus remove a major threat to his Villages.

He realized that great concessions would have to be made to the structure of society along the basic lines of its existing divisions, particularly its class structure. Specifically, Owen distinguished four main classes: the parish paupers, the workers, the artisans with some property, and the rich.

The parish paupers included the infirm, the aged, the children of the poor, *and* the unemployed, and these would be "advantageously combined in certain proportions into each 'Parish Employment Settlement.' " (There was to be no parish relief from any other source.) The second class consisted of the workers without property who would combine with the rich or fourth class. The latter would supply the capital, from 1,000 pounds to 20,000 pounds to employ profitably the second class. This working class would be voluntarily indentured for seven years and might at the end of that time receive 100 pounds (or 200 pounds after twelve years), and enter the 'voluntary associations' of the third class. This was the artisans and tradesmen with some property, i.e. between 100 pounds and 2000 pounds. (Classes 3 and 4 formed 'voluntary associations', while the working class was 'indentured' and the paupers administered.)

In addition to the paupers' villages, other Villages of Union therefore, would consist either of individuals of Classes 2 and 4 (workers and the rich would be together) or Class 3 (artisans with property). Agriculture would be the main occupation. The Villages of Union would have a regime of abundance, for there would be an extensive use of machines while at the same time economies would be achieved through communal cooking and living arrangements. Savings would be possible, through which, in modern terms, communal kitchens, day nurseries, and kindergartens, could be secured. In fact, there would be a large surplus of products, which would be exchanged among the Villages of Union, valued according to their labour content. This improvement in the standard of life due to the spreading use of machinery, would result to the great benefit of the working class, without any reduction in the profits of the employers. The capitalist would be attracted to the scheme by the possibilities of cheap labour which a working class, settled and self-supported on the land, could offer. For the worker, the long-term attraction of the 100 or 200 pounds at the end of seven or twelve years, would keep him voluntarily indentured and provide a stable labour force.

The pauper villages too would become self-supporting, and would be supplied with qualified instructors and administrators to direct the establishment.

Essentially, the whole of society was taken in under Owen's second or modified scheme. As he said, "The whole frame of society may remain as it is." Gradualism would rule the day. "The institutions of our forefathers, erroneous as they were, must not be handled with violence, or rudely touched. No: they must be still preserved with care, supported, and protected, until the new state of society shall be far advanced in quiet practice."

By pooling their resources in collective living, Owen thought that the Villages of Union would be cured of the delusions of individualism which are the bane of all existing religions. Soon the motive of gain would disappear. "It will be quite evident to all, that wealth of that kind which will alone be held in any estimation amongst them may be so easily created to exceed all their wants, that every desire for individual accumulation will be extinguished." The machine would cease to be the enemy of the worker, and become his backer and ally. The workers' life would prosper and unfold, while the existence of the rich would contain no more than the pitiable iniquities of the parasite.

At the same time, the basic frame of society, the market system would remain since profits would be required out of which payment of capital sums to the indentured workers would be made and there would be no nationalization of industry.

Although his postulates might lead to socialism, Owen didn't aim at a socialist society. He refused to consider taking anything from the rich or endangering law and order in any way. Instead, there would be gradual accumulation and distribution of capital, and stable employment.

The old state of society would continue to exist peacefully alongside the new, but it would become immediately apparent how inferior it was and the problem would be to restrain the influx to the new society: "the old state of society will not bear one moment's comparison with the new; and that the only real practical difficulty will be to restrain men from rushing too precipitately from one to the other." The transition would be voluntary and peaceful. It hinged on the triumph of example.

Owen was thus the originator of one of the most important ideas in the history of socialism. Toward the end of the nineteenth century when Marx (who held Owen in high regard) wrote his *Critique of the Gotha Programme* he said that there must be a period of transition based on the demonstrable superiority of the communist example. This became a key doctrine in the German social democratic movement and is of crucial relevance even today.

The emerging market system placed a fatal obstacle before the scheme. Goods produced in the new institutions would simply create more unemployment in the private sector, which was the essential criticism Daniel Defoe had made of Bellers' plan in 1704. The trade depression could not be overcome in this way.

The whole scheme ran counter to the economic developments culminating in the Poor Law Reform Act of 1834. The capitalist class needed an unhampered, mobile labour force, and Owen's indenture scheme would restrict change and efficiency for stability and employment. The movement toward a self-regulating market system, including a free labour market, was pressing forward.

Moreover, it soon became clear that none of the unemployed and paupers would enter such a scheme unless compelled by the parish authorities. Owen had excluded compulsion from the start and the parish authorities refused to act. Also, no organic community could result from linking the unemployed and unemployables in a common fate "as a community of work and expenditure."

For the other classes, no association existed for carrying the scheme through. What would induce investors to entrust their capital to the Village administration outside their direct control, and how was the product to be divided up among the various groups in the community? The secret of successful collective ventures lies not so much in increased numbers as in the strength of voluntary association of which there was none here. These and other questions excluded the ultimate possibility of such a solution.

Owen had compromised a great deal in formulating his second plan. He realized that the only way to begin was precisely with those elements which he hoped mankind would later transcend: the rich with their profit motive, and the division of society into classes, and partisan groups. He had to acquiesce to these aspects of society if his villages were to have any possibility of being started at all. His recognition and incorporation into his second plan of these real, and for him abhorrent, features of the society around him was a lesson.

His hope lay in education—that if he could only make a start, his schools and the self-evident truths of his scheme would win the day, and divisions among men would eventually disappear.

However, what might have been a practical plan to deal with the village destitute in 1696, when Bellers propounded it, was, in 1818, only a ditch dug by children on the beach to stop the tide. The ocean of capitalism that was headed by the juggernaut of the machine, was breaking in upon mankind.

After a few years, Owen saw that he was making no progress toward starting a Village in England. The New World, he thought, might perhaps offer a more suitable locale for his plan than the Old. In 1824 he left for America to inspect a site of 30,000 acres and a village, which the Rappites, a religious sect of German peasants, had put up for sale. He purchased the area and a year later formed the Co-operative Community of New Harmony. However, the difficulties were insuperable. Quarrels and dissension rent the community, whose members were from widely varied backgrounds. It split into several smaller groups and the venture dissolved in a few years. The discipline and control which Owen could maintain in his factory village of New Lanark was altogether lacking here in a voluntary community. Owen lost the bulk of his fortune—about 40,000 pounds—and returned to England in 1829.

In the meantime Owen's doctrines had been taken up principally by the new and growing trade union movement. Since the repeal of the Combination Acts in 1824 the workers had been free to organize. Owen founded the modern trade union movement and became its leader virtually against his will. In his Report to the County of Lanark, Owen had already put forward the principles of labour as a standard of value, and in 1832 he founded the National Equitable Labour Exchange where producers' co-operatives could exchange goods on the basis of 'labour time'. The idea of a private issue of notes was by no means unusual at the time, and for a while the "Labour Notes" were circulated in London without difficulty. However the venture failed during the trade crisis of 1834. Owen intended the "Labour Notes" to replace the gold standard, but he did not realize that setting labour hours on commodities in a market system (which set its own prices) was doomed to failure.

The Grand National Consolidated Trades Union was formed in 1833 and consisted of a number of guilds of craftsmen, artisans, retailers and other 'trades' along with the working classes. At one time it claimed a membership of almost a million and formed one of the largest social movements of the day. The purpose was "to form themselves into lodges, to make their own laws and regulations—for the purpose of emancipating the industrious and useful classes from the difficulties which overwhelm them." Owen kept to the idea of the economic autonomy of the labouring class.

The workers and artisans wanted a general strike but he insisted on gradualism and non-violence from the start: "All the individuals now living are the suffering victims of this accursed system, and all are objects of pity; you will, therefore, effect this great and glorious revolution without, if possible, inflicting individual evil. . .without bloodshed, violence or evil of any kind, merely by an overwhelming moral influence, which influence individuals and nations will speedily perceive the uselessness and folly of attempting to resist."

The power of this new trade union alarmed the manufacturers, and after a year of strikes, lock-outs and prosecutions the 'Grand National' was shattered. The National Building Guild, organized to provide employment and "superior dwellings" for the various members of the building crafts, did not fare much better.

The one movement to survive, of all the many that came forward in his name was the consumers' co-operative movement started by the 'Rochdale Pioneers' in 1844 with a small store in Toad Lane. Owen however, was little interested in this venture which ended up as the largest consumers' association in the world and was the most enduring organization of the Owenite movement.

The later years of Owen's life were occupied for a while by the unsuccessful experiment of establishing a Village of Union called Queenwood in Hampshire. Owen was appointed Governor and began erecting extensive buildings and a fine school, when the financial strain on the enterprise proved too great and forced it to give way.

Owen died at the age of eighty-seven after writing a splendid autobiography which reiterated his views as firmly as ever.

Owen was a true hero of the age: philosopher, friend of kings, multimillionaire, a Ford, Nobel and Carnegie rolled into one. In this favoured position and in his absolute dedication to mankind, lie the key to his depth and comprehensive perspective.

From the first, he saw the import of the machine and read man's future in its lineaments. In that naked dawn, technology revealed its essentials to him. He never envisaged retreat or defeat but faced up to the reality with all its implications. He held on to the machine whether it was to bring salvation or would be accompanied by everlasting suffering. Either humanity would be saved or salvation must be given up as hopeless. In any case, reason had gone to its limit and complaint was of no avail.

Owen's efforts were swept away by the onrushing forces of a burgeoning market society, man's initial response to the machine. For some, the postulates of this society were regarded as the limit of human initiative and valour. But Owen saw beyond the market to a society built on different moral foundations. What he reiterated was his recognition of a truth indelibly stamped on our consciousness in a technological civilization—the transcending reality of society for man's inner existence.

His life was a personal testament to this truth. His initial determination was boundless and heroic but implicit in it was the resignation to bear up to the unavoidable. But before man could resign himself to those evils of the machine which were intractable, the limits had first to be tested.

The standard that Owen set leaves us in awe.

August 1958

GEORGE GRANT

> Upon the rivers of Babylon,
> there we sat and wept:
> when we remembered Zion. . .
> How shall we sing the song of the Lord
> in a strange land?
>
> *Psalm 136*

The year 2000 these days, glows brightly in the distance. Its sanguine supporters remain undeterred by current upheaval or prospective revolution. Technology is the balm to make the wounded whole.

But there are dissonant voices outside this world of positive thinking. George Grant's new book, *Technology and Empire*, is not about the external revolution—the third world, imperialism, poverty or participatory politics. It is about an internal revolution and one that we have lost—the destruction of man's inner life in a technological society. The outer man has won spectacular victories over nature; the inner man, while hardly being aware of his loss, has suffered something ultimate and irremediable.

Grant is not a revolutionary, he is a prophet and he calls us to account for what we have done to the world, in the biblical terms of good and evil. He is no naive fundamentalist for he knows our century and its origins in that incisive and sweeping way which is given to very few. This is no milk-and-water sermon about morality lagging behind technology; no insipid call from the research establishment for more 'research' in the social sciences. It is a universal cry in a technological jungle which is already triumphant and irreversible. For Grant, our century is a paradigm of ultimate deprival; we cherish the idols of efficiency and liberalism, the pragmatism of our political and economic order, and all of it is empty of significance.

Grant's is a moving plea, evocative, passionate and deeply human. It sounds those hidden chords in all of us that could turn atheists religious and socialists conservative, and have them discover that against the common condition, their own divisions are insignificant.

The theme is not new. A powerful literary tradition has sounded this note many times: something central and precious in the life of man has eroded and we are helpless before an autonomous and runaway technology. Huxley, Orwell, Karel Capek, Kafka, Beckett, Dudintsev, Sartre—the list is long and eminent, each with his own form of allusion and indirection, but all pointing to a negative utopia. But we have a segregated compartment in our mind where we can isolate and contain the early warning signals from literary quarters. Are they merely products of the imagination? Literary licence?

Grant sounds the same message in a different key, but this shift from art to life has yet to find an adequate vocabulary. It is a shift from allusion to present condition and from warning to lament. It is a lament not for a nation, but for mankind; a Pilgrim's Progress in reverse. It is not a nostalgic reverie for a mediaevalism that never was, nor for a world of taboo, magic and superstition, of class cruelty and master-slave exploitation. It is not about the evils or benefits of capitalism. It transcends all of these but we barely have the vocabulary to stand outside and view our deepest selves. Gropingly, we search for metaphors such as 'deprival'; we formulate disturbing questions: What, if anything, is there to seek beyond the liberal virtues of freedom and equality? Was there ever something else?

Technology and Empire is a collection of five essays and an epilogue, four of which have been published previously. The most notable essay, "In Defence of North America," is new and is first in the volume. It is a masterful apologia and a powerful indictment both, and no Canadian has written with such sweeping insight on this subject before. Grant moves beyond the perspectives of both Louis Hartz and Jacques Ellul to trace the origins of the American destiny in the interweaving of history, ideology and technology. He writes as a Canadian closely identified with the North American experience:

> we are still enfolded with the Americans in the deep sharing of having crossed the ocean and conquered the new land. . . the majestic continent which could not be ours in the way that the old had been. . .because the very intractability, immensity and extremes of the new land required that its meeting with mastering Europeans be a battle of subjugation. And after that battle we had no long history of living with the land before the arrival of the new forms of conquest which came with industrialism. . . .There can be nothing immemorial for us except the environment as object.

While for Hartz, America is frozen as a Lockean 'fragment',

for Grant, it is shaped by a Calvinist Protestantism of the seventeenth century. Grant has in mind not only the connection between Calvinism and capitalism which Max Weber expounded, but the "deeper level of the matter which is the connection between Protestant theology and the new sciences." The connection is complex but its essence— following Troeltsch—was:

> the emphasizing of the individual and empirical, the renunciation of the concepts of absolute causality and unity, the practically free and utilitarian individual judgement of all things. The influence of this spirit is quite unmistakably the most important cause of the empirical and positivist tendencies of the Anglo-Saxon spirit. . . .

Benjamin Franklin provides a perfect illustration with his public virtues drawn directly from the Protestant ethos and his scientific drive a prime example of Troeltsch's analysis.

The moral and historical climates of America were highly favourable to the development and diffusion of technique. This diffusion was required in the subjugation of the environment and came to be regarded as an exercise of freedom. The drive of technology was so powerful because its purveyors could identify their activities with a beneficent progress and with the liberation of mankind. A sense of 'unappeaseable responsibility' became the secular version of Calvinist predestination.

The end result is a spiritual wasteland:

> . . .an immense majority who think they are free in pluralism, but in fact live in a monistic vulgarity in which nobility and wisdom have been exchanged for a pale belief in progress, alternating with boredom and weariness of spirit; when the disciplined among us drive to an unlimited technological future, in which technical reason has become so universal that it has closed down an openness and awe, questioning and listening; when Protestant subjectivity remains authentic only where it is least appropriate, in the moodiness of our art and sexuality, and where public religion has become an unimportant litany of objectified self-righteousness necessary for the more anal of outer

managers. . . .

America is a close-up of our global destiny as the technological society spreads. There is no 'saving remnant' in Grant's vision and no way out:

the drive for radical change in this society tends only to harden the very directions the society is already taking. . . the source of revolutionary fervour (arises) finally from a further extension of the very modernity which has brought us where we are. . . .

Radicals are caught in an insoluble contradiction:

They want both high standards of spontaneous democracy and the egalitarian benefits accruing from technique. But have not the very forms of the bureaucratic institutions been developed as necessary for producing those benefits? Can the benefits exist without the stifling institutions? Can such institutions exist as participatory democracies?

Little can be expected from social scientists either. They are deluded by their claims to 'objectivity', specialized to the point of myopia by their vested interests, and act as dilettantes picking 'values' in a fabian garden. Grant's essay on the university reads like an Epistle to the Philistines. Research factories are the order of the day:

If one has steady nerve, it is useful to contemplate how much is written about Beowulf in one year in North America. One can look at the Shakespeare industry with perhaps less sense of absurdity; but when it comes to figures such as Horace Walpole having their own factory, one must beware vertigo.

The essay, "Religion and the State," shows up the kind of Christianity which is taught in the schools as a "facade of tradition" which "serves the passing interest of the state without really serving the interests of the churches." "Tyranny and Wisdom" is a commentary on the debate between Leo Strauss and Alexandre Kojève about the universal and homogeneous state. The debate and commentary about this ideal of the liberal internationalists centres around the question of whether such a world implies nothing less than an appalling global tyranny. The debate is highly technical and Grant's commentary is inconclusive on the main issue, while touching only incidentally the major theme of the rest of this book.

On the question of the future of Canada, Grant is less passionate than he was in his *Lament for a Nation*, but no less resigned to the end of an independent Canada. She has no alternative vision to sustain her and is bound to be swept into the American vortex:

> To most Canadians, as public beings, the central cause of motion in their souls is the belief in progress through technique, and that faith is identified with the power of leadership of the English-speaking empire of the world. . . . The very substance of our lives is bound up with the western empire and its destiny, just at a time when that empire uses increasingly ferocious means to maintain its hegemony.

But prophecy is one thing and policy another; they can in fact point in opposite directions:

> Nothing here written implies that the increasingly difficult job of preserving what is left of Canadian sovereignty is not worth the efforts of practical men.

> It is a dim candle to light the way.

We were seduced by liberal ideology and now we suffocate in the grip of the cast-iron maiden of technique. Grant offers little to qualify his message of total despair. Is he the ultimate realist among us?

In the century and a half since the onset of the first industrial revolution, we have been given reasons to doubt the double-barrelled determinism of ideology and technique. Some lessons of that experience may be revealing. The official credo, derived from English political philosophy, pictured a society of atomistic individuals seeking their just reward on the market, with laws of property and contract guaranteed by the state. The feeding of the new machines with raw materials and labour required at the time, that both man and his habitat be governed by self-regulating labour and land markets respectively. Their disposition was to be solely the verdict of the mindless new order known as the market economy. Left to its own devices, the supply-demand mechanism for the 'factors of production', produced the disastrous dislocations of the early industrial revolution. Had matters rested there, ideology and technology would have produced a negative utopia matching any of Grant's deepest apprehensions.

But this was only the beginning of the first round, and the "fictitious commodities" labour and land were still to be heard from in their own right. The countervailing and spontaneous reactions of a society arising to protect itself, created the human and social history of that century. The extension of the market for genuine commodities was accompanied by its restriction in regard to 'fictitious' ones and created a 'double movement'. Trade unions, child labour laws, factory legislation, and later, minimum wage laws, zoning regulations and housing standards intervened as an institutional buffer in this unprecedented attempt to cast society into a mould suited to the needs of the machine.

There seems little room in Grant's view of the world for the role of institutions as mediators between ideology and technique and for being acted on in turn by both. Before this first century of 'modernization' was over, even more substantial institutional and moral forces were released. It became the age of universal suffrage, the beginnings of mass literacy and mass education, the flowering of civil liberties and the freedom of the press. Some of the developments are to be ascribed to the reigning liberal ideology, others to the reaction against it with roots in a Western moral heritage that was older. Certainly it was the century of the birth of socialism.

Who could have predicted this outcome? The assumptions of liberal ideology were only a tissue of shallow fictions on the nature of man and society, but because they offered permissive ground for the spread of the machine, they were, in a sense, wrong for the right reasons. But neither the moral nor institutional history of that first-round of industrialization was contained within the bounds of the liberal premises. We can hardly expect these premises to last a second round which is now underway.

The new wave of globe-girdling computer and communications networks and the octopi of multi-national corporations are phenomena far more implacable seemingly, than the institutional enormity of the market economy. Countervailing institutions and the indigenous traditions of nation-states are not so clearly suited to become the protective barriers in the second round. The requirements of control, co-ordination and expansion of the system create a proliferating bureaucracy which operates as an anonymous tyranny for which no one can answer.

But the reaction nevertheless escalates in proportion to the spread of the technological society. There is a global explosion of moral passions in which we seem to have discovered, virtually for the first time, social wounds that are as old as mankind itself: poverty, racism, inequality, national oppression and exploitation and our intolerance of them is fierce and unbounded. The phenomenon is universal. Our universities and churches will never be the same, and we may witness, for the first time, the resignation of a Pope. In the early throes, these movements are often blind or groping. But can we rule out a creative institutional and moral transformation out of the anguish and upheaval? Will total despair turn out to be as myopic a verdict in 1969 as it was in 1820?

It is precisely the fact that we cannot answer this question either way that produces the basic tension of the technological society. No one knows the limits to which it can be reformed, nor indeed, how. For some, this provides a precarious but sufficient basis for hope without illusion and for action.

But I doubt that all this reaches the core of George Grant's complaint, the sense of ultimate deprival. The term is a metaphor, but a metaphor for what? Grant is barely articulate on this question and the reader can only attempt with some hesitation, to reconstruct his meaning.

When Grant writes that "technique is ourselves" and that it "comes forth from and is sustained in our vision of ourselves as creative freedom," he goes to the heart of the question of technology. But he has eminent predecessors. For McLuhan, technology is the extension of man in a literal but far-reaching sense. For Marx, the concept of externalization (*entausserung*) refers to the projection of man through his technology but also through his laws, his art and his institutions. A theory of technology as the projection of man, helps to explain the irreversible impetus which the technological thrust has acquired.

Marx follows up the moral implications of his theory in the specific critique of capitalist alienation (*entfremdung*). Grant fails to do likewise, but one can imagine that his sense of deprival must be linked in some way with his view of technology. To recognize on the moral plane that 'technology is ourselves' is to stagger under the burden of an immense responsibility. We can no longer dissociate ourselves from, or contract out of the vast network of compulsion and anonymous tyranny that the technological society creates. We ourselves are its source when we opt for the reign of the machine. We cannot escape through non-recognition, the burden of what we do to others. We are helpless in the defence of that citadel of conscience which is the core of inner life and the foundation of religious existence as we have known it.

Grant's inarticulate anguish and despair may be fore-shadowed in the single sentence

I could not face the fact that we were living at the end of Western Christianity.

May 1969

KARL POLANYI, 1886-1964

In his Foreword to *The Great Transformation,* Professor Robert M. MacIver wrote of Karl Polanyi:

Here, at a crucial hour, is a fresh comprehension of the form and the meaning of human affairs. . .he is shedding a new illumination on the process and revolutions of a whole age of unexampled change.

Born in Vienna in 1886, Karl Polanyi grew up in Hungary and studied philosophy and law at the Universities of Budapest and Kolozsvar, Rumania. During his student days he founded a broadly-based radical student movement, the Galileo Circle, in 1908 at the University of Budapest. It had an eventual membership of about 2000 and attempted to introduce the liberal ideas, absent from the archaic curriculum, that were essential for the creation of a modern democratic nation. Members of the movement volunteered for popular education among workers in the trade unions. The members of the Galileo Circle were prominent participants in subsequent political events in Hungary such as the revolutions of 1918 and 1919.

Karl Polanyi was called to the bar in Budapest in 1912 and served in the Austro-Hungarian army during the First World War. In 1919 he moved to Vienna and there he married Ilona Duczynska in 1923. Their only child, Kari, was born in the same year. From 1924 to 1933, he was foreign affairs editor of *Der Oesterreichische Volkswirt*, the leading economic weekly of Vienna.

Under the rising tide of fascism, he emigrated to London in 1933 and lectured for the Workers Educational Association and for the Extra-Mural Delegacies of Oxford University and the University of London. He was active in the Christian Left and was joint editor of *Christianity and the Social Revolution* (London 1935) which contains his study "The Essence of Fascism."

He visited the United States on several occasions to lecture on international affairs for the International Institute of Education. In 1940 he was invited as a resident scholar to Bennington College where he wrote *The Great Transformation* (1944), the most complete statement of his social philosophy. Not since Adam Smith had shown the market to be the pivot of a newly-emerging economy, had anyone penetrated more deeply into its social ramifications. The social history of nineteenth-century response to the machine took the form of a double movement. The attempt to extend free markets for genuine commodities included also the attempt to encompass the factors of production, labour and land, within the workings of the self-regulating market economy. But labour and land were together the constitutive elements of society—man and his environment. Thus the attempt to embed society itself within the economic process gave rise to a spontaneous countermovement to protect its substance and thus to restrict the operation of an economic system running automatically in its own grooves. Socialism and the trade unions were early examples of this countermovement. The emergent stresses and strains brought about the collapse of market civilization in the upheavals of the 1930's. The 'Great Transformation' is the present challenge of re-embedding the institutions of the economy within society after this initial response to the machine had failed.

In 1943 Karl Polanyi returned to England and in 1947 was invited to Columbia University where he served as Visiting Professor of Economics from 1947 to 1953. He was co-director of the Interdisciplinary Project on the Economic Aspects of Institutional Growth from 1953 to 1958. The result of the interdisciplinary work was the volume *Trade and Market in the Early Empires* published in 1957. Professor Polanyi was joint editor and a contributor to this volume. Continuing the work of *The Great Transformation,* a new conceptual apparatus was developed to extend beyond the traditional economic questions about the efficient allocation of resources in a market setting. The general frame of reference in this interdisciplinary approach was "the place of the economy in society." Comparative and developmental studies of early economies in their market and non-market variants required general redefinitions of basic terms such as trade and money and of the economy itself. Trade, as old as mankind, was detached from its more recent market variant. 'Administered trade' was carried on in that universal precursor of the market institution, the 'port of trade'. Thus the study of the empirical process under which livelihood was organized meant a departure from the traditional perspective where all economic activity was viewed either as an imperfect or perfect version of market activity. The existence of alternative patterns of economic organization—reciprocity, redistribution and householding—was confirmed.

As a social philosopher concerned with freedom in an industrial society, Karl Polanyi left us the concept of 'the reality of society' as an alternative to the atomistic individualism that symbolized the market society's view of itself. Once mankind had opted for a complex industrial society which generated great centres of power, the absolute priority of conscience and inner life could no longer be upheld. Power was sustained by opinion and in a radically new way we were compelled to compel. But neither could the demands of conscience be relinquished prematurely. Resignation to the reality of society was only possible after the search for the limits to which society could be reformed. Our metaphysical freedom is then suspended, but our concrete freedoms and civic liberties would be assured. The freedom we relinquish is illusory but the freedoms we gain are real.

On his retirement from Columbia in 1958, Karl Polanyi moved to Pickering, Ontario, and was co-editor with his wife of a collection of prose and poetry from Hungary, *The Plough and the Pen*, published in 1963. The English versions of the poems were rendered by a number of Canadian poets.

Before his death on April 23, 1964, Karl Polanyi had completed a manuscript on West African economic history, *Dahomey and The Slave Trade*. He was also the founder of the new international journal published in Canada, *Co-existence,* "for the comparative study of economics, sociology and politics in a changing world."

Karl Polanyi was a socialist all his life, although never associated with a political party.

He touched very deeply the lives of a generation of graduate students at Columbia University. His selfless charm, his originality and his immense intellectual courage are his life-long gifts to those who knew him.

June 1964

Points of Departure

14

WATTS: AN AMERICAN DILEMMA

America today presents a conundrum. The Great Society is moving ahead at a startling pace—civil rights legislation, aid to education, the 7.5 billion dollars to housing and urban renewal, the 1,900 pilot projects launched in the War on Poverty, Medicare for the aged, and tax reform constitute an extraordinary success. In sharp contrast stand the 'leaderless' negroes, rioting in Los Angeles, Chicago and Springfield to whom the salvation promised by The Great Society seems irrelevant. And in foreign policy, America remains the despair of its friends and the source of perverse satisfaction to its enemies—the helpless mire of the war in Viet Nam, the ill-conceived intervention in the Dominican Republic, the now-muted obsession with Castro, and the blind spot on China.

Yet present domestic and foreign policies are not, by most Americans, regarded as inconsistent. The cast of mind which has produced both lines of policy is the subject of some excellent historiography that has recently appeared.

The critical issue within contemporary America is, of course, civil rights. The great gains that have been made under Presidents Kennedy and Johnson have exceeded even the predictions of optimists five years ago. The present position of the American negro should be seen against the background of the oppressive severity of American slavery. As Stanley Elkins convincingly argues in *Slavery: A Problem in American Institutional and Intellectual Life*, the Americans created the most extreme slave system that had ever existed in either the Old or New World. The slave was a straightforward item of property, without any social or human status in society, and there were no avenues for manumission, as there had been in both antiquity and in Spanish-American slavery. The extremity of this slave system was matched only by the moral absolutism of the abolitionists in the north. From that confrontation sprang the first of the modern total wars—including a scorched earth policy. A moral victory was won, although with few social and political gains. It then took a century for actual gains to be realized. Elkins's portrait of American slavery is also a portrait of the fundamentalism of liberal America—the commitment, not to the art of the possible, but to the solution of total justice at any price. The dogmatic abolitionism of the nineteenth century was echoed once more in the demand for unconditional surrender in World War II and by the post-war branding of Communism as an absolute evil.

This ethic of the liberal absolute was not, however, the product of native soil. Louis Hartz in *The Founding of New Societies* shows how new societies in North America, South Africa, Latin America and Australia are "fragments" of various parts of the Old World. As fragments, these societies are cast in an ideological mould at birth which, in their succeeding history, becomes "a moral absolute, a national essence, a veritable way of racial life." The United States is the liberal bourgeois fragment *par excellence*, the physical embodiment of the Lockean philosophy and liberal ideology. "Born free," Americans must be allowed to become equal. American history is then seen as the fulfillment of this original destiny: e.g., Jacksonian democracy, the New Deal, and presently The Great Society. The ideological leaven pervades the search for the solution to ills such as segregation and poverty, and the search, Hartz suggests, "cannot tolerate an accommodation of degree."

But the fragment does not only shape domestic destiny. It becomes a true *Weltanschauung*, a window on the world. The liberal ethic proclaims (in Hartz's terms) that "the world is really one," and on a recalcitrant planet, this ideology provides the citizen "with a shield against the Saracen, [and] the only imaginable moral way of dealing with the man outside the West." The very dogma that compelled America to fight a civil war a century ago has inhibited American political responses toward a solution of the Cold War and today blocks a solution in Viet Nam. It is not, as some commentators have noted, that the war in Viet Nam threatens The Great Society (the immediate evidence is to the contrary), but the very success of domestic ideals may increase the desire to protect and project The Great Society in the international sphere. Not only Rostow's 'takeoff' into high mass consumption, but liberal conceptions of freedom and order are envisaged in this American dream for the world.

Hartz is pessimistic about the possibilities for America to meet and to live with alien ideologies and societies on the globe. Yet he is not a determinist about the future and leaves a vague message of hope: "the new generations emerging in the fragment [find] the old alignments. . .increasingly empty." The final words of his introductory essay tell of an "imaginative renewal [which] with all its trauma, is today the mark of the new era that the fragment enters."

Hartz does not specify who these new generations are that may inspire an imaginative renewal. He certainly does not name the American negro. Negro history is simply part of the history of the American fragment, and the negro's efforts today, Hartz believes, are geared to assuming his rightful place within it. "The Negro is today," he suggests, "implementing the peculiar millennium that the interior of the Enlightenment promises. . .he is working with what has always been the *one* 'revolutionary' factor in the national history" (italics added).

Hartz is open to question on his interpretation of the negro experience. While the negro would wish to secure all the rights that middle class America has to offer, his discontent may have different roots and consequences than Hartz suggests. The recent riots offer a sufficient basis for doubt that the negro's goals are identical with those of The Great Society. These riots symbolized not only race war and a war between generations, but also a class war as evidenced by the massive destruction of (negro as well as white) property as the primary goal. "This is not a color problem," declared H.H. Brookins, the minister of a Los Angeles negro church, "it's a class problem." Yet for Hartz, the absence of class conflict is the hallmark of the true liberal society, and 'classlessness' is at the centre of President Johnson's rhetorical vision of The Great Society. But the heart of the matter lies in the past.

Historically, the paradox of why American slavery ('liberal slavery') was the harshest of all, is adequately explained by Hartz (just as by Elkins). In a bourgeois community,

> where the Negro is either an item of property or an equal human being, a free Negro under conditions of slavery is an enormous paradox. How can an object of property be 'free'? Or if it can be free, it must be human and hence all Negroes must be free.

By contrast,

> the Latin-American [feudal] fragments, by absorbing the African like the Indian into their status system, indeed by creating that system out of their ranks, were saved from the radical oscillations of egalitarian morality.

While ideological history can indeed go far in illuminating actual history, the danger of reification always remains. In the case of the negro, Hartz mistakes the concept for the reality. It is precisely because the negro was regarded as 'property' that he has a social history and outlook which is not that of the white fragment. It was one thing to treat the negro as property but quite another to expect no more animate and human consequences from this experience than that of actual property. In the present countermovement, the negro belatedly re-enacts a pageant reminiscent of the early Industrial Revolution, when labour in general was treated as a veritable commodity and rebelled against this status through the trade union movement and political action.

Social history is contained as much in the reaction to ideology as in its fulfilment and such reactions may take unexpected directions.

The negro in America is being invited, albeit partially and in anguish, to take his place in the white fragment. But is the liberal ideal of 'equality of opportunity' enough? The week in which voter registration was launched in the South was also the week in which negro riots erupted in the West and in the North. It is not the liberal ideal of equality of opportunity which is the watchword, but at least, the much more substantive 'equality of condition'. Yet much still remains to be explained.

The negro district of Watts in Los Angeles, where the riots erupted, is by no means a typical urban slum found in the East. There are no rat-infested, crumbling tenements and littered streets. There has been no major influx of negroes into this district during the past five years. It is an area of individual, small, rented homes, many surrounded by lawns. While there is a higher rate of congestion, crime and unemployment than in the rest of the city, the municipal administration has done a great deal toward alleviating existing complaints. Biracial committees with large budgets have been set up and only month ago a *New York Times* correspondent reported from Los Angeles that

> The past year has been marked by an array of unspectacular but extensive efforts toward social harmony that have been substantial enough to ease militant frictions.

A partial explanation is offered by James Farmer, the executive director of CORE who states:

> The old way won us the right to eat hamburgers at lunch counters and is winning us the right to vote, but has not basically affected the life of the average Negro.

Is the problem then merely a matter of time—until the programme of The Great Society is successfully implemented? Does this programme itself meet the aspirations of 'the average negro'?

The most eloquent and profound voice of the American negro, James Baldwin, does not concur:

> I cannot accept the proposition that the four-hundred year travail of the American Negro should result merely in his attainment of the present level of the American civilization. . .the white man is himself in sore need of new standards which will release him from his confusion.

The negro in America falls out of Hartz's fragment—and thus out of its current embodiment in The Great Society—because he brings to bear a different social and spiritual history. Whatever importance one puts on the racial difference *per se* (and on the political impact of the rise of the new African states), the difference in race has had concrete social consequences that have created a distinct destiny for the Negro in America in the past, a destiny that has acquired a momentum of its own for the future. Baldwin's hope is that the two fragments will merge:

> The black and the white deeply need each other here if we are really to become a nation—if we are really, that is, to achieve our identity, our maturity as men and women.

American historiography may feed our pessimism about America's future, but the pessimism must be qualified—'absolutism' is never absolute and 'fragments' never entirely immobilized. Nor, after the Watts riots, can we easily retain any romanticism about the spiritual renewal that the negro may bring to a new America. Baldwin's The Fire Next Time is a warning as well as a hope.

Yet we should also take serious note of Baldwin's other warning—the possible lack of compliance of the negro in American foreign policy where it touches non-white peoples: "There are some wars (if anyone on the globe is still mad enough to go to war) that the American negro will not support."

In this perspective, one can sense the fundamental importance of Martin Luther King's stand against American foreign policy in Viet Nam and his attempt to swing the civil rights movement behind such a position. This effort is by no means assured of success. Dissenting voices from the N.A.A.C.P. have already been heard. But little hope remains that America will be influenced in its Viet Nam policy by its allies—and certainly not by its enemies.

The negro, and those allied to him, may be the only substantial influence that can press for peace in Viet Nam. For
the long term, this influence may become a political force to
convince America to abandon its traditional moral absolutes
in the international sphere for a commitment to genuine coexistence with alien ideologies and ways of life.

Hartz writes that America must rediscover its roots in
Europe. America may instead broaden its view of the
diversity of modern life through its confrontation with its
'Africa within'. For America is not one fragment but two—one
white and one black, one liberal and one tribal. On the creative
merging of the two may depend the success both of America's
domestic and of its foreign policy.

With Mel Watkins
September 1965

CHILE

A week spent at Vina del Mar, Chile's gracious old-world
vacation resort, does colour one's view of the world's first
freely-elected Marxist government. Few placards, posters and
slogans were apparent at the end of September. The palms
rustled quietly in the early spring breeze while the ocean surf
nonchalantly tumbled along the shores in an off-season
mood. Everyone was waiting somewhat anxiously for Senor
Allende's reign to begin.

Some eighty or so academics and government officials from
about a dozen countries bordering the Pacific rim, had
gathered for the 'Conference on the Pacific'. The Conference
was an attempt by the Andean Countries of Latin America
to explore the basis for a new relationship with other countries
on the Pacific and so try to get out from under their close
dependence on the United States.

But nervous undertow or not, at Vina del Mar the Chilean
bourgeoisie paraded everywhere in full flower. One had the
sense of the last remaining pocket of old-time elegance and
perfect manners—perhaps what France had looked like at

the turn of the century in the days of 'la belle époque'. It all hit home the evening the Chilean Navy invited the Conference participants to dinner. The Navy has, as I recall, about one and a half military vessels which it can deploy in a crisis. But there they were to greet us at their country club and swimming pool—admirals replete with gold braid, perfect English accents and beautiful wives in evening gowns. We were royally entertained by the most literate and gracious naval cortège one could imagine. The irony of history was somehow at work: the most perfect bourgeois society moved on, at its very peak, to the next stage. . . .It had all been written, but it had never happened that way before.

During the many working sessions of the Conference, one word sooner or later came to the fore among all the Latin American commentators: *dependencia.* It was the core problem to which all discussions of political, social and economic conditions returned. How then, could the Latin American countries bordering on the Pacific reorganize their external relations to each other and to other Pacific countries so as to create new political and economic ties to supplant the overriding American connection?

The initial discussions with the dozen or so countries represented at the Conference were not very hopeful. The developed countries such as Canada, Japan and Australia were able to outline increasing trade prospects with each other under various common-market type arrangements. But the best that could be foreseen for countries such as Chile or Peru was some marginal or associate status within these larger agreements. The only concrete scheme that looked hopeful was the arrangements that the Andean countries had embarked on to help themselves, in particular a trans-national development corporation under the joint auspices of the governments of the Andean Pact—Chile, Peru, Bolivia, Ecuador and Colombia.

The following interviews were taped at the end of September at Vina del Mar, prior to the installation of Senor Allende. The first interview is with Guillermo Atria, the deputy minister of mines. Senor Atria is a very young man who received part of his training in the United States. He seemed to be totally self-assured and a very skilled negotiator with the American copper companies. In the light of the present renewed concern in Canada over the ownership of our natural resources, the successful Chilean technique of 'progressive nationalization' merits careful examination of both its financial and its political aspects.

Our second interview is with Jacques Chonchol who has acquired an international reputation as the architect of the Chilean land reform programme. Toward the end of the interview he sketches out the broad economic setting in the rest of the economy which is required to back up a thorough land reform programme.

The general impression I had from many conversations was that Chile and Peru together, at the present time form the most exciting social laboratory in the world with unusual innovations being tried in many areas. The overall feeling was one of great hope and great energy being deployed in these countries. I also felt that we could benefit from a great deal of 'external aid' from our Latin American colleagues. Call it *dependencia* or call it independence—it seemed that we were moving in the same direction.

1. Chileanizing the Copper Mines

Rotstein: Senor Atria, Canadians have been very interested in recent months in the policy of the Chilean government with regard to the Chileanization of the copper mines. I wonder if you could start by giving us a little background. What was the general situation in the Chilean copper industry as you saw it, say several years ago?

Atria: The copper policy was born during the previous election campaign in 1963 and 1964 when Frei ran as a candidate for the presidency. During these two years there was a technical group which prepared a different policy to be implemented during the Frei government. In the economic sphere, the most important problem we had was, fundamentally, the deficit in our balance of payments. That created great difficulty in obtaining foreign credit. On the other hand, we had this real problem of lack of productive capacity to increase our exports in order to improve the balance of payments. Now in Chile, we do not have many industries that could help with this problem. We had one main industry, that was the copper industry. This industry provided about eighty per cent of our foreign exchange and about twelve per cent of our fiscal revenue. We could say it's about six per cent to seven per cent of our Gross National Product. So this was *the* industry we could look to as the main tool for the government. And this was the role we wanted it to play during our government.

Rotstein: In that case, should we assume that the objectives, then, were twofold: to increase the foreign exchange that might be available from copper, and secondly to provide a basis for generating capital for development of other industries? Were those the objectives?

Atria: Yes, and of course the political objectives of gaining more independence through the possibility of controlling our own resources, and the possibility of defining the areas in which we wanted to invest.

Rotstein: Could you tell us what percentage of the industry was foreign owned?

Atria: Well, I want to talk about the big mines. They are Chuquicamata and El Salvador owned by the Anaconda Copper Company. And then we also have the El Teniente mine that was owned by Kennecot Copper. Along with the Andina Project and the Exotica mine—these were the major copper mines. Eighty per cent of the copper exports were under foreign control.

The measures we undertook were designed to increase state participation in the ownership of the copper mines. Secondly, a huge investment was made in order practically to double our production and increase our exports. Then we wanted to increase the refining capacity in a substantial way. The fourth point was that the commercial policies were to be defined by us. This meant that we were able to participate in the decisions and in the commercial approach in selling more copper. Now we sell all the copper according to the policies that the *Corporacion del Cobre* (the Government

Copper Corporation) fixes and all the export contracts are approved by the *Corporacion*.

On the other hand we also wanted this industry to be integrated into the national economy. This mainly meant that in all this huge development, such as the investment of 700 million dollars for the expansion programme, the purchasing of materials and equipment should be done in Chile both for the expansion and for regular supplies.

Rotstein: And did you find, in practice, that the large companies were bringing in their machinery and other requirements from abroad? Was that the point?

Atria: They bought about forty per cent of their normal supplies in Chile. They're now actually buying over seventy per cent of their supplies in Chile. Our policy was designed to give an impetus to national industry in order to acquire the technical capacity and efficiency to compete with imported goods. And this went all the way from very small supplies, up to the huge cranes and refineries. The cranes and refineries are now built here, you see, and they are even thinking of exporting them at present. So this is one of the objectives that was not directly connected with the copper industry but had an effect on the rest of the Chilean economy.

Rotstein: Could you tell us about the actual steps that were followed from the time of Mr. Frei's election. What was actually done?

Atria: Well, we first drew up an agreement with Kennecot about the programme of the El Teniente mine. This meant that we acquired fifty-one per cent of the stock. These shares are held by the *Corporacion del Cobre* and the *Corporacion* has representatives on the Board of Kennecot. On the other hand they have general control as a state agency that controls commercial affairs in the copper industry.

Rotstein: Can you tell us more about this government corporation? The *Corporacion del Cobre* has holdings in existing mines and is it also the government monopoly for copper export in Chile? Is that correct?

Atria: No, it's not. It has a double function. It is a holder and on the other hand it controls. . .it is a controller. This does not mean that the copper companies do not export by themselves, and have their own contracts. They sell directly, but they sell under conditions fixed by the *Corporacion.*

Rotstein: Does it set prices for the export of copper?

Atria: We are actually selling now at the L.M.E. (London Metal Exchange) settlement price. And this price is the one that all the contracts of the different Chilean companies must follow to sell abroad. The L.M.E. is an international commodity market that operates in London. We concluded that this was the most accurate price to follow. But for instance if Chile wants to change the price policy it can change it. Before L.M.E. we had producers' prices. It was the same price as the Americans had. When there was a big difference apparent, we said that this market in London would be the one that set the price as far as Chile is concerned.

Coming back to the El Teniente mine, we agreed jointly to the expansion programme that is going to increase production from 180,000 to about 280 to 300,000 tons per annum of refined copper.

Rotstein: Is the refining now done in Chile?

Atria: Not all, but we have increased enormously our capacity.

The next project was the Andina project. This was a new mine. This new mine was owned by Cerro del Pasco. We agreed with them to participate in a joint venture and at first we held twenty-five per cent of the stock. Owing to the increase in the amount of money required for the investment, we increased our participation in the stock and we now actually have around thirty per cent.

Rotstein: Could you tell us in both cases, Senor Atria, on what financial terms the stock was acquired from Kennecot and from Cerro del Pasco. Was there an actual investment of capital by the *Corporacion del Cobre* or was there some other financial means to acquire this stock?

Atria: We acquired the stock, that is fifty-one per cent for 80,000,000 dollars and Kennecot was to use that money coming from us for the expansion programme. Then in the case of the Andina project, we have now actually, as I have said, thirty per cent of this mine which produces about 67,000 tons of refined copper. The owners of the Company, Cerro del Pasco, are American. Then we come to the Anaconda Group. This Anaconda Group was the largest producer in Chile. And they did not agree originally to state participation. They only agreed to the expansion programme. That meant that their capacity was to increase substantially. So this was how things began. There is another new mine in the Anaconda Group. It's Exotica, just near Chuquicamata and it's going to produce around 110,000 tons and in this mine we have twenty-five per cent of the stock also.

Rotstein: And once more you contributed a certain amount of finance as your portion?

Atria: Yes exactly. As things developed there was an enormous rise in copper prices, due to a shortage of copper and a great increase in consumption and because of the Vietnam war. Also, the big American copper strike reduced their stocks and created lots of problems in the internal American market. On the other hand, we as a government had changed the price policy from the producers' price to the L.M.E. This finally meant that conditions had changed totally from what we had used as a basis for the negotiations with Anaconda. And since things had changed, we opened negotiations again with Anaconda, and we agreed on two main points. First, there was the purchase of fifty-one per cent of the stock immediately to be paid out of future dividends in twelve years' time and with six per cent interest. We also had a contract to buy the rest of the forty-nine per cent but we have an option to choose the time when we will do it.

Rotstein: Could you tell us, Senor Atria, whether this participation in Anaconda is backed up by legislation? Is that a matter of Chilean law that Anaconda must sell its stock to you or was this really the subject of negotiations and pressures by the government but without legal sanction?

Atria: Let's put it this way: the Government through *Corporacion del Cobre* has the possibility of creating this joint venture.

Rotstein: I see; it is in the terms of reference of *Corporacion del Cobre* that it has the right to participate?

Atria: No, they can create or participate in any copper company, but this does not mean that we needed to force this through the law. This does not operate that way. We had to go through negotiations. Anaconda understood our position and were willing to talk about the subject and they agreed to·sell fifty-one per cent of their stock.

Rotstein: But they were not legally forced to do so?

Atria: They were not legally forced, and we also reached an agreement about the other forty-nine per cent of the shares. This means that the Chilean state will eventually own one hundred per cent and the time is to be determined according to what policies we make. The other agreement that we reached with the Anaconda group, specifically with the Chilean Exploration Company (a subsidiary) was that we had state participation as preferred dividends when the price of copper went over forty cents a pound. This is very important because, as I told you before, the prices when this negotiation began were different from the ones that were in force when the second negotiation began.

Rotstein: So if I understand that agreement, it was the right or the ability of the state to participate in dividends when the price of copper rose above forty cents a pound?

Atria: Yes, as preferred dividends to the state-owned shares. When the price is over forty cents a pound this means that the profits increase. Well, in this situation the state-owned shares receive a preferential dividend. They receive more than the rest of the shares.

Rotstein: Looking back on this policy now, at the end of the Frei government, what is your feeling generally about it? For example, do you feel that it was an adequate policy? Do you feel it went as far as it should have gone?

Atria: Firstly, I think we did more than we had planned in our programme, because we now have the certainty that we will own eventually one hundred per cent of the two biggest mines, that is Chuquicamata and El Salvador. Secondly, as to our balance of payments, we have a surplus of 400 million dollars now and that is a fact.

Rotstein: And most of the 400 million dollars surplus you would ascribe to the income from copper?

Atria: Yes, there is no doubt about it. On the other hand the programmes are completely fulfilled. The expansion programme is now in force. We inaugurated this year several Andina projects, as well as the El Teniente, Chuquicamata and El Salvador projects. And we expect annual production to increase about 100,000 tons from this year onwards.

Rotstein: So if I understand you correctly, you feel quite satisfied that the actual achievements fulfilled the programme as it was originally conceived?

Atria: We exceeded the programme.

Rotstein: Since this policy has been so successful, could you envisage applying this policy to other minerals? Does Chile have other important minerals and do you see this as a model for a more general policy?

Atria: Of course we can use some of the measures we've taken as a model for others. Joint ventures are not only for copper. We have joint ventures for almost any kind of industry, for manufacturing or for minerals. Next to copper we have iron ore and we are actually producing around eleven million tons and we have projects to increase our production of it almost to twenty-five million tons. Of course this depends on our financial resources and this would require a new agreement, because conditions in copper are absolutely different from the conditions in iron ore. Our importance as a producer of copper is much larger than as a producer of iron ore. On the other hand copper is scarce and it's controlled by four countries that have created a group (exporting countries group), and they control eighty per cent of the exports. So this changes absolutely the terms of reference between copper and iron ore.

Rotstein: Do these four countries exert a substantial influence on the world price? Is it in effect, a price that depends upon the agreement between these four countries?

Atria: Let's put it this way, these four countries are selling copper under almost the same commercial conditions. We have created this to have more or less common policies in order to affect the copper industry. We meet normally two times a year and we discuss what is happening in the market, what are the best conditions and all that and we try to have sort of one face to the world. This, of course, is a new experience and we are very happy with it and it has had great achievements. These four countries are Chile, Zambia, Congo, and Peru.

Rotstein: May I return to an earlier point? In retrospect, there seem to be two forms of financing to take over the copper mines. One is the Kennecot model where government funds were injected into the enterprise. The other is the Anaconda model where the government shares were paid for out of future dividends. Have you any view about the relative benefits of either model?

Atria: You always come out with what you have paid for. I think that the means by which you buy are not as important as what you really pay.

Rotstein: In other words, are you saying that you pay for it one way or the other?

Atria: Yes. If you see that paying with future dividends is more than you would pay if you had the cash down. . .

Rotstein: I see, you would make a purely pragmatic decision on this question of how to finance the government shares?

Atria: Yes, you have a whole range of possibilities. For instance you even have the possibility of the law—expropriation at a given price. That's another possibility, but it depends on circumstances. I wouldn't have strong feelings about it. It's not a matter of principle.

Rotstein: Could you tell us what policy Mr. Allende has put forward in regard to the copper mines? What he would propose to do at this point?

Atria: Well, I haven't participated in policy making. I just have the references given by the press. And the press says that they want to nationalize all the big copper mines. Actually this would be one hundred per cent ownership by the state. I don't know what would be the means or the prices they would pay. This is the political side.

Rotstein: Do you have the feeling that, on the basis of past experience, this general policy is feasible? On the basis of your experience, is Mr. Allende's policy a practical policy?

Atria: I can't really give you an answer to it because once again you come to the feasibility of what you're going to do. You have priorities, and it depends on which other priorities

Senor Allende would have in mind. He might have in mind development, he might have in mind economic independence, or he could have in mind the possibility of increasing employment. It depends on what are his objectives.

Rotstein: If he goes ahead with this scheme, do you foresee any political difficulties? If he makes this one hundred per cent nationalization his first priority and he goes ahead with it, do you think there are any very great political difficulties with the copper companies, or any other political difficulties standing in the way of his achieving this policy?

Atria: I should be a prophet because this is about what might happen in the future. You come always to the same point; it's the way that things go on. . .I don't know how they will come out. For instance, what if he agrees with them to buy and there is no trouble? It could be.

Rotstein: If you don't mind giving us the benefit of your own experience, from the Canadian viewpoint it was always feared that if we tried any sort of similar policy, the mining and exploration in Canada would cease and the companies would leave and they would create important political difficulties for us. Have you, in your past experience, found anything of that sort?

Atria: We have had no political difficulties. This has been dealt with between the companies and the state. On the other hand, as we acquired new resources, increased our income, we found that what was done by the companies that were receiving that income, can be done by us. We continue to explore and we are continuing technical and scientific research and we are going to do it by ourselves. We now have the possibility of doing it.

2. Land Reform

Rotstein: Mr. Chonchol, could you tell us a little about your educational background and your previous experience in the area of land reform?

Chonchol: I graduated as an agricultural engineer from the University of Chile. After this I did some studies of economic development in E.C.L.A. (the Economic Committee for Latin

America, a U.N. Agency)—you know E.C.L.A. has a lot of studies on economic development in Latin American countries. I also went for a year to England to the L.S.E., and subsequently to France to the Institut de Sciences Politiques in Paris and also to the Institut Agronomique. Afterwards I worked in the Ministry of Agriculture here in Chile in different sections and also with the F.A.O. I was in Cuba for two years at the beginning of the Land Reform as an assistant on land reform problems for the Cuban government.

Rotstein: This was after Castro came to power?

Chonchol: At the beginning of the Castro regime, from 1959 to 1961. Later I was also in different Latin American countries. I was a general expert for agrarian reform problems in Latin America. When the government of the Christian Democratic Party came to power in Chile, I took the job as Director of one of the executive agencies of the agrarian reform program centered at the Institute of Agricultural Development and Cattle Breeding.

Rotstein: Could you tell us what year that was?

Chonchol: This was from the beginning of the Frei government (1964) till the end of 1968.

Rotstein: Could you tell us the way you perceived the agrarian problem in Chile? How did you define the problem at the beginning.

Chonchol: The problem of agrarian reform in Chile is a very important problem, and very similar in some respects to the general development of agriculture and agrarian problems of other Latin American countries, but with some differences. One of the differences is that the proportion of the population that is engaged in agriculture in Chile is relatively small compared with other underdeveloped countries. Here in Chile we have more or less three quarters of the Chilean people living in cities and only one quarter of the population which depends directly on agriculture. This is a proportion comparable to more developed countries. Second, we don't have in this country very rich resources for agriculture. Chile is a very big country not in terms of other Latin American countries, but say in terms of European countries. But a large proportion of the total land in Chile is not suitable for agricultural production or for cattle breeding. We have a total extension of 750,000 square kilometres of land. This makes seventy-five million hectares of total land. Of this seventy-five million hectares, not more than five million hectares is arable land—less than ten per cent of the total. You can add to this five million hectares of other land that can be used for cattle breeding or for forest production. But in any case, Chile is not a very rich country from the point of view of agricultural development. But we have some advantages. We have in the central valley of Chile conditions very similar to northern California. It is irrigated land with a very good climate suitable to Mediterranean production—fruits, vegetables, wines and such things. Moreover, we are placed in the southern hemisphere. When you have your winter, we are in summer, and vice versa.

Rotstein: Is this arable land already irrigated?

Chonchol: Chile is a very long country and we have large differences in rainfall. In the north, there is no rain at all. In the central part of Chile there is good rain, but it is concentrated in winter and we have no rain in summer. In summer, we need the snow which during the winter accumulates in the Cordillera of the Andes and which melts during the summer. This gives irrigation for the central part of Chile. In the south of Chile we don't need irrigation because we have too much water. It's like the north of Europe.

Rotstein: But is the irrigation completed? Do you need to extend the irrigation?

Chonchol: It is necessary to extend the irrigation. We have now only 1,300,000 hectares irrigated and we should have two million or maybe a little more. We have some possibilities for extending the irrigation and we must do it. But the other problem is to transform some of the actual agriculture we now have in the irrigated lands to a more intensive agriculture. Generally speaking our agriculture has been a mixture of cereals and extensive cattle-breeding. We need to change this to a more intensive type of agriculture such as fruit, wine, vegetables, and also more extensive forms of animal production not only for internal consumption but also for export. A good climate and our geographical position give us the possibility of being a relatively important exporting country of some Mediterranean types of products.

Rotstein: The immediate objective, then, is agricultural produce for export?

Chonchol: The real objective is food for internal consumption, say wheat for instance. But we can get wheat in two ways: producing all the wheat ourselves or producing fruits, vegetables and wines, exporting these and then with the earnings importing part of the wheat we need. This is best for Chile. We can have more wheat if we use our limited resources for more intensive agriculture.

Rotstein: In many Latin American countries the major issue is that land is concentrated in the hands of a very few people. Could you tell us about the Chilean situation?

Chonchol: We have, more or less, living in the rural areas about 400,000 families. Of these 2–3,000 control eighty per cent of the good land. The rest was the peasant population without land or with very small pieces of land. This also means a concentration of credit and economic resources in very few hands. When the families go to the bank for loans, the banks—which work in a capitalistic way—ask for collateral or guarantees. The rich can provide guarantees, but the peasant who has nothing but his work has no guarantees. This concentration of land holdings therefore means the concentration of credit and the concentration of political power in the countryside. This created a social relationship in which many of the landowners who were the richest were exploiting the men who worked the land.

Rotstein: Are you saying then, that in spite of higher average incomes in Chile (compared to other South American countries), in spite of a more progressive political tradition, in spite of a more advanced industrial sector, you are still able to describe the concentration of land ownership in terms that are reminiscent of the most backward areas of South America?

Chonchol: Well, you see the problem is like this. We have in Chile political development, cultural development, and a developed democratic society but this modern political development has not been correlated with a democratization of the economic system. The wealth, the greater part of the banking system, most of the industrial sector, and most of the agricultural sector was concentrated in the hands of very few people. It does not seem very normal, but what is the reason? First, in the traditional economy, before all this development began, our main wealth was in agriculture and there you have the landowner and the poor peasant. During the present century there was industrial development which was concentrated mainly in the cities, and in some cities we had rival political groups emerge to the political power of the middle class parties which, during the last thirty to forty years, have become a very important political force. But these parties also represent much more the interests of the middle classes, and not the interest of the peasant population. Many of the political, social and economic transformations that the country has had in the past few years, and also industrialization itself have been for the benefit of these middle groups. But the rural sector remained very traditional throughout. There was a gap between the advancing organization in the cities, and what was happening in the hinterland.

Rotstein: Could you tell us a little about the social conditions, the social relations of the peasant to the landowner? For example, was he paid wages? What were the conditions of his employment, his work and his housing in this case?

Chonchol: Well, you see, first of all it was a very traditional relationship (it has changed to some degree now) in which the peasant was very dependent not only for work but for all his living conditions on the landowner. In the traditional system, the peasant lives on the same farm, sometimes for generations. He receives the right to cultivate a piece of land, the right to have a house, which was not his house, but which was given to him by the farm. He receives the right to have on his farm some animals of his own. He is paid partly in money and partly in kind. This means that he lives in very poor conditions. He was not a very cultivated man and he didn't know what was going on outside in society. He depends on his relationship with the owner not only for his livelihood but for everything. For instance, if he needs money now because of the marriage of a daughter or for any special occasion, it's the owner—the latifundista—to whom he goes. If he has anything to do with the state, it is through the latifundista. It is a personal relation in which he is a minor. It is very paternalistic.

Rotstein: I take it that you were as much concerned with the social conditions and the social relations as the economic conditions?

Chonchol: Both. The idea was that it was necessary to disrupt, to break this paternalistic link to give the peasant the possibility of being a citizen, to give him a set of different conditions to make him a member of modern society.

Rotstein: Have you any figures on the average income, more or less, of the peasant population? Can you compare it to the national average income in some general way?

Chonchol: The national average income in Chile is 5–600 dollars per capita. The average income in agriculture is about sixty per cent of the national average. But you have huge differences within this average between the landowner and the peasant, as much as seventy to one. Many peasants are living at the level of fifty to one hundred dollars per year.

Rotstein: What was your initial program when you began? What kind of land reform plan did you start with?

Chonchol: Well, the idea of the Frei government was first to establish a limit on the quantity of land that people could own. This is why the agrarian reform law has a maximum limit on the concentration of land. All the land in the hands of one family that exceeded this limit, could be expropriated and distributed to the peasants. The idea was to force a limitation on the size of the farms with two objectives. The first was to have land to redistribute to the peasants. Secondly, for many years we were living in an inflationary situation and the best investment for people was to buy land. When the landowners had more money they bought more land and continued to concentrate ownership without improving the land. Our idea was that the people who were in agriculture should invest in improving the agriculture. The idea then was to keep a limited sector of capitalistic agriculture and together with this a peasant agriculture owning land and having the help of the state in supplying credit, and many other things. This scheme was developed. But the targets fixed by the government were not accomplished. The idea was to give land to 100,000 families. At the end of the Frei government, it is necessary to recognize that for the first time in the history of Chile, the process of agrarian reform has properly been started but clearly we will have no more than 30,000 families of peasants who received land in this way.

Rotstein: How much land was actually redistributed?

Chonchol: If you take the irrigated land (because total land is not relevant) a little more than twenty per cent of the irrigated land.

Rotstein: And your feeling is that you fell far short of what you had hoped?

Chonchol: Yes. We think that the problem is to create a new form of agriculture in which all land in Chile is reorganized. We want to guarantee to each peasant the right to have his house and a piece of land—what we call the 'garden'—for some private cultivation. The rest of the land should be in a co-operative system. We want to organize a system where all the land and all the related commercial and marketing and industrial sectors linked to agriculture will be in the hands of the peasants and organized as co-operatives.

Rotstein: What has your experience been thus far in organizing co-operatives?

Chonchol: It's quite difficult to generalize, but I think it is necessary to combine smaller groups of agricultural production inside the bigger co-operatives and link them to other sectors. I want to give you an example. We have created a co-operative in one part of Chile with a little more than 1,000 peasant families but all these are in different geographical regions and they don't form one agricultural production group. Inside this co-operative for instance, there are different groups which are producing broiler chickens. Well some of these groups have five, some have ten, others have twenty families. Each group is an enterprise for producing broiler chickens. But the co-operative also includes a slaughter house and also provides chicken feed. So inside this co-operative there are groups producing the chickens, other groups have the slaughter house, others produce the feed for the chickens. So you have incorporated not only the agricultural production, but also the related production inside the same group.

Rotstein: This seems to be a very ambitious plan. You propose to approach peasants who have been very dependent for a very long time, perhaps not all of them literate, with no experience in business, in management and accounting, and you would suddenly expect a great deal from them. In practice, how did this work out?

Chonchol: In our experience, the ability of the peasant, is much greater than people think. Even with all these limitations, they are much more intelligent, much more willing to change conditions. Until now, they never had the opportunity. If you give them the opportunity, they very quickly change. They need a certain kind of assistance and the role of the government agencies is to help them in the transition. But when they start, they very very quickly change their mentality and this condition of working in groups gives a dimension, a force which they don't have as isolated peasants. Now you need at the beginning, it is true, technical assistance, financial assistance and economic assistance, but this is perfectly possible in our country. We have a lot of people who have been preparing for this and who were not used, and the many peasants themselves can be used in this.

If there is political will and if there is a certain minimum of resources, I think, at least in the case of Chile, that we have enough human and technical resources for developing this process which must be done by the peasant with some help at the beginning from all these groups.

Rotstein: Could you give us a concrete idea of how many people you were able to send into the field to work with the peasants and with the co-operatives? How many were there in your section at your disposal?

Chonchol: In my institute for instance we had more or less 3,000 people working: social workers, agricultural engineers, veterinarians and so forth.

Rotstein: Mr. Chonchol, could you tell us generally how you would evaluate the progress of this programme now—at the end of the Frei regime?

Chonchol: If you want to make an evaluation, you can say that now, for the first time in Chile, a programme of agrarian reform has really been established. During this regime, they spoke a lot about agrarian reform but they have not done anything, at least not at the start. As the Frei government itself developed, the process grew slowly, due largely to interference by right-wing forces and also because the government was pursuing an ambivalent policy. It was a very reformist government from a social point of view, but it thought that the economic development of Chile needed to be based on the bourgeoisie, on the private entrepreneurial groups. Because of this need for keeping the confidence of the bourgeoisie, the social programme began to lag more and more.

Rotstein: But then you are pleased with the quality of the reform and the character of the reform as far as it went?

Chonchol: It is necessary to make some changes because (now) we have a lot of experience, but I think it is necessary to continue this process in a much more intensive form.

Rotstein: Could you tell us to what Mr. Allende is committed so far by way of agrarian reform? What has he promised?

Chonchol: He has promised a more intensive programme of reform, and also—this is very important—in his programme he is not only speaking about agrarian reform, but he is also speaking about making other changes in other sectors of the economy. To nationalize the banking system, and to nationalize the great industrial monopolies of the Chilean economy. And this is, in my view, the absolute complement of agrarian reform, because it is not possible in modern agriculture, even if you have the will or the power, to change all the relations of property *inside* of agriculture if you do nothing *outside* agriculture. You must take into account the relation of what is happening inside and outside. The real problem in modern society is not land, but people who produce inputs for agriculture from the industrial sector, the people who buy the raw materials of agriculture for sale to the consumer, and the people who are financing all these processes. I say that agrarian reform cannot be ended at the door of the latifundia. It must be developed in other sectors of the society, because if you don't do this, there arrives a moment when agrarian reform is cut off.

The problem is not to give a piece of land each to 100,000 families—our original goal—but to change the whole structure of agriculture and the relation of agriculture with the rest of the economy. That is much more important.

Rotstein: Finally, can you give us an idea of how much land should be redistributed in such a situation, or to put it differently, do you foresee the continuing existence of a capitalist sector of landowners of some size together with the new distribution of land to the peasants?

Chonchol: No. I see only a modern peasant agriculture but not a capitalist landowner agriculture.

Rotstein: So you would hope to see a total redistribution of the land and you would be prepared to continue the co-operative idea which was started?

Chonchol: Exactly.

November 1970

ITALY: THE STRIKE AT FIAT

Industrial unrest is now widespread in Europe and above all in Italy. In Canada, we receive only vague and perfunctory reports of what is going on and analysis in any depth is almost non-existent. Much of this unrest falls outside the realm of the traditional demands for higher wages and some of it has opened up an entirely new set of issues in the relation of workers to management.

I visited Turin a few weeks ago, mainly to see at first hand what the strike at Fiat was about, and went to the local headquarters of F.I.M. (the Federation of Italian Metal Mechanics). The union is housed in a new two-storey building at the end of a small street directly across from the Mirafiori plant of Fiat which employs some 50,000 workers.

A long interview followed with the head of the local Franco Aloja, a young man of about thirty. (The staff at the union headquarters were all in their twenties and thirties. I was told that union leaders at all levels were paid salaries that were no higher than the average wage at the plant—a refreshing innovation compared to the North American scene.)

From the beginning of our talk, one phrase came through that is symbolic of the strike—*making automobiles in a different way*. It summed up graphically the new mood that now prevails, taking nothing for granted in the established industrial order: neither the stringencies of the assembly line, the sacrosanct management prerogatives, the ordering of the workday, nor the authoritarian relations of management to the labour force. Everything was being questioned in the name of a more democratic and more human industrial order. To paraphrase the short-lived Czech motto (although they did not use it), the underlying theme seemed to be 'industry with a human face'.

Even though the average wage at Fiat was only about $50 a week, low by our standards, wage demands were regarded as of secondary importance among the demands of the union. Specifically, the workers, through their elected delegates, want a voice in the organization of production, in the speed of the assembly line, in the conditions under which new machinery will be introduced and the rate at which it will operate. As Aloja put it, the speed of operation should not be based on some general statistical standard set by the stop-watch people working for management. It should be based on the human situation and possibilities of the particular group of individuals involved in the work. Work speeds, in short, should be tailored to the individuals who are doing the work.

The main thrust of the workers' demands falls into the realm of what is generally called 'industrial democracy' or 'workers' control'. The unions at Fiat have already elected 'delegates' from every section of the plant—from various points on the assembly line, the machine shop, the paint shop and so on. The delegates represent between thirty to one hundred workers and are the direct spokesmen of their group for negotiations with management. These delegates are subject to recall at any time by a majority vote of the section they represent. Together they form the 'Council of Delegates', covering the entire plant, which co-ordinates and puts forward the workers' demands. Continuity would be provided by an executive of this Council which eventually would subsume the role of the existing unions in the plant. The delegates now stand ready to negotiate directly with the management which has steadfastly refused to have any dealings with them.

I had a second interview with Alberto Tridente, the national secretary of F.I.M., a man of about forty who had spent some time visiting North American trade unions. "What we are trying to combat," he said, "is the monotony and stupidity of the work in the automobile factory." He emphasized particularly that individual jobs should be enlarged and enriched by including a greater number of functions for each worker. The classic case of the man tightening a single bolt throughout the day must be eliminated even if it means new machinery and a reordering of the assembly line. There should also be increased attention to retraining and upgrading of functions for the individual worker. All incentive schemes should be abolished along with invidious classifications of workers by management. At Fiat for example, there are four main classes both of workers and of white collar employees. The union wants to abolish the fourth class immediately and move eventually to one homogeneous category.

Other demands include an elimination of the night shift, longer lunch periods (from one half to three quarters of an hour), more allowance for time off for personal needs such as for workers who are also students and are facing examinations.

Tridente spoke at length about the question of health care in the plant. He wanted every worker to have a health booklet registering his 'biostatistics', e.g. his absences from work and their cause, to note psychological and nervous conditions as well as physical health. He wanted independent health care by doctors paid by the state but under the direction of the workers themselves. "Health is not for sale" is Tridente's curt summary of this issue.

The most militant workers are those from southern Italy,

the *meridionali*, who are at the lowest end of the scale. They are in Tridente's phrase the 'white negroes' of the Italian labour scene and form a basic supporting group for this push for workers' self-management.

The strike tactics are ingenious. Every worker gives up three hours a week to the strike, but at sporadic intervals throughout the week as decided by his section, e.g. fifteen minutes on Monday at 10 a.m., all of Tuesday afternoon, a half hour on Friday morning and so on. Different sections of the plant strike at different times, thus effectively disrupting operations for management, but at a relatively low cost to the workers.

The pressure is beginning to tell on the Fiat management. While the head of Fiat, Giovanni Agnelli has a reputation as a progressive and forward-looking employer, his top management is entirely out of sympathy with the present thrust of the union. A strong public campaign is going on, ridiculing the union demands and warning that these innovations in the plant will price Fiat cars out of the world market. Since Agnelli has majority control over the dominant mass-circulation newspaper *La Stampa*, the unions have not, on the whole, had public opinion on their side. Still, the demands they are making are not entirely new to the Italian public. Other unions have already won this same battle in a number of companies such as Olivetti, Alfa Romeo, Innocenti, and Aspera, producing various industrial products. But these are smaller companies. A victory at Fiat, the largest single employer in Italy, would establish industrial democracy as an accepted feature of the industrial scene in Italy.

I tried to elicit from Tridente what the long-run aspirations of his union were. Did he see this battle, for example, in a larger ideological context, as a move towards a socialist society, or at least as a way of gradually eliminating capitalism?

These demands he said, were quite straightforward and should be taken on their own at face value. No longer-run scheme had been mapped out, and the future course would depend on the workers themselves. He took an entirely pragmatic line. He was also aware that other countries' experiments had to be taken into account. What they were attempting in Italy was quite different from the German workers' scheme of 'co-determination'—a token system—and also different from the Yugoslav experiments, which he felt, had grave inadequacies in failing to give democratic control to the workers.

Where, I asked him, had these ideas originated—was it from abroad? His answer gave full credit to the Italian student movement that had been in the forefront of the discussion for some years. Many students were now active in the plants and in the union and kept pressing for these demands.

At the end of my talks, I left Turin with the feeling of having had a preview of things to come before long in North America.

June 1971

A SUMMER ON THE ISLAND

Morning glories, roses and strawberries grow wild by the roadside. The road leads down to the sea and from the red sandstone bluffs the waves shimmer into the distance in five shades of opalescent blue and tourmaline. On the shore, there are clams for the digging, starfish, sand dollars, snails and crabs sauntering busily along the bottom of the ocean. White sand stretches for miles and along a further cove, there are mussels and transient schools of mackerel.

We had left the urban caverns of Toronto for the unexpected enchantment of Prince Edward Island. But unlike the current best seller, it was not 'future shock' that struck us, but the shock of the past. As the local society unveiled itself, we had a curious sense of being back in southern Ontario at the turn of the century: the stable society of small farms and old families; political faiths—Liberal and Conservative—as deeply embedded as religious faith. Smuggled supplies of liquor oil the election machine, double constituencies have carefully balanced teams of Protestant and Catholic for each party, an extended network of patronage keeps the party contractors and workers employed—until the government is thrown out and it's the other team's turn.

An Irish lilt inflects the speech with shades of an Ottawa valley accent: words such as 'filum', and 'elum'; strangers were 'from away'. First names such as 'Pius', 'Urban' and 'Parnell', were everywhere; an endless number of Acadian descendants with the surname Gallant were interspersed with the McLeods, the MacDonalds and the Kellys.

The Island is a Canadian garden before the ravages of the machine. Every turn in the road brings its classic portrait of neat ambling fields on the rolling hills topped by rows of pine trees running to the endless beautiful bays and beaches. Whether by a trick of the light or of the red soil, it is the greenest green one could imagine.

The radio plays country music all day and the Country Music Festival drew 5000 people to the Coliseum to hear Myrna Lorrie, Gary Buck, Blake Emmons and all the household names which were utterly new to provincial Torontonians. The Prime Minister made his appearance in the Coliseum that evening and drew respectful but moderate applause. He was hardly aware that he would be followed by Wilf Carter, the veteran of country music from Nova Scotia, whose reception by contrast brought the house down. It was a curious audience to observe if one was conditioned to the generation gap. People spanned the whole gamut, from three to seventy-three: young couples on a date, young marrieds with small children, ten-year-old boys and very old men.

There were other evenings of old-time fiddling and step-dancing contests, and the annual Charlottetown Festival known as Old Home Week. Harness racing was the other main entertainment carrying on essentially unchanged since the 1870's. The highlight of Old Home Week was the special race for the Gold Cup and Saucer. I had to learn an entire new vocabulary with mysterious words in betting such as 'exactor' and 'quinella'.

But everywhere there hangs a hidden apprehension that it can't last. The new game is called 'development' and its signs are spreading. Tourism is fairly well contained in the growing enclave on the north shore from Cavendish to Stanhope. But old houses are now being torn down for motels within Charlottetown itself. Several times every week, old farms are being auctioned off and one stumbles on the old bric-à-brac furniture as well as the tragic memorabilia—a framed certificate from J.L. Ralston after the loss of a son in the war; an old organ for evensong.

The Island is wrestling with a development plan which breeds in its wake the almost unknown phenomenon of massive social protest. Mid-August brought the farmers out on the tractors slowing the traffic to Charlottetown down to a crawl. I followed behind the tractor contingent and discovered, to my surprise, that these were young men. One could sense the simplicity of their message, that they refused to be phased out of existence by the plan which called for a reduction in the number of farms from 7500 to 2500. The official demands of the farmers were all about remission of gasoline taxes and reduced licence fees on trucks, but these seemed incidental. The farm economy based on the family farm had no future in the plan.

A new generation at the University of Prince Edward Island, some from outside the province, are carrying the message into the community: 'I have seen the future and it doesn't work'. Their own underground newspaper *The Square Deal* has made an important impact followed by a newer sheet called *The Broad Axe*.

The development plan is a classic of its kind, drafted by 'experts' and parachuted down from above. Its first function is to legitimize the granting of about $125,000,000 of federal funds, and a 'plan' is the price you pay for the money. But the population has no clear idea what will happen, and the reaction varies from passive resignation through apprehension to active mobilization against the plan by the farmers. After fiascos in industrial development such as Gulf Garden Foods which went bankrupt under very suspicious conditions, the attempt to establish industry on the island appears more doubtful than ever. Tourist complexes are to take the shape of the new multimillion-dollar Brudnell development with a swimming pool, golf course, bars and the 'kitten club' (real Bunny Girls). The land on which this new resort is built is alleged to have been sold to the government by none other than the Minister of Tourism. Other persons close to the Premier are also reported to be benefitting substantially from this 'development'.

The future of the Island is now discussed everywhere. One hears frequently the warning against another 'Coney Island'. Still others keep talking of a national park. What the people do need is better housing, better schools and better medical care. Other ostensible reasons for development are less obvious. The seasonal unemployment is high but the figures are misleading and unreliable. Lobster fishermen for example who work mainly in the two months of May and June have cleared about $6,000-$10,000 recently. Are they unemployed in any usual sense of the term?

Pockets of poverty and unemployment exist on the eastern shore around Souris and at the western tip, and alcoholism is marked throughout the Island. The Island has its severe human and social problems, but it seemed at least to this observer, that there was neither hope nor reason to recreate the doubtful melange of southern Ontario. Much will have to change on the Island if it is to stay the same, but by the turn of the next century we might want to restore in the rest of Canada what the Island has today.

September 1971

University and Society

15

UNIVERSITY AND SOCIETY
Address delivered to the African Youth Conference,
Syracuse University

University and society are in a symbiotic relationship. They are tied by an umbilical cord, but the feeding process runs both ways. One might even go so far as to wonder which of the two is the mother and which the child. Each requires the other for sustenance and self-renewal.

Our discussion today centres on African educational institutions in the context of Africa's developing societies. If I may define our concern somewhat more closely, the question is how African youth that come through African educational institutions may lend their best energies and abilities, their minds and their hearts to the urgent tasks of social and economic development we commonly call 'nation-building'. In the terms of the recent political analysis of David Apter—how will educated African youth undertake the tasks of the mobilization of social forces and the reconciliation of divergent interests required for a developing body politic?

There is no doubt that one of the major functions of universities everywhere is to provide for the personal development of the faculties of the *individual*. This is an objective we may well accept, but it does not form the subject of the present paper. We turn instead to the political and social role of the university as an institution in society. While Africa is at the centre of our attention, I hope through some brief reflections and comparisons to add a few insights which derive from contact with universities in the Soviet Union, in Peking and in the province of Quebec.

Societies, as Louis Hartz has pointed out, are defined by their stellar political values. New societies in particular, he suggested, are locked in the web of values implanted at the time of their creation. In that sense, the core political values become a birth cell out of which the body politic grows and is shaped, virtually in the same way that human beings develop according to the genes they have inherited at birth. His illustrations from the new societies of the United States, Latin America and South Africa are telling indeed. Whether born of a revolution or of a vision of society peacefully implanted on new soil, the die of future development is cast at birth. These core political values are what we term in this paper 'ideology'.

Professor Hartz has not, however, as yet applied his theoretical model to the new African states. If he had, some stringent difficulties would become apparent. First, the revolution in Africa, the emergence of independent states, has been conspicuous by the absence of an explicit and distinctive body of ideological principles as the guiding light and touchstone. Nkrumah and Sekou Touré have borrowed heavily from conventional Marxism with very little innovation of their own. Léopold Senghor and Julius Nyerere have stood out as humanist socialists but their contributions have still to become widely accepted and are far from developed political theories. The African revolution emerged instead in the exceptional circumstances of a unique hiatus in world politics. External political factors forced the issue and thus the African revolution—if you will forgive this overly broad designation—is still engaged in an intensive search to define itself.

This absence of an indigenous ideology compounds many difficulties. If we accept the view that African universities were grafted on society under the external impetus of colonial and ex-colonial administrations and cast in a Western mould, the absence of indigenous ideology is one of the serious obstacles to their integration in domestic society. One can go further perhaps and point to the possible danger of their role as a bastion of that most pernicious of all forms of colonialism—the indelible marks left on the spiritual life and politics of a people by virtue of the lasting intellectual effects of a colonial inheritance. Too often has the phrase 'the Africa within' been bandied about in literary circles. Too little attention has been given instead to the effects of 'the England within' in Africa. As long as poetry centres on Wordsworth's English daffodils, economic history on England's industrial revolution and political science on the two-party system, Africa will continue to bear the scars of her 'England within'. Fortunately this battle is being won, but the graduates of the system continue to bear its marks.

Perhaps an anecdote will suffice to make the point. A colleague of mine with much experience in African universities tells the story of a series of lectures which had been specially prepared for an African university class on agricultural development in Africa. To this professor's chagrin, one student came up after one of the lectures and asked: "When sir, can we get on to something we know, like Venice in the sixteenth century?" And most of you are aware of the famous litany of the French school system which Africans learn by heart: "Nos ancêtres les gaullois, ils avaient les yeux bleus et les cheveux blonds."

On one level these are humorous anomalies. On a deeper level, they are the heavy burdens of the African educational system. Malaise among any body of youth today is born essentially of one factor: frustration. The latent idealism and commitment that we expect of young people and which is natural to all societies, is stillborn or turns sour if the world appears blocked to them at every turn in the achievement of their important goals and aspirations.

This frustration and even careerism of African youth today derives from many sources—corruption in domestic politics, the slow pace of economic development, the inability of the civil service and the private sector to absorb the kinds of graduates now being produced. But I wish to focus on yet another source of this frustration. The ideals and goals that form the intellectual environment of African universities as well as the attitudes of the students seem curiously irrelevant to the travails and aspirations of their societies. Many things are responsible, but the chief of these, I believe, is the fact that the African revolution has yet to articulate its own indigenous ideology. From its own soil, there is yet to be born the goals, aspirations and particularly the political values formulated in a coherent body that we designate here 'ideology'. To create this ideology is the real task of the African university.

The chief concern of some of the African educators with whom I have talked has been the maintenance of standards at their universities and the fear of deterioration of the calibre of intellectual life. No doubt this is an issue of the first importance, but I wonder if it is not, in fact, an expression of several different problems which lie behind this fear.

At the risk of oversimplification, at least two separate issues are involved. First, there are the functional requirements of modern education comprising all the technical and bureaucratic skills which are necessary for every industrial and industrializing society: engineering, medicine, commerce, etc. These are the tangible and obvious requirements toward which education must be directed for the development of African society. But there are less obvious and perhaps equally important requirements of which we are only slowly beginning to be aware. These are revealed as the result of much of the new work in political science by Apter, Almond, Verba, Easton and others who have been examining the politics of developing societies. In the process of their analysis, I may add, they have also provided as many new insights into the 'invisible' tendons and muscles of our own political culture as they have of the new developing political systems. What does emerge from these studies is that every political society has its own characteristic mechanisms for producing cohesion, handling stress and conflict, legitimating and instituting new proposals and policies. In a political sense, these societies pivot, moreover, on distinct norms of political behaviour and political role expectations.

These political norms, and values are basic to every society; they are not merely a matter for exhortation—for the secular preaching of party newspapers or independence day speeches. These norms and values are as functionally significant in their own way in making wheels turn as the bridges, roads and factories.

And as I suggested earlier, these analyses of the new political science, have been equally illuminating about the political anatomy of all societies. General models have emerged and in the context of these models we have begun to appreciate the particular and time-bound character of our own political norms.

But there are further implications of this work as well, for the role of universities in society. The specific culture-bound assumptions that characterize Western universities become as apparent as those that characterize Western political cultures generally. Examine some of the usual principles one hears in Western universities: the school and university should be apolitical or neutral in their orientation. They should be an arena for dissenting voices, free speech and an enclave where the individual can pursue the research dictated by his conscience and scholarly intuition; good citizenship and civil liberties should be fostered. But on further examination of this particular cluster of values in our educational system, it turns out that our democratic practices and civil liberties are in fact education toward a certain group of *political* goals. Thus there is a fundamental ambiguity involved in claiming that our educational system is apolitical when what we really mean is that these are the specific norms required for the functioning of the liberal democratic state. Unless we are committed to the universality of such values for all cultures, we begin to see that all education is intrinsically political in character in one form or another.

From a historical perspective we can see that Western educational practice has evolved from a mediaeval era when education was subordinated to religious ends, to a liberal plateau in the eighteenth and nineteenth centuries which was preoccupied above all with the danger of political bondage— of the servitude of education to a political tyranny. Liberal values have for so long *seemed* both universal and self-evident that we have not hesitated to use them as our final criterion of judgment with reference not only to African universities but to African states as well. Some would argue that the recent episodes of political repression in African universities are a vindication of the need for precisely the liberal values they advocate. But I suggest that an alternative interpretation might well centre on the political disparity or strain between Western political values that were implanted in African universities both by Western educators and by those trained in Western universities, and the extreme stresses of the very different political realities in these states. A liberal yardstick fails to contribute substantially to an understanding and analytic penetration of the relevant issues. This is not to gloss over actual instances of political repression in the universities. But I suggest that we would become far less certain about our yardstick if we began by noting the particular and time-bound nature of Western liberalism as it is expressed in our hopes and goals for African universities. We would be much better off, I believe, in understanding the stresses in the relation of African universities to their societies if we recognized the arbitrary and time-bound criteria we are using to judge the issues.

It may be of some significance to examine the question of the political ideology of an educational system in relation to three societies in the grip of rapid social change.

As many of you may be aware, a significant political movement in the direction of greater self-determination is rapidly gaining ground in the province of Quebec. It is highly significant that this movement has received substantial impetus and leadership from university quarters in Quebec. Some claim can be made in fact, that the major influence in shaping this revolution has come initially from the social science division at the Université de Laval which, in the early 1950's was headed by Professor George-Henri Lévesque. Several generations of graduates trained under Lévesque have now assumed the key posts in the Quebec civil service which has now become perhaps the most competent and imaginative provincial civil service in Canada. New proposals for social welfare legislation, for increased autonomy under Canada's federal system, and for a complete revision of the educational system have come from this group.

The essence of the problem in higher education has been as follows: Quebec has had several hundred small Catholic colleges, the *collèges classiques,* which were staffed by Roman Catholic orders. These were explicitly religious colleges devoted in substantial measure to teaching theology and Catholic philosophy to high school graduates. The ideology of these institutions thus centred on conservative and religious political norms and had the effect of preserving in Quebec a right-wing traditionalist Catholic orientation extolling the rural virtues of the devout Catholic peasant—the 'habitant'. The graduates of these institutions then went on to study at the various professional faculties such as law, medicine and engineering at the two larger universities, the Université de Montréal and the Université de Laval in Quebec City.

The 'Quiet Revolution' as it arose originally in Quebec evolved a different set of political norms—those of an urban-industrial society, moving politically to the left and increasingly nationalist.

The old ideology of the *collèges classiques* was inappropriate and strongly inhibiting to this new movement. The ideological battle shifted therefore to an institutional struggle centred on secularizing the educational system, curbing any expansion in the *collèges classiques* and developing undergraduate studies instead at the large universities to begin to replace these Catholic junior colleges. The student body in these larger universities has joined the now not so "Quiet Revolution" with enthusiasm and gusto. They have been a constant prod to the Quebec provincial government, and have, for example actually labelled the student newspaper at the Université de Montréal as 'the largest socialist bi-weekly in the world'. These students have provided a growing stream of able and committed graduates to the civil service and to the government corporations.

It is, to my mind, a successful illustration, in a general sense, of what we would hope that African universities could become. It provides a clear example of the role of newly articulated ideology in mobilizing the energy, idealism and commitment of youth in the service of a developing society. The functional requirements of an industrial society are also being well served. Expansion in the faculties of science, engineering, and the social sciences is taking place at a very rapid rate. Yet the key factor in this mobilization of youth is the overall political atmosphere at these universities—the norms, the goals, and the aspirations which we term here 'ideology'.

A substantial contrast in the role of ideology in the educational system is provided by the University of Moscow. I was privileged to visit the Soviet Union for six weeks in the spring of 1966 and had some extensive contact with students and staff.

A dominant impression of my visit was the existence of a formalized and to some extent ossified, ideology taught in the undergraduate curriculum. Most of the undergraduate student body takes two courses in Dialectical and Historical Materialism—known locally as 'Diamat' and 'Histmat'. I gathered that these were the conventional doctrines of Marxist philosophy being taught here and somewhat of a bore among the undergraduates. I had the impression moreover, that the attitude of the state and the university to the students was overprotective and sheltering—as if they were susceptible to strange intellectual viruses from which they must be shielded. The result, I felt, was a certain undertone of glumness, a vague restlessness and disinterest and on the whole, not a very live or stimulating atmosphere at the university. Ideology then had become a matter of sheltered, formal exclusive study.

Yet there were in Moscow a very alert group of intellectuals, spirited, thoughtful and stimulating. These were connected, not with the university, but with the institutes of which there were several dozen in Moscow. The members of these institutes were full-time research workers in economics, politics, philosophy, history, etc. and had achieved the equivalent standing of our Ph.D. They had then, in a certain sense, been 'turned loose' to pursue their own researches and had extensive access to foreign materials, journals and books, and were quite prepared to talk freely to foreigners. They were not, in my view, greatly hampered by the under-graduate ideological training and were, in general, fairly pragmatic in their outlook. I had the impression that these institute members were the fount of new ideas and practical solutions to the country's problems. The circumstances of daily life themselves drew from them effective contributions to the country's social problems. I sensed moreover a deeply-rooted patriotism and commitment to their country and to its development. Formal and doctrinaire ideological training had done them no harm, although it seemed to make of undergraduate life something less than it should be. From what source did their positive commitment to their country's development come? I was uncertain. It may have derived from the traditional patriotism of the Russian people. It may have derived even more from their pride in the Russian revolution. But it was not clear at what level, if at all, their undergraduate training had reinforced this commitment.

My final example derives from a brief visit to China and to the University of Peking on the very eve of the Cultural Revolution of 1966. China, as is well known, is now blanketed throughout by the vigorous and total affirmation of a set of ideological principles linked to the works of Chairman Mao-Tse-Tung. The slogan one hears very often is "Let Politics Take the Lead." I took it to mean that ideology must take precedence over technique.

I had a long and interesting conversation with the vice-chairman of the economics department, Professor Wu. I gathered that the main subject on the curriculum of the economics courses was the study of the works of Chairman Mao. Other authors which the students read included Marx and Lenin. I wondered to myself whether the functional requirements of training economists were being radically subordinated to ideological issues. (It was a question which occurred to me often while in China.) My visit to the University ended with a trip to the Economics Department library. I expected to see only volumes of official Marxist authors. To my surprise, every volume and journal which I myself was using at the University of Toronto was present in the library. Clearly while "Let politics take the lead" was the watchword, the functional requirements of training economists were also somehow being met. There appeared to be a substantial overemphasis, in my view, on ideology in the interests of mobilizing the Chinese people, but technical training I thought was not being neglected and perhaps in time a new balance would be struck.

The problems of mobilizing the best energies and the commitment of African youth to nation-building is, I believe, closely although not exclusively, tied to the ideological environment of the schools and universities. In my view, the educational institutions must be transformed from the present semi-artificial relationship to African society, in order to create and transmit those political norms and national aspirations which grow out of African life and experience.

In an ideological sense, a condition approaching anomie or normlessness exists at present. Many African leaders such as Kaunda and Nyerere have made the attempt to transform something of the indigenous African values to meet the present situation. I refer to the values of the co-operative, corporate character of traditional Africa. The task that is involved, I would call—with the rather pretentious phrase— *the transvaluation of values*. I mean the adaptation of these co-operative, corporate values which stand in contrast to Western atomistic liberalism and individualism—their adaptation to the requirements of an industrializing society in an African setting. This creation of an appropriate indigenous ideology should be the task of the university teachers and students. It will be a slow process. I have a feeling that the creation of this ideology will have much to do with a definition for the African situation of what has been called 'African socialism'. I do not know, however to what extent Western teachers can help to contribute to it.

But there is a concrete suggestion that I should like to make, which derives from a few experiments in Western experience. I refer particularly to the notion now being

discussed and experimented with in several places in the
United States, namely, *the free university*. In New York and
California, I understand that this is a highly topical educational venture at the present time. I think it should be tried
in Africa by Africans. The aim should be to extract from the
free spontaneous discussions of such a university environment
a definition of the goals, values and political norms to which
Africans are prepared to lend their mind and heart.

The very process of such a search may turn the African
university from a transplanted institution to one integrated in
the native soil. (And it is the absence of any form of educational experimentation which most impresses a Western
observer.)

Other previous experiments in the West should also be
examined for possible lessons that are relevant. Such experiments as the Antigonish movement in Nova Scotia and the
Folk Schools of Denmark may have many useful lessons to
offer, particularly for adult education.

In the end, Western scholars and friends of Africa may
have to adopt new attitudes and yardsticks. I believe the
concept of coexistence which we tend to think of only in
relation to Communist countries, may be a significant notion
for our relations with Africa and with the "third world"
generally. The best of the Western political heritage is not
necessarily the appropriate set of norms for Africa. More than
simple tolerance is involved. A recognition of the historical
and cultural limitations of our experience is crucial, and with
it the attitude that the lessons of Africa may have much to
teach us about ourselves. For Western educators, this may be
the real test of our moral calibre and our humanity.

October 1966

THE TORONTO TEACH-INS

Communication in a New Key

The real teach-in was not on the podium of Varsity Arena
but in the grandstand. 6,000 persons, mainly U. of T. students,
had suddenly come alive. They applauded, booed, gave
standing ovations and asked questions with a quick intel-

ligence and flair that had never been dreamt of in the lecture hall. Could these be our own laconic and withdrawn students?

True, the world was brought to their doorstep, the anguish and pain of the Dominican Republic in the person of Andres Lockward, the militant Marxism of Cheddi Jagan, the wit and thrust of the American academy through Z.K. Brzezinski, the poetry of an Old Testament prophet in the person of Staughton Lynd, and many others—Cambodians, South Vietnamese, Patrick Gordon Walker and Adolf Berle, *Pravda* and the French Communist Party. Students spent the entire weekend at it—five general sessions and two seminars— and for three days they changed the face of education at Toronto. I doubt that we shall ever be as successful in the classroom. Did some of this contagion spread over the radio hookup to Dalhousie, McGill, Western, U.B.C.? And what was the source of enthusiasm—a mere manifestation of political partisanship, an old-fashioned rally of the left?

On the face of it, the organizing committee of the International Teach-In at Toronto took great care to present a 'balanced' programme and exerted yeoman efforts to obtain qualified speakers to present official American viewpoints. The committee succeeded as well as anyone could in the present climate in Washington of growing hostility to the teach-ins and reluctance to send official speakers. (This reluctance was also echoed by the Chinese and the Viet Cong, and, at the last moment, an effort by the committee to secure unofficial representation for Hanoi, produced the unfortunate administrative bungle of the 'Myerson affair'.) Nevertheless, on the formal count of 'balance' in viewpoints or of fairness to complex issues, the Toronto teach-in largely met its own criterion of an 'educational' rather than a 'protest' event.

But a recognition of the formal political balance hardly tells the story. The Teach-In remained shadowed by ambiguity centring not on the balance of the programme but on the reaction of the audience and on the significance of the Teach-In as a whole. The exploration of that meaningful ambiguity has only begun. If there was a sense of 'protest' in the very atmosphere of the Teach-In, against what or whom was it directed?

Some of the 'protest' centred not on the political content, but lay in the technical form of the medium. The teach-in is a new medium of communication at the university. The technology is the loudspeaker, the radio hookup and the mass student audience. These are 'hot' media, particularly in the university environment where serious messages are in print and the audience is expected to keep quiet and take notes. An atmosphere of live instant reaction—including 'protest'—is inherent in the medium and could not be eliminated no matter how careful the political balance among the speakers. The continued emphasis on the 'education' objective of the International Teach-In by its organizers must be seen as an attempt to 'cool down' a hot medium, but only rigor mortis could have eliminated the general sense of protest as well as the enthusiasm and spontaneous ovations.

If a rationale is to be sought for the new medium, it lies, one may presume, in an implicit conviction among all those who chose to participate, that present channels of communication are inadequate. The pace of change today has made obsolete the concept of the public as passive recipients of information and decisions who should be heard only at election time. The continuing blunders in a world increasingly run by experts have cast doubt on the standard conventions that diplomats should talk only among themselves. The view of the university as an ivory tower from which the real world can be seen only dimly has already been destroyed by the successes both of professors as consultants to the military and of students in the civil rights movement. Perhaps the spontaneous involvement at the Toronto Teach-In is a long-delayed answer to the muffling effects of the cotton-wadded bureaucracy that now sets our foreign policy. In that sense the Canadian teach-in is a legitimate successor to the national outcry recently heard against the Merchant-Heeney 'wallpaper' philosophy.

But it is more than that. The teach-in is an attempt to stake out and consolidate the new ground of political discussion opened up by the thaw in the Russian-American Cold War. Only in retrospect do we begin to sense the numbness of political thought and action imposed by the compelling and pervasive fear generated by the Cold War. The post-war period was (and in part, still is,) an era when criticism was suspect and the raising of questions was tantamount to political opposition. It was thus the function of the teach-in to re-establish and legitimize a moral basis for dissent.

Those still haunted by Cold-War constraints, and responding with the old reflexes to the freeze in Chinese-American relations, may regard many of the political viewpoints expressed as dangerous anti-Americanism. (This seems to be the most recent view of the White House.) Press commentary in Canada on the International Teach-In has, in part, centred on this issue. This is hardly surprising. In the Canadian environment, the Teach-In was bound to touch latent chords of anti-Americanism. Historically, anti-Americanism has been contained in Canada by channelling it along narrowly economic lines and by always discussing Canadian-American relations in isolation from the world. The Teach-In created unease—which the press was only too ready to exploit—because it violated these rules of the established game. In effect, the possibility was raised that the war in Vietnam may be more relevant to Canadian-American relations than the automobile agreement. In any case, a frank appraisal by Canadians of America's global position must transcend the usual issues in Canadian-American relations.

The International Teach-In was planned as an educational activity. "Educational movements," Kenneth Boulding writes, "have to be low-keyed, respectful of existing legitimacies, and tying into them wherever possible, and chary of arousing counterprotest." It is also possible to agree with Boulding that "the task of the peace movement is fundamentally educational rather than protest," or as he qualifies his position, "a strategy of limited protest and extensive education."

Perhaps the fundamental task ahead for the teach-in movement is to educate toward a commitment that stable peace is possible—that political solutions can be found as alternatives to military solutions. In Canada it may mean a reversal of the old attitude of leaving foreign policy to the experts and diplomats. It will fall, at least in part, to the academic community to demand a public accounting, to judge the arguments and the information and not least to insist on open discussion of the premises on which foreign policy is based. We may discover in the process that such an 'academic' community will spread far beyond the boundaries of the university.

The Ivory Microphone

After the furor raised by the first International Teach-In over its alleged exploitation by anti-Viet Nam demonstrators, news coverage of Toronto's second international speakfest was understandably hypersensitive to any manifestations of political bias. It is true that Hirendranath Mukerjee, an Indian Communist M.P. did take a paragraph of his speech to attack American warfare in Viet Nam, although *The Globe and Mail* in emphasizing with Warhol-like photographs his "passionately anti-U.S. speech," missed the more significant point that this pro-Soviet Communist had given a remarkably conciliatory appeal for an understanding of China's excesses. It is also correct, as the C.B.C.'s documentary on the Teach-In showed, that there was a strong clash over the value of the Red Guards, David Crook, a resident of Peking, giving them the dubious accolade of being some of his children's best friends while the British Labour M.P. John Mendelson denounced them as an indication of 'organized irresponsibility'. Throughout the four sessions, in fact, the audience acted as emotional referee, some sections appluading pro-Chinese statements, while others approved points criticising the communist system. While the Teach-In speakers were deliberately chosen on the assumption that 'the experts disagree', one surprising result of this transmuted ivory tower was the consensus developed by the twelve speakers.

Even on the explosive issue of the 'great proletarian cultural revolution', discordances in value judgements between fellow travellers and travelling Fellows did not obscure a basic agreement on why it is occuring. Many splendoured Han Suyin (the major crowd gatherer in the eyes of the organizers) defended the Red Guards not just as a morally enobling school for Chinese youth but as the current expression of the Chinese revolutionaries' preoccupation with fighting the poisonous roots of creeping embourgeoisement. While Stuart Schram, a political science professor from Paris, pointed out that the campaign against the party apparatus by this ersatz youth movement was without precedent in Communist political history, he nevertheless concurred that this latest activation of the purge mechanism was consistent with the spirit of the Maoist revolution in its obsessive fear that the past might rise up to suffocate the New Society.

This view that the emphasis on ideology regardless of efficiency is a domestic political development has important international implications. It was no surprise to hear such a defender of the People's Republic as the writer Felix Greene affirm that China's foreign policy presents no threat to the outside world despite its support for national liberation wars. What made this assertion about China's lack of aggressiveness more telling was the same point made by three of the academic papers: one must distinguish China's flamboyant ideology from its cautious practice to appreciate the overall defensiveness of China's diplomacy (David Mozingo, of the Rand Corporation); because of his strategic faith in final victory but tactical prudence in committing his forces, Mao insists on letting local revolutionaries fight their own battles (John Gittings, English student of the Chinese army); as for its national interests, China wants primarily to stabilize its relations with neighbouring countries in order to build up its own military and economic base (Shinkichi Eto, professor from Japan).

While the panelists agreed that introversion and domestic development epitomize China's policies, it did not follow in their view that there is no current danger of war. On the contrary, Han Suyin's conviction that the point is near in the Vietnam escalation when the Chinese will feel obliged to intervene in defence of their vital interests was corroborated by Eto's affirmation that China will react in force when it feels threatened. The general impression of impending war with China was strengthened by Gittings's demonstration that the Chinese are more obdurate than the Vietnamese in their hostility to the Americans and by Mozingo's opinion that the

Chinese believe they will undermine the forces of imperialism in the long run in combat with the Americans.

To accept both the defensiveness of Chinese diplomacy and the real possibility of China entering the Viet Nam conflict was of course to call into question the rationale of American policy. While the non-committed in the audience could have dismissed as anti-Americanism Felix Greene's or Hirendranath Mukerjee's denunciation of U.S. policy in Viet Nam, it was impossible to discount the cumulative alarm voiced by the other contributors. It was striking to hear the American policy of 'forward containment' labelled as inappropriate and reckless by scholars like Mozingo and Gittings. Mendelson pointed out how President Johnson's hard line is bolstered by American public opinion's anti-Communist psychosis. Chester Ronning, Canada's senior statesman of Chinese affairs, declared the traditional non-recognition policy to be based on two assumptions long since proven false: Mao's puppet-like dependence on Moscow and Chiang's imminent reconquest of power. No less impressive was the repetition of this view by such pro-Soviet figures as the Indian Mukerjee and the Yugoslav diplomat Leo Mates in whose view an isolation policy designed to fence China in can have no positive result. Even Charles Burton Marshall's sardonic defence of his government's position managed to convey the impression of the unreality of official American thinking.

For all the ruffled feathers that Marshall roused, there was even general agreement on the final point on which the Teach-In closed, the relevance of the debate to Canada. As he is now a professor rather than a policymaker for the State Department, his designation of Canadian recognition of China as no more than an eventual footnote in diplomatic history may not have been intended as scornfully as it was interpreted. While Chester Ronning agreed that this obvious step would in itself hardly solve the problems of China's relationship with the outside world, it was essential both to save our own souls and as a first step to create a new climate of confidence in world relations to China. Thus, for all its emotional static, the Teach-In's message was loud and clear.

As a new medium of communication, the Teach-In in Canada is still in an experimental phase, though it already appears to be a very powerful instrument. The China Teach-In linked ten Canadian universities from coast to coast through a radio hookup, was carried live by twenty-six radio stations in Canada and the United States to an estimated audience of two million, was covered by some fifty members of the press from many countries and by both Canadian TV networks. A normally print-bound audience of 3-5000 responded spontaneously to the spokesmen for and critics of China, questioned the speakers from the floor, and witnessed a vigorous exchange among the experts, unobtainable in books and articles.

While the teach-in phenomenon had originated in the United States as a protest movement organized by Americans against their government's policy in Viet Nam, it has quickly been adopted and adapted around the world including Great Britain, Scandinavia, Australia and Japan. While these teach-ins have centred on an urgent international issue the temper of their proceedings has fallen somewhere on the spectrum between education, debate and straightforward protest. The Canadian Teach-In has adopted an 'educational' label and has, up to a point, lived up to its claim. The addresses of some of the academic speakers—Schram, Gittings, Mates, Mozingo and Eto—could have been presented to a learned societies' meeting. In addition, the week preceding the Teach-In had scheduled some thirteen lectures, films and symposia which were attended by overflow audiences.

Much of the press and student reaction to the Teach-In was favourable, but criticism reminiscent of last year's discussion was also raised (cf. previous article). This criticism centred hardly at all on the substantive issues the speakers had raised (one newspaper suggested that the audience should have shown more 'scornful incredulity' with regard to some benevolent defences of the Red Guard) but on the *format* of the Teach-In—its 'lack of balance', 'emotionalism', its 'anti-Americanism', whether it was more 'protest' than 'education' and whether the university should have been involved in such an event at all.

The Teach-In committee was concerned with 'balance' from the very moment it began to plan its programme, but how was this equilibrium to be defined, and even more important, how could it be achieved? Should it be primarily geographical balance with regard to the different positions taken on China in various parts of the globe? Should a pro-Communist but anti-Chinese speaker be balanced by a pro-American or anti-American speaker? Should a teach-in on *China* (or any other major international topic) necessarily have an equal roster of pro- and anti-American speakers? And would the Americans come? The list of American invitations—and refusals—to the Teach-In eventually read like a distinguished who's who. Should speakers be selected who were dryly 'academic' or who would present their views with impassioned conviction? Clearly the programme committee's decision could not be foolproof.

The charge of 'anti-Americanism', the most sensitive nerve of Canadian public opinion and Canadian foreign policy, was applied even to very specific criticism of certain American *policies*—an entirely different matter. The demand for 'balance'—a desirable objective in its own right—seemed to suggest that there should necessarily on every issue be an equal number of pro- and anti-American views. Nevertheless, the criticism of the Teach-In, even if exaggerated, deserves to be taken seriously for some important issues lie just beneath the surface. For behind these and other criticisms lay the implicit assumption that a substantial and direct influence on public opinion should be avoided, or at the least neutralized by some ideal format; that a teach-in *per se* should not influence public opinion and policy in any particular direction if it claimed to be 'educational'. If the teach-in was to shelter under the umbrella of authority and legitimacy of the university, then it must retain an aura of academic detachment and remain simply an impartial arena of free speech. At the root of the unease was the feeling that this classical ideal of the liberal university had not been achieved, and had likely been violated either openly or furtively.

What we have begun to realize however, is that the ideal

itself may be an illusion and that the very operation of such an international forum as the teach-in, amplified by the full coverage of the media, is bound to have an effect both on public opinion and foreign policy in its own right, no matter how perfect the 'balance'. In the present instance, for example, George Bain hit on the central issue when he wrote in *The Globe and Mail*:

> Last week's teach-in at the University of Toronto was not conceived with the purpose of pushing Ottawa one way or the other—the aim was to instruct rather than give vent to protest—but the total effect can only be to heighten the pressure (for Canadian recognition of China) which the Minister (Paul Martin) is already aware of.

This is what really underlies much of the malaise and ambiguity surrounding the Teach-In, even though the issue may be called 'balance' or even 'education vs. protest'. At the least, public opinion will be aroused and exert a stronger pressure on our decision-makers. But the effects may be in a very specific direction. (Anyone who watched External Affairs Minister Paul Martin uneasily trying to defend Canadian policy towards China at the end of the C.B.C.'s hour-long report on the Teach-In would have recognized how correct George Bain was.)

There is little point in sustaining the comfortable illusion that the teach-in is like any other university educational activity except more massive in scope. Nor is the solution to be found in a change to 'cooler' labels. (President Bissell suggested that the teach-in was really a "community seminar.")

Because it is a new and powerful medium, the unease about the teach-in is understandable up to a point. Traditional channels of moulding public opinion—newspaper editorials, radio and TV commentaries—have known and fairly predictable effects and we feel at home with them. They provide well-worn channels of debate and rebuttal, and of communication to the politician.

The teach-in's overall effects and influence are still being assessed and its subject matter and rules of procedure still being formulated. Until these become generally known and accepted, unease and criticism (under different labels) will likely continue.

But none of this means that the teach-in should suspend operations in the meantime, nor that the university should cease to endorse it. In a country where serious public debate has often been diffident, halting and impoverished, the teach-in's success can only be accounted for by the fact that it has filled an important need and offers some creative possibilities. We should welcome the addition of the microphone to the ivory tower and demand of the teach-in's organizers only the traditional integrity and responsibility of the academy.

With Mel Watkins, November 1965
With Stephen Clarkson, November 1966

THE MAKINGS OF A PRESIDENT

For well over a century since Cardinal Newman, university presidents have had as their avocation, the weaving of semi-sacral utopias for university audiences. Presidents have usually enjoyed an unchallenged monopoly on campus in the unending search for *The Idea Of A University.* Successful aspirants in the search became presidents in their turn and carried on the tradition. Sermons, visions and myths about the university nourished the souls of academics, students and patrons alike and created a community devoted to yesterday's tomorrows.

This idealism served more practical functions as well. It provided psychic compensation for an absurdly underpaid staff. It also mesmerized the students with visions of spiritual community and intellectual liberation; it shunted youthful energies into beer and skittishness, and into such opiates of the classes as fraternities, vaudeville revues, and the Whiffen-poof Song. When the president performed his task well, he imbued his constituents with a life-long nostalgia. Grateful alumni and captains of industry returned on football weekends for booster shots and kept the collection plate moving. Everyone basked in the university's aura of a prestigious never-

never land.

There were certainly exceptions but as a general rule, the more distinguished the university president, the more conservative were his utopias and, not surprisingly, the more authoritarian was his tenure.

But these are all matters of the past. The trouble with students these days is that they have begun to weigh up the old utopias against the modern realities, and what is worse, have begun to produce more modern utopias of their own. They rudely interrupt this game of solitaire and, without having been asked to join, insist instead on playing poker. University presidents are, understandably, rattled. Is this simply a new round of the *folies de la jeunesse*, or have the intruders come to stay?

Some historical musings come to mind after reading President Bissell's new volume of selected addresses delivered over the past decade, *The Strength of the University*. While the present University of Toronto was chartered in 1906, its structure, he tells us, reminds him of more ancient times. In a mixture of candour and whimsy he refers to the university as resembling a "feudal monarchy," and "a model of the *ancien régime*." Was this a portent, I wondered?

As I recall the era, the chartered companies of that time also had problems not unlike the modern university. Their overseas trading monopolies were being challenged by free traders who insisted on their own rights to trade and by quite different rules. Cries of anarchy and chaos went up from the established order and epithets such as 'interlopers' were heard. But the chartered companies had had their day and they rapidly disappeared. Free trade was a more timely and more democratic approach and it soon became the new orthodoxy. Instead of the predicted chaos, world commerce flourished as never before.

But all this is an unsettling digression. Bissell's essays are elegant reading although some who are less well conditioned to academic high-mindedness may find them on occasion soporific. The style conveys the winning qualities of the man— an urbane wit, a detached charm and a pleasant irony. Although a conservative, he has excellent antennae for the world around him as it begins to bear down heavily on the university. The decade in which these essays were written has been a period of enormous change and these essays reflect the way in which he has been able to lean with the prevailing winds.

Like most of his distinguished predecessors, Bissell is at heart a weaver of classical utopias. The university, he tells us, is "of all man-made institutions, an act of faith, a perpetual experiment, a search for the ideal." In his own terms he is a conservative romantic:

> There is also a conservative romanticism that sees institutions not as repositories of human error and perversity but as the means by which we maintain our ties with the generations and our sense of the glory and beauty of the human spirit. Universities have often inspired such romanticism in the past. And they continue to do so today.

It is a timeless view able to take in stride even the new student radicals for as Bissell tells us stoically they are "part of that recurring cycle of protest against reason, order and selectivity that constitute the classical virtues."

Bissell has political theories to match his philosophy and his view of history. "Direction," he suggests "must come from those who have familiarity, knowledge and a sense of affectionate identification." The university is the *last place*, he feels, where full-scale democracy should prevail, where "quantitative ideas should be given the dignity of doctrine."

The good old days must have been very good, for they had about them a "general atmosphere of unvexed liberalism," while university government ran smoothly as "a polite agreement among gentlemen." These are the lovely echoes of *la belle époque!*

But as the twentieth century overtook the university, life became considerably less unvexed. From without, the government loomed threateningly by becoming the largest single benefactor of the university committing tens of millions of dollars of public funds toward expansion plans and operating costs. Bissell stood vigilant on 'academic freedom'. And where in untroubled days he proclaimed the classical virtues of the university as a haven for individuals to pursue their own insights and eccentricities, he now discovered "institutional freedom, because at this time the area of stress has changed from the individual to the institution." It is a partial discovery, for Bissell's institutional freedom is only a doctrine of resistance to government pressures. It is a freedom not to be exercised except under duress. The twentieth century will have to press further before the university will discover where and how it will take a stand *qua* institution.

There is at least one instance of a missed opportunity. The University of Toronto might for example, have exercised its institutional freedom by excluding manufacturers of napalm from recruiting personnel on campus. Instead, it claimed, among other reasons, that it could not distinguish manufacturers of napalm from manufacturers of nickel. No such difficulties were encountered apparently in distinguishing among the students between 'activists' and 'saboteurs'. The outlook for the new doctrine of institutional freedom is not exhilarating. One hopes that should governmental pressures increase, the doctrine would not have atrophied in the interim.

Berkeley came and went, followed by Berlin, Columbia, Paris and virtually every other world capital one would care to name. On the U. of T. campus, our own student radicals loomed from within. It was on the issue of student radicalism that classical standbys were found wanting. Charges began flowing from the President's office directed against the brand of idealism and the imputed methods of the student radicals; they were, he claimed, romantic neo-Marxists, carried away by moral fervour and some even, committed to violence. A newspaper battle was on with the students, tensions began to escalate and to some, it appeared that the President had lost his cool.

An examination of the record casts a quite different light on his charges. Take moral fervour for a start. In the President's discussion of the multiversity, moral fervour was the one answer he offered in order to contain its more pernicious effects. At the University of Toronto, he cited the existence of the religious colleges which "endow intellectual energy with moral fervour and purpose."

It could hardly be the romanticism which he found unacceptable, for he too was a self-declared romantic, although of a different vintage.

As for the charge of violence, the President holds a particularly weak hand. When student violence occurs at a university, it is usually the final stage of a process of escalation, and in this respect Bissell already bears a serious responsibility. He was the first to flaunt violence on the University of Toronto campus. Amidst some casual qualifications the following thinly-veiled threat appears in his last annual report:

> I think for instance that the university community should only as a last resort summon police to the campus. . . . [When patience, wit and humour] have ceased to be effective, it must act with firmness and resolution.

Surely the President exaggerates the power of positive humour. Nor would it be unreasonable for the students to expect that their discussions with the President be taken seriously.

Compare Bissell's position on violence with one of the most prominent radical voices, that of Stephen Langdon, the president of the Students' Administrative Council:

> The ultimate means by which a significant societal institution such as this university can be changed, I believe, is by major non-violent confrontations in the form of a complete opting out of the university's educational process . . .in which the student body refuses to any longer comply with the current method of operations of the university.

The difference in moral horizons is striking. Langdon opens up a whole vista which was previously invisible: the possibility of genuinely new institutional innovations which are not hopelessly compromised from the start by the politics of an archaic and unwieldy structure; innovations which will not be ruined by violent means of achieving them. The plans which the students have announced for building and administering a large coeducational residence including educational facilities, offers one concrete example of what Langdon has in mind.

Finally, Bissell's charge of neo-Marxism, is as puzzling as all the rest. Assume for a moment that the following is a fairly typical credo of student radicals of the 'saboteur' brand:

> The student body may choose to become a subservient ally of the university; or it may, confident of its invulnerability, assert its independence, and become a force for 'skepticism, emancipation and pluralism'. The student body 'holds the critical cards', and if it plays the game resolutely and intelligently, can release the university from bondage based upon the maintenance of tension and the titillation of desire.

The passage has an authentic revolutionary ring to it. Who is the author of this raving piece of 'neo-Marxism'? With a few (admittedly perverse) substitutions in wording, it is none other than the president himself. Having been influenced by Galbraith's *The New Industrial State*, he has attempted to update his university utopia to suit the times and seized on the corporation as villain. The original passage reads as follows:

> The university may choose to become a subservient ally of the corporation; or it may, confident of its invulnerability, assert its independence, and become a force for 'skepticism, emancipation and pluralism'. The university 'holds the critical cards' and if it plays the game resolutely and intelligently, can release society from bondage based upon the maintenance of tension and the titillation of desire.

There is more to all this than fun and games. How realistic is the President's outlook? Corporations are more likely to encircle universities than the other way around. This is the gist of a widespread critique of Galbraith's position. In Canada moreover, the same group sits on the Boards of both institutions.

We are so bemused by these reveries about the university that we fail to realize how unwieldy and inefficient are its day-to-day operations. The university as presently constituted, is hardly capable of performing its own housekeeping properly, much less releasing society from bondage.

One might imagine that the Canadian corporate elite which is represented on the Board of Governors could run the place properly. A great deal could be overlooked if they had brought to bear some real ability, imagination and efficiency. But it is a unique business class in the Western world; its most dramatic achievement has been to preside over its own liquidation. Whatever time it could spare from selling its enterprises to the Americans, it has devoted to the neglect of the university.

Lest the reader imagine that I am grinding an axe of my own, let the president put the case in more modulated tones. He speaks of complex problems

> that could not easily be resolved. . .in a Board that often lacked the knowledge, and usually the time, to deal quickly and effectively with many serious issues.

There is much evidence to support this view. Take the proper planning of facilities for a start. While many new buildings have been built, more often than not, they are discovered to be too small, even before they have been opened. Furthermore, a forecast of space requirements was carefully prepared several years ago by university departments, and then promptly filed away and forgotten by the administration. Today, there is a first-class crisis in office space.

The architecture of the new buildings in turn, is a sea of unalleviated mediocrity; the damage is irreparable for at least the next quarter of a century.

Clerical and administrative personnel at the university are, as a matter of long-standing policy, paid lower salaries than the going rate. The result, with the exception of a few able and devoted people, is a network of incompetence and a high turnover of personnel. The accounting division, for example, has been a shambles for years.

It is ironic therefore to read that

> The operating budget of a large, complex university is far in excess of that of many principal corporations in Canada.

Surely the members of the Board of Governors would not

tolerate for an instant in their corporations, the kind of regime for which they are responsible at the university. Would the students do worse?

Stepping back for a moment from the scene at the University of Toronto and looking at the larger issues involved, we should note at least one great surprise. It has become commonplace to bewail the impersonality, the meaningless and tread-mill existence inherent in the institutions of a technological society. Nobody expected the amazing reaction that came in the second round: an explosion of moral passion of literally global proportions.

Forces of such dimension and tenacity necessarily have powerful political consequences. They are diverse in their effects and seem everywhere to take on the local colour of indigenous complaints.

Antiquated and inflexible institutional structures are least able to stand up under such powerful stress. It is beside the point for those at the head of such institutions to plead their good intentions and their willingness to reason and to compromise. If their institutions are brittle or unwieldy, if the change they offer can only be very slow and very partial, then the normal course of political escalation begins and violence may be the final result.

This is a rough but not I think, inaccurate description of the situation on university campuses today. Even when university administrations proffer the best of intentions and unlimited good will, we cannot expect these political forces to disappear on that account alone. If anything, the situation becomes more intractable, as the actual rigidity of these institutions becomes apparent.

At the University of Toronto as a result, the administration has developed a siege mentality which is sometimes accompanied by pleas of good intentions and at other times by paternalism, low-key epithets and threats.

The administration's strategy is unimaginative and inadequate. The President has proposed a committee of staff, students and representatives of the Board of Governors to prepare a plan for a single body to govern the university. He proposes to come up with a new plan in one year's time.

This should certainly be tried, but there are two major difficulties which I doubt can be easily surmounted. First the committee is to seek a general consensus among a remarkably diverse group in a short period of time. The president overlooks the lessons of the Macpherson Report published last year whose committee was more homogeneous. Some rather limited proposals were made, and the committee reported that

> larger questions than the ones we have dealt with. . .[are] less susceptible of rapid consensus.

Among the recommendations of the report are another "special committee. . .to study these long-range problems." It is unrealistic to imagine that a committee which will include radical students and ultra-conservative Board members will do better.

Secondly even if the committee eventually agrees on a more democratic structure, the basic educational environment of the university to which the student radicals object may be little affected. The present educational process itself has lost much of its meaning for them.

It is even more doubtful that a general consensus can be reached in this area. Nor is a general consensus necessary. Why should the rest of the students be offered such courses or seminars as "Doctrines of Alienation from Hegel to Ellul," or "The Sociology of the Dispossessed," if they have no interest in them?

What I would propose instead is the creation of a new and semi-autonomous college on campus as a home for student radicals. It would engage in much-needed experiments in more democratic organization and in a variety of educational approaches, and offer the courses that radicals want. It would take advantage of the federated structure of the University of Toronto, and obviate the need for general and centralized solutions which both sides are now seeking and which may be very difficult to attain. We have had reasons in the past for nurturing Anglicans, Catholics and United Church members in their own colleges—why not radicals? They should be permitted to seek their own state of grace and may have much to teach the rest of us.

Student radicals address themselves passionately to one of the central issues of our time—whether the institutions of a technological society can be made more just, more human and more democratic than they have been. No one has answers to these questions. Why not run such an experiment at the university—a 'free college' for perhaps a five-year period?

Student radicals are a fringe of the academic community but have an importance far beyond their numbers. For it is the fringe that tells us what is happening in the silent strata of the median. They are a DEW line which suddenly throws our entire environment into high definition.

If they decry what is shoddy, inflexible and oppressive in our institutions, if they are long on criticism and short on solutions, they also force the rest of us to confront our own apathy, indifference and premature resignation.

The task is certainly to find ways of averting violence, but also to turn this immense moral force into creative channels.

I suppose that most of us at the university are utopians in the end, although we do not always share the same visions. Yet every once in a while, we do meet each other in the higher strata. President Bissell commends the following passage to us from Robert Hutchins, and it is a good meeting-point:

> If education can contribute to a moral, intellectual and spiritual revolution then it offers a real hope of salvation to suffering humanity everywhere. If it cannot, or will not, contribute to this revolution, then it is irrelevant and its fate is immaterial.

September 1968

THE RIGHT TO SURVIVE

*Opening Remarks to the Conference on
the Canadianization of Post-Secondary Education, Toronto*

The theme of this conference on the Canadianization of the university is, in a sense, highly artificial. Where, in any other country of the world would it be necessary to call a conference to support the *national* content of the higher educational system? The very need to have such a discussion is indicative of the peculiar dilemma which we are in.

We have all heard the brusque complaint that a preoccupation with 'preservation of the national identity' and the 'Canadian content' of the educational system are highly introspective and neurotic concerns—a national exercise in navel-gazing. The task of a nation, some would maintain is to *live*, not to brood about its identity.

On the surface there is much that is valid in this complaint. A rough comparison can be made to the biological processes of daily life on which we depend. They are not in fact, a subject of constant reflection, of concern or of introspection except by inveterate hypochondriacs. For example, none of us go around all day thinking about our breathing apparatus, even though breathing is vital to our daily survival. We breathe normally, naturally and unselfconsciously. And many would assert that in the content, the curriculum and in the administration of our Canadian universities, the process should indeed be as natural and straightforward—that the constant fear about our identity is artificial. But consider what happens when there is something wrong with our breathing, when something is amiss with our respiratory system. Then nothing preoccupies us as much in our day-to-day existence, as this particular complaint.

Similarly I would like to suggest to you that this country is increasingly in trouble on a wide variety of fronts that affect its day-to-day existence. We cannot any longer take for granted the social processes of daily life, of cultural activity, and of economic decision-making. The national process of self-expression is sharply curtailed. We are in precisely that artificial condition which produces the need for a conference such as the one we have today.

I have spent some time over the past few years talking about the problems of our economic life, particularly the shift of decision-making to the United States by virtue of the high degree of foreign ownership. It is not a subject I propose to pursue today. Instead I should like to confront what may be a more serious problem: the question of whether the values of this society, the continuity of its culture, the right to pursue its own processes of social change at its own pace, are not in fact being seriously threatened. At bottom, this question runs to the heart of our national survival.

The legitimacy of this concern is often undermined by three or four objections that are usually offered whenever the question is raised. Let us examine these in turn. Objection number one, is that learning and culture are in their nature international. Thus we are bound in this view, to create a parochial enclave with second rate scholars and ideas if we concern ourselves primarily with a Canadian focus. I suggest however, that you ponder this question further. You will discover that no production of culture derives from anything resembling an international environment. The Abbey Theatre is Irish, the New York School of Painting is American, the orchestras in Salzburg are Austrian, Chekov and Dostoyevsky are Russian, and we could go down the list. Culture and ideas emerge out of a national subsoil. It is consumption that is international; production is national. To fail to take account of what is happening in our universities in Canada is to relegate our cultural future to consumption of other peoples' culture for an indefinite period and to produce little of our own.

The second issue that has been raised as an objection to the kind of concern before us today—the overpopulation with foreign professors—is that it violates, of all things, 'human rights'. We are told that we have legislation on our books, and a moral commitment to non-discrimination among individuals. Every case, we are told, should be judged strictly with reference to the professional ability of a person as is required in a liberal democracy. I would suggest to you, without challenging the validity of these liberal values of our society, that they are premised on a situation where national rights are not in jeopardy, where the continuity of the society is not at stake. Where a fragile culture is threatened either with erosion or with being swamped by the tide of information, entertainment, methodology and personnel coming from outside its borders, a different set of priorities must prevail. Unless we are able to assert and to balance the rights of community with the rights of individuals. I suggest to you that we are headed for substantial political disturbance. We must now become conscious of premises and of assumptions which have not traditionally been raised in the context of a liberal democracy because our situation is unusual and because our condition is both urgent and artificial.

A third objection maintains that if Canadian universities are in trouble, in the sense that a growing proportion of personnel and curriculum is not centred on Canadians and Canadian culture, then we have nobody to blame but ourselves. Our own helter-skelter expansion brought this about. The implication is, therefore, that we lie back and do nothing. I am prepared to accept the first part of this argument but I am not prepared to accept the second. The fault in this area must clearly be put at the doorstep of a short-sighted educational establishment unconcerned with the long-run implications. It was a monumental absence of foresight but it makes the task of repairing our situation more urgent rather than less.

The sponsors of this conference are not here to assume the role of casting the first stone. Regardless of what has happened in the past, and accepting our share of responsibility, there is a major problem of national significance to which we must devote our attention. Our purpose is not to express vindictiveness nor to find a villain either domestically or in the United States. Nor is our purpose here to sidetrack our discussion into one or another set of global philosophies. What we owe to ourselves, what we owe to our educational system and what we owe to this country is a discussion of the possible, the feasible and the necessary; what to do, and how to do it in the situation in which we find ourselves.

I am reminded at this time of a tourist who got lost on a back road just outside of Collingwood and couldn't make his way back to Toronto. Soon he spotted a local farmer nearby and asked him the best route to Toronto. The local farmer looked puzzled, scratched his head, thought awhile and said "Well I'll tell you, if I were you, I wouldn't start from here." I am afraid that today, we have to start precisely from here. The problem should not be centred on the historical exercise of discovering the villains of the piece, but on the practical exercise of planning for a different kind of educational future.

In opening this conference we should draw attention to a number of individuals who, breaking the conventional wisdom of the silent majority within the past two years, have raised the question of Canadianization to a national issue at great cost to themselves. Much recrimination has since come their way. The issue was unpopular, it was uncomfortable, it was unwieldy, it threatened all kinds of liberal premises. Speaking personally, I find that now that the issue has received national attention, now that governments are concerned with what is happening, now that directives are issued from the Ontario Department of Education and other Departments of Education that focus on this problem, we should give credit to people such as Robin Mathews, who began to draw this to our attention. Those who break the silence of the conventional wisdom often have much ignominy heaped on them.

Our educational dilemma occurs in a global context of the dramatic spread of multinational corporations, mainly American corporations, around the world. Aside from the economic questions they raise, there are legal and cultural questions as well. The spread, extraterritorially, of American law, involves, for example, the claim by the U.S. government to primary jurisdiction over some forty billion dollars of U.S. holdings in this country. The projections for the future are ominous. At present rates of growth, in less than twenty years, American domestic companies with their multi-national subsidiaries abroad will control some four fifths of the world's resources. We are heading for a situation where *I Love Lucy* will become the fare for forty countries in forty languages. We are headed for Walt Rostow's ideal, a world where Colgate toothpaste is the hallmark of 'high mass consumption'. These projections cannot be allowed to determine the future. It is a future that must be stopped. And therefore I suggest to you that we meet today not with a sense of guilt or a sense of the awkwardness of the problem, but with a sense of the full legitimacy of a society's right to survive. This must be given at least equal weight with liberal atomistic premises of individual rights and non-discrimination. We should pursue our discussions with neither guilt nor vindictiveness, in a realistic appraisal of the alternatives before us for the future and the course of action that is practical and feasible.

March 1971

The Unknown Student

16

*Annual Spring Lecture to
the Thomas More Institute, Montreal*

Canada, several commentators have told us, is a country without myths. I suppose what they mean is that our national image of ourselves is not shaped and enriched with the power of myths such as those of our neighbour: George Washington's crossing of the Delaware, the Boston tea party, Abe Lincoln's birth in a log cabin and his Gettysburg address, the covered wagon pushing toward the Western frontier, and the cowboy.

We are undoubtedly the poorer for it. The only equivalent we have to the cowboy is perhaps the Mountie—the lonely symbol of central authority in the barely inhabited and dour areas of this country.

But a country needs its myths. They are the national parables that tell us what we are and what we can aspire to be, milestones of the past and beacons for the future. Without an awareness of its native myths, Canada has lived vicariously on the myths of others. The American myths have effectively, if informally, been woven into our childhood. But a more active role has been played until very recently by the myths of England: Canute's turning back the waves, Alfred's burnt cakes, Harold's eye at Hastings, even Wordsworth's arcadian daffodils and the sun which never set on the

British Empire. But these are the incidental features of a colonial existence. They remain in Canada, 'the England within'.

It would not be correct to say that Canada has had no myths at all. Perhaps we have not been so conscious of them. In English Canada at least, we have soothed the troubled conscience of the conqueror's role by the sentimental myth of the joint heroic deaths of Wolfe and Montcalm. But this myth of heroism has not been enough to overcome the liabilities of both the conqueror and the conquered. The moral aftermath of the Conquest for this country may still be the greatest roadblock to the building of a common future.

But my subject here is not French-English relations. I am concerned with one little-discussed Canadian myth of the recent past, and I wonder how this myth can be turned into a guidepost for the future. I should also like to say a few things—hunches if you will—about the moral framework of that future society whose threshold we have now crossed— the technological society.

But anything we can say on this important subject still borders, I am afraid, on vagueness and on the mutual confrontation of our intuitions. We must still enter the subject through side doors and discern approximate shapes in the gloom.

My theme is "The Unknown Student." The phrase may evoke some self-evident associations, for it derives from that major symbol of the First World War, the unknown soldier. And it is this myth which may be one of the side doors through which to enter the main arena we have chosen. For although Canada has few national myths, I would venture to suggest that one of the strongest is the way in which we remember the First World War—enshrined as it was and still is in the countless war memorials in virtually every large and small town in this country. You have all seen them, bronze and stone figures, bayonets poised, and at the base of the statue, the aging brass plates listing the names of our soldiers who fell in the service of their country. In our larger cities these darkening statues are joined by the large grey armouries. Together they remind us now of a past which quickly settled like a mist over this country and still retains its hold today. The Unknown Soldier has become the symbol of that past, not only for Canada but for many countries who fought in that war. Yet its hold remains strong in Canada in particular, because we sense, in a way, that the First World War was a traumatic moment in Canadian history. As Professor Lower has pointed out, "Canada entered the war a colony, she emerged from it close to an independent state." It is no coincidence, in my view, that a renewed interest in the First World War both in England and in the United States has been echoed in Canada by a series of books on the war, particularly the great battle at Vimy Ridge. The recent volume by Lieutenant Colonel D.E. MacIntyre is perhaps the most dramatic presentation of the story of Vimy and its significance for Canada.

I will bypass the larger meaning of the event itself but focus on the symbol that we have held to in the past half century—the Unknown Soldier.

60,000 Canadians died on the field of battle, and perhaps an equal number died later of their wounds. We could only respond to these lists and lists of names through a symbol — a nameless individual who was to embody the essence and meaning of this event. Only through anonymity itself could we do justice to the numbers involved. Only in this way could we achieve an adequate human response and express the gratitude, devotion and honour of the entire country. It is remarkable how effective the symbol was. But it was always an anonymous symbol, and it is precisely this characteristic which gave it its strength and its humanity.

Perhaps we are still too close to the mood and atmosphere of this national myth to see it clearly. There is nothing more difficult, as Marshall McLuhan has pointed out, than to understand our own environment. For those who may think that I am exaggerating the present power of this myth in Canada, I refer you to the celebration of the fiftieth anniversary of the Battle of Vimy that took place recently in France. As you may recall, the celebration was caught up in a diplomatic *faux pas*. We gathered from the newspapers that it had been badly handled, that some unforeseen error had been made. In particular there was inadequate recognition of the role of the French government and its sovereignty over this particular area. Some commentators attributed the problem to the sensitivity of the French. Much was made of De Gaulle's touchiness, although it soon became clear that on our side we had invited the Duke of Edinburgh to participate without prior clearance and consultation with the French.

While there were undoubtedly French sensitivities involved, we have given far less attention to the other side of the coin, namely, our own sensitivity. I suspect that the key to the incident may well lie in the fact that Canadian minds were still bound by a myth of Vimy which by now had itself taken on a timeless, and in fact an extraterrestrial significance. We had lived with and cultivated this myth for half a century and we had virtually ceased to realize that Vimy was an actual place, located in a specific country. For us it had become a symbolic enclave perched halfway between earth and high heaven—the real proof of its mythic character. It simply had not occurred to us that more terrestrial procedures had to be followed in a ceremony being held on the sovereign territory of another country.

What relevance does such an issue have to the present, or indeed to the future? The link, I must admit, is entirely personal. I am occasionally reminded of this myth in my day-to-day activities as I teach at the University of Toronto. The University, as you may be aware, now has about 23,000 students. Sometimes as I deliver my lectures, and look out over a sea of faces at a class numbering in the hundreds, I am confronted with many unsettling questions. I sense the impossibility of getting to know personally, or indeed having any inkling of the students sitting in the lecture hall before me. Our contact throughout the academic year is distant. For me, most of the students remain anonymous.

It is not a problem which can easily be solved. There are the possibilities of new techniques, the use perhaps of TV in the class-room, the extension of office hours, the creation of more lecture and discussion groups. But I am not sanguine that this problem can really be solved by any of these techniques. I discovered that, strangely enough, the larger the class, the fewer the students that have particular problems or questions which they wish to discuss personally. During my office hours I would sit for hours on end, and no one would show up. The large university and the large class creates in itself a pervasive atmosphere which is not easily bridged by new technical devices and small adjustments. I am beginning to suspect that we may have to give up the ideal that is so firmly rooted in our minds, namely an attempt to restore in some way, the personal relationships of the small class, the traditional 'student-teacher' relationship. I suspect that to a large extent, the anonymity of this class-room relationship will persist and that it will become the standard setting in which university teaching will be carried on.

The passing, at our larger universities, of the old classical ideal of personal teaching is a matter of deep regret. But it also produces many gnawing questions for the present and for the future. At what level, for example, should these lectures be pitched—to the top twenty per cent of the students? Or is that too high a standard? Does our commitment to the democratic character of this type of class-room situation call for a more popular or least-common-denominator approach and a much lower standard of instruction?

Most important perhaps, is the question of the interaction between student and teacher. It is this dialogue or feedback which sets the level, the direction and the creative type of learning experience on both sides, which we value most. How is teaching to be carried on in its absence? What is to sustain the sense of purpose or commitment, the morale, the live enthusiasm of the lecturer?

I regard these questions as setting, in a broad sense, the moral framework of the class-room. But I will confess that these are not questions to which I can give adequate answers. In my own mind there is little more than a half-formed solution. As I stand on the lecture platform confronting a sea of student faces, the only answer I can give to some of these troubling questions is a symbolic one: the unknown student. I sense that many of the thoughts and ideas of the course will be received in very different ways by different students; they will be absorbed, used and remembered in ways which I cannot know and will never know. In the absence of a class-room dialogue or response, I cannot be aware in what way I shall have had any influence on them.

The situation I have been discussing is not a novel one, and there are similar class-room experiences that we have all been through both as students and teachers. But we have generally soothed our conscience by some notion that this was an unfortunate departure from an ideal: we would keep the ideal before us in the hope that things would get better. Perhaps more money and more teaching staff would be found. But it is the realism of this ideal which is now in question. I think there is something basically new and very likely permanent in having to teach in this environment and to teach in it with a degree of resignation as to its continuing character and its limitations. The atmosphere which I am describing applies not only to the large classes, but pervades even the smaller ones, when the institution itself is large and creates its own general atmosphere. However, this sense of resignation I refer to is not a resignation of responsibility, nor a feeling that in any crucial sense the moral relationship to the class is weakened or suspended. In some ways, in fact, the responsibility has increased because of the sheer number of students involved.

But there is only a symbolic answer to the central questions which every teacher must face: to whom is he speaking, to what purpose, and how much of himself does he leave with his students? The teacher, I feel, can only fall back on a symbol—one that he must shape for himself. I suggest that he lectures to the unknown student, and he must construct for himself the human shape of that student. The teacher must anticipate the chords to which such a student will respond, the direction in which he should be moved, the level and degree of responsibility he must take for the influence he will necessarily exert on this student.

But having done all that, the student in the end remains anonymous, and the lecturer's image of him not clearly testable. There will be little or no feedback, yet the anonymous class-room does not preclude a human solution. It does, however, pose a stringent challenge to our inner resources to produce that symbolic solution and to live with and sustain it.

The dilemma in education is not unique. It is just one example of an important facet of modern society. The growth of the non-personal or purely functional human relationship may be its most pervasive moral characteristic. In the large corporation, in government, in our social welfare schemes, in our large apartment buildings, in the electoral process, even, I might venture to add, in our religious institutions, the personal association is being increasingly displaced by the non-personal, the functional and the anonymous relationship. It is a characteristic feature of the mass society. The problem is vague and unsettling. Sometimes we blame red tape and bureaucracy, sometimes the large city, or most frequently, just the plain problem of the size of everything.

In any case, we tend to regard the problem as an external phenomenon, somewhere 'out there'. But this may not be entirely true. The phenomenon may be strongly rooted inside each one of us. Anonymity has another side to it, a new search for privacy, even a kind of freedom. We all tend to draw inwards and circumscribe the segments of our life in various ways. For example, it becomes a matter of poor taste to discuss our religious views in the office, and a matter of equally questionable taste to discuss business in church. This process is politely called 'discretion', but it is only another aspect of the general trend which I have been describing.

Some insist, perhaps correctly, that the heart of the matter lies not so much with bureaucracy but with the new media of communication. I sometimes think that the dilemma must be most sharply focused in the case of the journalist, the broadcaster, and the TV commentator. The characteristic problem they face is the presentation of ideas to a vast sea of persons whom they shall never know nor meet, from whom they have only infrequent reactions, and where they must continually wonder, I imagine, what effect and consequence their public articles and statements have on the anonymous shifting sea of public opinion.

I am reminded as well of the advice of one of our most eminent musicians, Glen Gould, who has heralded the end of the traditional concert and made a virtue of artistic expression through the new media, citing in particular the enormous success of recordings and tapes.

The situations to which I refer, are undoubtedly familiar to everyone. There is nothing essentially new in what I am describing. What I do seek to question, however, is the moral stance that we have taken in the face of this total new environment which begins to surround us. I suspect that it is time for us to ask some basic questions about all these events. What do these new situations portend for our inner life, for the responsibilities we must assume, the situations that we create, the nature of the creativity to which we should aspire, the kinds of intuition that we can draw upon?

In attempting to find answers to these questions, we fall back on the moral codes and moral framework in which most of us have been brought up and educated, in the great religious traditions of the West. But these may not be adequate. Our moral codes refer to relationships which are essentially direct and personal, to a moral environment which is in essence small. Examine, for instance, the personal relationship invoked in the work of Martin Buber, the 'I-thou' relationship. We have centred our moral insights and premises on the *personal* character of the relationship of individuals and generalized this to produce a morality of the neighbourhood. Even our concept of 'the person in community' refers implicitly to a small group. We tend to generalize to larger environments by some implicit assumption that what transpires between two people or among a small group of people, can be in some simple way multiplied for society as a whole. I am not, I hasten to say, questioning the importance of these relationships. I am suggesting however that as all of us cross the threshold of the technological society, we begin to be hemmed in by a different environment, and the old morality of the neighbourhood fails to meet the challenge.

For most of us the challenge is disturbing. Apart from a vague sense of fear and discomfort, we have no clear sense of direction in this new environment. We grope quietly for some restoration of a classical ideal. Even the reform of our social institutions as well as the expansion of our religious insights are, in Marshall McLuhan's phrase, seen through the rear-view mirror. I think it is time to take stock of the broad dilemma which we face, which is at bottom a moral dilemma.

The potential benefits of the new society are immense and should not be neglected or negated. The opportunities for self-development, education, security, a higher standard of living and the prospect of greater equality are obvious. Whatever liabilities follow are admittedly much more vague, intangible, and some would even say irrational. However, certain things can be recognized and agreed upon by all. First, we have left a world of essentially personal relationships, ones that we still cherish, for a world of massive simultaneous involvement. We are all participants in a world where the media have virtually eliminated time. There is instant awareness and global response.

It is a world we never made. It just happened under the compelling and almost irreversible momentum of the new technology. I cite for example the testimony of Dr. J. Robert Oppenheimer in 1954 when he was being questioned by the U.S. Atomic Energy Commission about his role in the decision taken in 1949 not to produce the hydrogen bomb:

> "I do not think we want to argue technical questions here," he said, "and I do not think it is very meaningful for me to speculate as to how we would have responded had the technical picture at that time been more as it was later.
>
> "However it is my judgement in these things that when you see something that is technically sweet, you go ahead and do it, and you argue about what to do about it only after you have had your technical success. That is the way it was with the atomic bomb. I do not think anyone opposed making it; there was some debate about what to do with it after it was made. I cannot very well imagine if we had known in 1949 what we had got to know by early 1951 that the tone of our report would have been the same."

We are deeply committed to what Robert Oppenheimer has

called the 'technically sweet', and none of us would seriously imagine that we could now abandon entirely the main directions of the path on which we are set.

I have tried to suggest that in the first instance, the problems we are now confronting should not be regarded simply as an endless series of temporary irritations and nuisances to be cured by simple devices or new techniques. Let us face the difficulties squarely. The web of society is more closely meshed, the rules, institutions, and pressures of society close in on us and leave less room for manoeuvre. Many of the rules, the red tape, the sense of pushing continually uphill towards an unknown peak, the massive alienation, derive in large measure from the new forms of organization, and the tasks of control and co-ordination. We hear unending complaints against 'the establishment', a bureaucracy as helpless and anonymous as any other. There is a pervasive sense of oppression which comes from the new structure of society. Yet we are all aware that we cannot buy a railway ticket back to the integral and placid societies of the mediaeval period; nor even to the period of the flowering of individualism of the eighteenth and nineteenth centuries. Individuals and small groups may opt out but there is no way back for most of us, if only because of our own wishes and commitments. However we may slow down or reorganize the technological society, a moral commitment to progress remains and that seems in some irrevocable way linked with the machine.

We are all sponsors of the new regime and most of us devote our day-to-day existence to making it function. Virtually every decision we take is bound to affect others; our daily tasks give rise to both direct and anonymous control of persons and situations. Our integrity demands that we act according to our own moral standards and that we be able to live with the consequences of our actions. But these consequences now fall outside the orbit of our control. We want to resist fiercely the manipulation by faceless persons; but we cannot bear the responsibility of the manipulation that we ourselves generate. We remain responsible without knowing the degree of responsibility nor the final outcome of the rules, constraints and pressures to which we have given rise. The compulsion we create is impersonal. We drop stones into the sea and do not know which distant shore the waves will reach. Our conscience and our freedom have been compromised not only by what is done to us, but even more by what we do, wittingly or unwittingly, to others.

The anonymous society must evoke from us a morality and a response appropriate to its complex character, so that meaning and significance can be re-defined in the new setting. The mass society is not amoral and certainly not, in my view, immoral. But the nature of a new faith required to sustain our activities in society, to give them meaning and purpose, has to be boldly examined and re-defined. We will have to create, in this new 'tribal world', new myths to sustain us, as ethos, as attitudes, as roads to the future.

Admittedly, the anonymous society evokes a humanity which is, in a sense, abstract. But the abstraction has become the reality. I know that the bonds which tie us together, whether conveyed by the sound waves of the microphone, the small dots of the TV screen, the print of the large newspaper, or by Telstar—this humanity is present and must be recognized. Otherwise we should become victims of an anonymous despair which would undermine the basic activities of our daily lives.

A fear sets in, and a peculiar kind of courage is required. We are bombarded with impressions which the new media of communication fire at us in endless salvoes. We must sort these more quickly, respond instantly, decipher the urgent from the trivial, the manipulations from the genuine pleas, and pursue the moral intuitions which we cannot relinquish. In an immediate sense we are all, in this new era, *unknown students*.

May 1967